The best of

Woodworker

A SELECTION OF PROJECTS FROM OVER 90 YEARS OF THE WORLD'S BEST WOODWORKING MAGAZINE

Compiled by Zachary Taylor

ARGUS BOOKS

Argus Books
Argus House
Boundary Way
Hemel Hempstead
Herts HP2 7ST
England

First published by Argus Books 1994

ISBN 1 85486 101 8

Cover photograph by Manny Cefai

Explanatory note:
As the projects contained in this book are produced in facsimile from
the original magazine articles, some pages contain continuation text
from articles not selected for this book.
This irrelevant text has been tinted.

Due to the age of some of the material used in the production of this book,
the print quality on some pages is poor.

Printed and bound in Great Britain by BPCC Wheatons Ltd., Exeter

Contents

Introduction

The commissioning editor for Argus Books, Beverly Laughlin, was once part of the *Woodworker* editorial team and during that time she became a staunch fan of the magazine and of woodwork. It was she who proposed this book and I was honoured to accept the delightful task of editing it.

I began by contemplating the shelves full of magazine archives in my office. Since 1901, "Woody", as we affectionately call it, has been at the forefront of woodwork magazines, in fact, for most of those years there were hardly any other journals published on the subject. Rather than tax the reader's powers of calculation, let me say that there have been more than one thousand *Woodworkers* produced in its time and here was I, faced with the business of selecting from it, the most appropriate material to accord with the title. The weight of the assignment began to dawn as I drew from the ancient chronicles first one, then another example, seeking suitable features for inclusion. 'Spoiled for choice' was a phrase that came swiftly to mind and I appeared to be on the threshold of the definitive example of that old adage.

Channelling some kind of formula into a plan I decided that there should be samples from every period since the birth of the magazine, taking in the 1st and 2nd World wars; the coming of man-made boards; power-drills and instant glues.

It seemed reasonable to reproduce the pages in facsimile of the originals, in order to show changes in style, and format. Interestingly, in the early editions, the editor found it necessary to only mention, in passing as it were, such things as "There is a haunched tenon joint connecting A and B", indicating how well informed on woodworking joints the average contemporary reader must have been. But, remember, they had *proper* woodwork lessons at school in those days!

Rather than use articles advising on practices using inferior or outmoded techniques or equipment, I have chosen to include projects that contained information about constructional and technical matters. Again, the problem was to decide which dresser, which bookcase, etc, etc, since over the years many examples of the same items were available.

The validity of designs in furniture such as pine kitchens, still as popular as they were ninety years ago; the basics of techniques in tool application and of sharpening methods; tips for safety and hints on better workshop practice, were all there in abundance and variety, contributed by some of the greatest authorities on woodwork. All I had to do was to choose...

So, here it is. Arguably the ultimate project book on the subject in its age. Others may have chosen quite differently. I am conscious of the fact that there is an enormous amount of material that I had to leave out. Maybe I'll go for a sequel...

Enjoy it, with my good wishes,

Zachary Taylor

ZacharyTaylor
Editor of *Woodworker* since 1992

Why do Windows Rattle?

"**B**ECAUSE it is impossible to prevent them," is often said ; but this is not true, and, if properly made, windows will not rattle. In Fig 1 are shown three different sections of sashes, the only difference in them being the

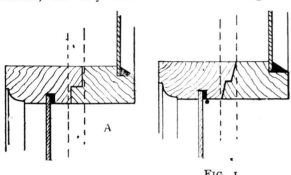

FIG 1.

method of fitting the meeting rails together. A is rebated, B bevelled, and C a combination of the two. The dotted lines show position of parting bead. If the meeting rails are made of such a width that the sash fastener on pulling them tightly together, also pulls them tightly to the parting beads, window sashes will not rattle, but if, as is usually the case, when the meeting rails

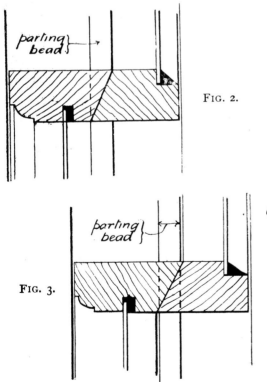

FIG. 2.

FIG. 3.

are close together, there is a space of half an inch between the stile of the top sash and the line of the stile of the bottom sash, and the parting bead is only three-eighths of an inch thick, then there is nothing to prevent the windows shaking with

considerable noise in the slightest wind. On the other hand, if the stiles of the sashes are within three-eighths of an inch of each other, and the parting bead is the same thickness, the fastener will pull all tight together, and no matter how high the wind is, the windows will be silent.

Figs. 2 and 3 show a section of the sashes made in the right and wrong way respectively, and if any one who is bothered with noisy windows, will take the trouble to remove them from the frames, and alter them until they fulfil the conditions given above, they will be relieved of the nuisance.

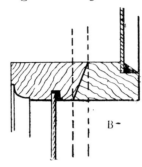

A Useful Book=Rest.

AMONGST the various little accessories which conduce to one's convenience and comfort may be enumerated an adjustable book-rest. Being endowed with vertical proclivities, most of us who have a liking for books readily appreciate any medium which will maintain a volume at a suitable angle to the eye so as to

FIG. 1.

A USEFUL BOOK-REST.

leave one's hands free for writing or other purposes, since it is always something of an effort to peruse a book lying horizontally, especially when the print is small. Therefore, we think that such of our younger craftsmen as seek a simple and straightforward subject for the exercise of their skill, might do worse than try their hand at the construction of a book-rest, for its introduction to the household will doubtless receive a ready welcome from those privileged to use it.

As the quantity of wood required for our purpose will be small, it is suggested that either solid walnut or mahogany be used for the most satisfactory result, although a sufficiently durable article could be made from pine, if preferred. Fig. 1 is a perspective view of the subject of this paper ; Fig. 2 is a front elevation of the same ; Fig. 3 a back view, and Fig. 4 a cut showing supporting struts in position, all of which, with the remarks and sizes which follow, should make the setting out a matter of the simplest moment, note being taken that the measurements given are for the smallest serviceable size. Taking Fig. 2, length from A to B may be

flange of hinge. The length should be 4 ins., width 1⅛ ins., and ' thickness ⅝ in., with 1 in. brass hinge, to which the lower and adjusting position of strut F is screwed. The length of F should be 4¾ ins., same width and thickness as upper part ; but the lower 1¼ ins., bevelled to ⅛ in., so as to afford a secure stay when entering any of the saw-tooth nicks in G. It will be seen that G is hinged to the centre of the lower edge of back, so that F, when not in use, lies flat over the hinge and in a line with E, G again folding as flat over this as clearance will permit. This will be seen by comparing the action indicated in Fig. 3 and Fig. 4. The length

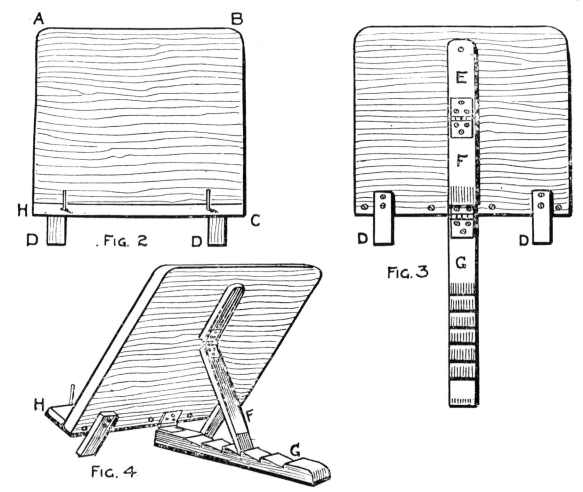

DETAILS OF BOOK REST.

11½ ins., with the corners rounded 1 in. each way ; B to C should be 10 ins. over all, out of stuff to finish ⅝ in. thick for hard wood, with ⅛ in. extra allowed for pine. The two supporting feet, D, D, give clearance for the saw-tooth strut when adjusted. These are better seen in Fig. 3, the length being 2¼ ins., out of ⅜ in. stuff, to overlap the back 1 in., and be fixed by two screws in each, carefully entered to avoid splitting. The upper part of back strut, E, Fig. 3, is a fixture, being secured in position by a screw at top and the three screws in upper

of G should be 10 ins. by 1⅛ ins. by ⅝ in. thick, and the saw-teeth nicks may start 3 ins. from hinge, being cut at intervals of 1 in., and to a depth of half the thickness of the stay. Five or six will be sufficient for this size stand, and the extreme end of G may be rounded for the sake of finish. Returning to the face side, it will be necessary to fix a strip 11½ ins. long, 1 in. wide, by ⅜ in. thick, as seen at H, Figs. 2 and 4, to prevent the book slipping. It should be glued along and flush with the lower edge, and be further secured by four screws, as shown in Fig. 3. To

How to Make a Toy Motor-car.

By " ALTHORP."

WHILST rambling through the various toy emporiums during the late festive season, the student of child-life must have been deeply impressed to see the rapturous delight of the youngsters of all ages and social conditions as they saw, examined, or criticised in almost impossible words the many ingenious examples of the toy-maker's art. Mechanical movement of the most crude form, or of the most highly developed scientific mechanism, invariably brought forth spontaneous admiration and enthusiasm from young and old.

The enormous development of the toy-making industry—especially on the mechanical and scientific side—is another of the wonders tireless inquisitiveness to fathom the unknown, the same love and reverence for old and favourite dolls, is just as manifest to-day as with us or our forefathers.

Who has not watched the care bestowed by the little mother on " baby " dolly in preparation for the morning or afternoon call, or for sweet repose, or on the washing and ironing of the many clothes, many of which are mere shreds of past glory, without giving a passing thought to childhood's days, and inwardly expressed the desire to assist in the true development of man ?

The means to effect this desire may be meagre, but leisure moments may be available, and it is our object to present a ready and effective way to add pleasure and profit to all who find the ennui of life intolerable.

The home manufacture of children's toys is at once simple, fascinating, and cheap, and may

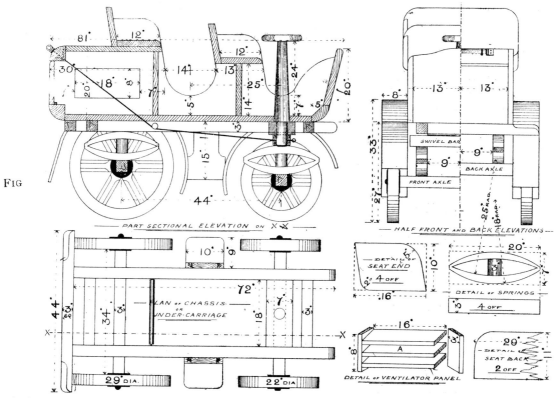

of the latter years of the Victorian era ; yet possibly in no other department has progress been more pronounced than with the doll and its surrounding equipment. A complete revolution in the design and build of the doll's house is apparent ; the furniture almost equals, in variety of design and ingenious construction, that of a modern villa ; whilst the carriages, from the cane or wicker type to those of the latest American models, are indeed creations.

Yet with all these marked developments, the cause—i.e., the child—remains in palace or cottage exactly the same. The same exuberance of buoyant animal spirit, the same restless, be carried out with the minimum of tools, and without causing much (if any) disturbance of the home arrangements.

Assuming that financial considerations precluded the purchasing of one of the latest forms of dolls' carriages, let us work out the problem of how best to satisfy the desire to aid " Little Mother " in her efforts to do her duty to " Baby," and to enable her to be up-to-date in the outdoor means of locomotion. The old draw-waggon is dilapidated ; the go-cart is shelved for the perambulator, which, in its turn, has had to give way to the motor-car, notwithstanding the fact that the latter, in its simple form—*i.e.*, devoid of any actual motor-propelling agency—is only an alteration of outline design of the carriage pram.

A careful perusal of the drawings, aided by the illustration of the finished car, will prove that nothing of any great difficulty is being attempted, and, further, that the expenditure on tools and materials will not prohibit the trial. The task is well within the capabilities of the average "big brother" who has completed a course of handicraft in wood at any of the elementary or secondary schools, and should not be beyond the powers of "Mother," provided she can "hit a nail on the head."

Bearing in mind that one of the chief essentials in the manufacture of children's toys is strength of construction, to enable them to withstand the rough usage which will certainly be applied in some outburst of innate irritability of mind, we must not forget that, as a general rule, far more care is taken of a fragile toy "made by father," than of those of a similar type purchased or obtained from other sources.

The box form of the design of the motor-car is calculated to give the maximum of effect with a minimum of labour, coupled with rigidity of construction — the absence of unsupported

simple numerals, which represent one-eighth of a standard inch as the unit standard of measurement ; thus a certain dimension reads between the arrow points 78·, the upper period point being the unit symbol ; the actual dimensions in ordinary measurement would be $9\frac{3}{4}$ ins., because $\frac{78}{8}· = 9\frac{6}{8} = 9\frac{3}{4}$.

If, therefore, it is desired to make the car proportionately larger, the standard unit is

increased accordingly. Thus, taking the above example, say we desire to make the car as large again as the model, we substitute $\frac{1}{4}$ in. for the $\frac{1}{8}$-in. unit, and read the dimensions

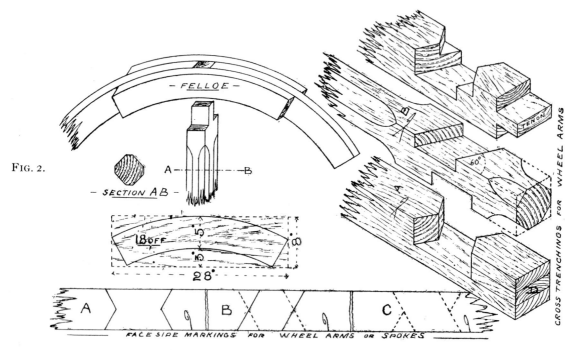

FIG. 2.

curves or scrolls will be fully appreciated—whilst the several detail elements, such as the elliptical springs, splashboards, ventilating panels, steering post, wheels, chassis, or undercarriage, are simple, yet effective and efficient.

A word as to the drawings. To enable the worker to build a car of any size from the drawings given, the standard dimensions of the model shown in the illustration are given in

given as 78 quarter-inches, or $19\frac{1}{2}$ ins., and so on, in any fractional proportion decided upon

If the worker will thoroughly grasp the simple elements of this method of measurement, no difficulty will be afterwards found to making strictly proportionate copies of any *undimensioned* sketches or drawings.

Having decided upon the size of the car required, proceed at once to make full-size draw-

gs of each element from the given dimen-
ns, so that you can see the whole work
rly on paper before cutting up the material
aper is far cheaper to make errors upon
n wood, and economy of pocket expenses
s one of the essentials of amateur work at
home.

The drawing completed, proceed to lay out
the body elements (cut each element out exactly to the outer line of the drawing, if considered necessary, and use each drawing as a
template) on a piece of ⅜ in. laned American
whitewood or Canary wood, being careful to
notice the *grain-way* of the wood (taken generally, the largest dimensions of any element or
detail denotes its length, and this should always
be placed with, or along, the grain-way—*not
across*), and leave sufficient space between each
outline to admit of the saw-blade (either tenon,
pad or bow) to pass between without cutting
into the outline.

Proceed to plane and dress up with file or
spokeshave the parallel and curved edges of
each side piece, and plane exactly parallel, and
of equal width, the two stretcher pieces, top
and bottom pieces, front splashboard, and rear
drop door. Remove the waste pieces from the
ventilating openings in each side piece by boring a small hole at each corner of the rectangle
marked, through which to pass the pad or bow-
saw blade, and finish each edge of openings
with chisel or file. Plane down the waste pieces
to ¼-in. thick, and build up the pair of louvre
ventilator panels, as shown on detail drawing
at A, to fit into the prepared openings ; mark
off the exact position of each stretcher piece,
bore for, and nail in place with, 1½-in. oval wire
nails, fit in the bottom piece, also the top,
bore for and nail in correct positions.

Work the curves on front splasher board,
fit it between the sides, bore for and nail in its
position ; prepare two 1-in. square pieces of
Canary wood ; cut these to length to fit in between the sides to make joint with the top and
bottom pieces at the rear end of car, and when
nailed in correct positions proceed to work the
corner curves to fit those on each side piece. Prepare one piece of 1¼ ins. by ¾ in. Canary wood,
cut to length, and fit it neatly to the lower
edge of front splash board and bottom piece,
nail in place, and work the curved corner as
before. Next build up the two seats, backs
and ends, and neatly round off the lower edge
of each end piece to fit against the sides.

Prepare the drop door to fit neatly into the
opening at the rear end of car ; round off the
outer upper edge, and attach to each side with
a fine panel pin to form a pin joint ; furnish
with a small knob or button, and finish off
flush with end of car. A narrow strip must be
fitted on the lower corner piece to prevent the
door swinging inwards.

Now carefully punch in all nail heads well

below the surface, and prepare the sides, edges,
and all available surfaces with fine sandpaper,
ready for painting.

We will next devote our attention to the
chassis or under-carriage.

Procure some ¾-in. square Canary wood in
lengths, and from this cut off the elements of
the chassis to the dimensions given ; the
stretcher pieces may be *tenoned* in if thought
advisable ; but if they are neatly butt jointed
and double nailed, the construction will be
thoroughly efficient. The axle-trees are prepared from the same material, as is also the
rear mudguard support. The latter may be
tenoned to the side-bars, but the butt double-
nailed joint will be equally effective. The
elliptical springs—certainly a misnomer in
point of resilience—are made from ¾-in. Canary
wood, bored out, sawn and filed to the given
dimensions and form (the centre piece being
fitted in and nailed through adds materially to
the strength ; but it may be omitted if desired),
and attached to the bottom side of the chassis
side bars for the rear, and to the swivel or fore-
carriage bar for the front wheels. Between the
chassis side bars is fitted the forecarriage bearing plate, through which passes the steering
post, when attached to the swivel or lock-bar
below.

The steering-post is worked out of ¾ in. square
stuff, shouldered as shown, and either permanently fixed to the swivel or lock-bar, or
attached by means of a draw-pin and chain, as
illustrated.

And now we come to probably the most difficult part of the problem—viz., the making of
the four wheels. No, we don't advocate purchase. Self-effort is our maxim ; therefore to
business.

The rims of the wheels fitted to the standard
model, as illustrated by the illustration, are
made in one piece, being cut direct from ⅜-in.
material with a special boring tool or cutter,
and the wheel arms, or spokes, simply overlap,
jointed through the centre of which is fitted
a short piece of bamboo or metal tube. The
spokes are to be neatly tapered and chamfered
from nave to felloe, and carefully fitted (not
forced) in the rim, and nailed in the desired
position. Thus constructed, no great difficulty is presented, and an effective and neat
job is secured.

But for those desirous of something more
orthodox, more nearly resembling the actual
artillery type of wheel almost universal in the
motor world, the following method of building
may be adopted :

The rim is built up of three 3-16th-in. layers
of six segments, or "felloes," the outer being of
equal length ; the spokes—six in number—
are fitted between the outer layers, and the
spaces between each spoke are filled in with

shorter segments, the boss, or nave, end of each spoke being tapered to make butt-edge joints ; or they may be overlap-jointed, as shown on the detail drawing ; or built up with three strips of 3-16th in. stuff, crossing each other at an angle of 60°, each end then being built up to thickness, as at D ; in either case, tenons must be left on the ends of end arms to fit in between the segments ; whilst on the face of each side are fitted covering discs to form the requisite boss through which passes the short length of brass tubing.

The outer rim segments being fitted to break joint with each other, and securely nailed together, a semicircular groove can readily be worked round the circumference with a round file into which a solid rubber tyre, or a piece of rubber tube (through which a stout piece of sash cord is passed, and joined to form a complete core ring), may be cemented in the usual way. The cross-section of the finished spokes should be elliptical. The building up of the wheels in this way takes some little time, but the result is much more satisfactory and correct in style. In either case, the inner surface of the rim should be neatly finished with file and glasspaper before the spokes are finally fixed. Care must also be taken to obtain the proper size of bamboo or brass tube, so that the wheels may run true and free on the shank of the screw axle pin.

Having completed the wheels, we can direct our attention to the ensemblement of the elements already prepared. Adjust the car body to the chassis, mark out and bore for three screws in each side bar, and attach body to chassis ; then prepare for the steering gear by boring a $\frac{1}{2}$-in. hole in the centre of the bearing plate, and through the bottom of the car. Bore a similar hole in the swivel bar exactly in the centre of its length and width, and fit the end of the steering post into each—fairly tight into the latter, and movement free in the former. Adjust the forecarriage to give a free swivel movement, and insert draw-pin through swivel or lock-bar, and post. Attach the axle trees to the springs with screws, and bore for and insert the screw axle-pins. A small metal washer should be placed on each side of the wheel boss before the wheels are attached. Round-headed brass screws (No. 14) will be suitable for the axle-pins. See that all details move freely in position, and that the alignment of the wheel tread is correct.

We next prepare the steps and step brackets to the dimensions given, and securely attach these to the side frames, ready to receive mudguards, which we next attach. Obtain some bent wood (such as is used for cheese-boxes), thoroughly soak some 2-in. strips in boiling water, and when sufficiently pliable, bend and securely bind with string, or by overlap-end nailing each piece round the outside of an 8-in.

or 9-in. stone jam jar, and let them remain at least twenty-four hours (until thoroughly dry) ; then remove, cut off the required length for each mudguard, and adjust each to its respective position. Smooth off the outer surface and edge of each with fine glasspaper, and fix securely to lower step and crossbars.

To give additional reality to the model, it will be desirable to provide means whereby the steering of the car may be operated by the child from the rear end. This may be done by means of two cords attached to the opposite ends of the swivel bar ; these pass under the carriage and up through the box part to the driving handle-bar, as fitted on the rounded rear top corner. By the careful adjustment of these cords—*i.e.*, fitting taut with two opposite turns round the handle-bar—the direction of the car is readily altered by a simple turning movement of the handle-bar in its fixtures.

Before fixing the seats to the car body, it may be desirable to add a little upholstery, either by directly padding the surface with layers of cotton wool or wadding under a covering of cloth or leather, the buttons being nailed directly through the stuffing and cloth into the woodwork ; or cushion work may be adopted—*i.e.*, the whole of the upholstery made separate and afterwards attached to the woodwork with gimp pins or tacks. In either case a strip of narrow gimp must be neatly tacked on all edges to give the necessary neat finish (after the painting or other decorations are completed).

Directing our attention to the latter, much artistic elaboration is unnecessary : a simple line of yellow on a dark chocolate ground gives a pleasing and effective combination.

Proceed to stop all holes and defects of jointing with dark putty, and apply a priming coat of lead-colour paint ; when dry, rub this thoroughly smooth with fine glasspaper, and then apply two coats of colour, allowing the first to dry thoroughly before putting on the second, and thoroughly rubbing down each application as before ; then finally, with a fine brush, apply the third coat, which should be of turps ground pigment, to which has been added a small quantity of varnish. When this is thoroughly dry, proceed to work the yellow striping, or stencil design. Finish off with oil copal varnish, and set aside to thoroughly dry in a place free from dust.

Do not attempt to test the progress of drying by finger touch : simply breathe upon the surface, which, if it remains bright, indicates that moisture is present ; but if a thin film appears to form, the work may be freely handled, and the upholstery trimming be completed.

For more ready reference as to method of procedure, the following is tabulated :—

1. Prepare working drawings to full size.
2. Lay out sides and details of body of car.

3. Prepare and cut out the curves of sides.

4. Plane parallel and true the other elements of the car body.

5. Build up and fit in louvre ventilator panels.

6. Fit stretchers, bottom and top pieces ; nail in position.

7. Work front splashboard curves ; fit in between the sides ; and nail in position.

8. Prepare material for ; fit between sides ; nail in and work rear-end corner pieces ; and also lower front splasher curve.

9. Build up the two seats as per drawing.

10. Prepare material for, and fit rear drop door.

11. Prepare car body for " priming " coat of paint.

12. Build up chassis, or under-carriage ; securely double nail all butt joints.

13. Prepare the elliptical springs, and attach one pair to chassis side frames (rear end).

14. Prepare swivel bar and bearing plate ; fit the latter between chassis side frames.

15. Work up the steering-post ; bore for attachment to swivel bar and through bearing plate.

16. Attach the other pair of elliptical springs to the swivel bar.

17. Adjust for free movement of fore-carriage.

18. Prepare material for the four wheels, solid or built-up pattern.

19. Ensemble all details ; adjust car body to chassis, axles to springs, wheels to axles, testing all separately for freedom of movement, where necessary, and for alignment.

20. Prepare step brackets and steps, and fix in position.

21. Prepare the bent-wood mud-guards, and fit each accurately in place.

22. Adjust steering by cords or lever movement.

23. Prepare upholstery for seats.

24. Dismantle wheels and chassis from body, and apply a priming coat of paint to each detail.

25. Give car body additional coats of paint ; rub down when dry ; add striping or stencil design ; and varnish.

26. Repeat ditto on all details.

27. Fix upholstery to seats, and finish edges with gimp.

28. If thoroughly dry, readjust and ensemble all details, and get ready for trial trip.

In conclusion, it is hoped that any technical points which may appear abstruse will not deter the amateur woodworker from exercising his powers, to the lasting pleasure and delight of the little ones, whose future depends very largely upon the influence and example of home.

Practical Hints on Box Making.

By Herbert Turner.

PERHAPS no idea springs so readily into the mind of the ordinary amateur than that of making a box of some kind, be it jewel case, writing case, workbox, handkerchief box, stationery box, photograph box, and so forth. They are useful as presents to our lady friends, as well as being extremely useful in themselves to us, and no wonder can be expressed at their popularity. This is sufficient excuse for the hints contained in this article, which will be of some service to those craftsmen who desire to make the boxes complete, quite from the beginning.

There are several traps into which the amateur craftsman can easily fall, and the professional craftsman will certainly not be the worse for a consideration of these traps, and for the hints which may enable them to steer clear of them. The craftsman's greatest attention should be given to the making of the joints at the corners of the boxes, the strength of the box depending much more on this than upon anything else ; and therefore the soundness of the method of making the joint, and the excellence of the workmanship, are two considerations of the very greatest importance.

Another almost equally important consideration is the quality of the wood and its state or condition. A lack of attention in this respect is often productive of disastrous results, and spoils what otherwise would have been an exceedingly fine piece of work. What a most annoying experience it is to find that after a great amount of time, and an equally great amount of tender care and careful workmanship, has been spent upon our work, our efforts have been rendered useless because of the shrinkage of wood that has not been quite dry enough.

Let us turn our attention first to the construction of the box. It is better to take an actual example, and for this purpose let us suppose we are making an ordinary handkerchief box, as shown in Fig. 1. This is just the ordinary type of box that is suitable for so many purposes. In size it will be about 7 ins. by 7 ins. by 4 ins. deep outside measurement. The thickness of the wood is the first consideration, and what this is will depend somewhat upon the kind of carving to be placed upon it, but chiefly by the object of the box. Boxes like this should be as light as is consistent with safety ; safe construction is quite the first condition, combined with the object of the box. The kind of ornament to be employed is a secondary matter, and should never be thought of entirely as the principal object of consideration. Ornament should be subordinate to the use and the construction of whatever article is being made.

MANUAL TRAINING.

MODELS FOR WOODWORK CLASSES.

A MEDICINE CABINET.

BY F. STURCH.

MANY woodwork teachers have found that the joints used by carpenters form the basis of a valuable series of exercises by which the use of the various tools may be

CABINET FINISHED.

learned. For example, such joints as the mortise and tenon joint, the halving joints, haunched tenon joint, housing joints, etc.

The ornamental and useful models which follow these should, as far as possible, be designed *to show the application of the above exercises*. Of course, the model to be made should be of good design and construction, and in addition to its usefulness should be suited to the strength and ability of the pupil.

Our present subject, the medicine cabinet, shows the application of some of the above-mentioned joints, viz.: dovetail housing, common housing, mortise and tenon joints. Useful practice in " setting out," shaping, glueing, etc., is also obtained.

This model looks well made either in American whitewood or satin walnut, with the panel for the doors made in walnut or sycamore respectively.

DRAWING.—The drawings comprise a front and side elevation, from which all necessary measurements may be obtained. These drawings should first be drawn to a convenient scale by each student.

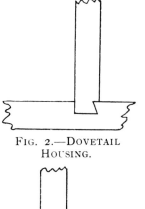

FIG. 2.—DOVETAIL HOUSING.

FIG. 3.—COMMON HOUSING.

The " cutting-out sheet " would appear as below :—

PIECE OF WORK : MEDICINE CABINET.
(*Allowance to be made for Planing.*)

Pieces.	Thickness.	Wood.	Part of Work.	Length.		Width.
2	$\frac{5}{8}''$	American Whitewood	Sides	2'	1"	7"
2	$\frac{7}{16}''$	,,	Wide Shelves	1'	9"	7"
1	$\frac{5}{16}''$	,,	Top Shelf	1'	9"	$2\frac{1}{2}''$
1	$\frac{3}{16}''$	,,	Back	1'	9"	10"
4	$\frac{7}{16}''$	,,	Stiles		$9\frac{1}{2}''$	$2\frac{1}{4}''$
4	$\frac{7}{16}''$	,,	Rails		$10\frac{1}{2}''$	$2\frac{1}{4}''$
2	$\frac{3}{8}''$	,,	Panels		$6\frac{1}{4}''$	$5\frac{1}{4}''$

Method of Procedure :—

1. Prepare the sides to correct width and thickness as shown in the drawing.

2. Set out the shaping with compass, rule, and pencil.

3. Plane up the wood for the shelves and shoot the ends square. The two wide shelves should then be dovetail housed into the sides (Fig. 2). The top shelf may be common housed (Fig. 3).

4. Mark out and make the rebates ($\frac{1}{4}$ in. deep) on the two wide shelves in the front and at the back (see end view).

8. Plane (and if necessary joint and glue) the board, or boards, for the back.

9. Prepare the wood for the door frames and

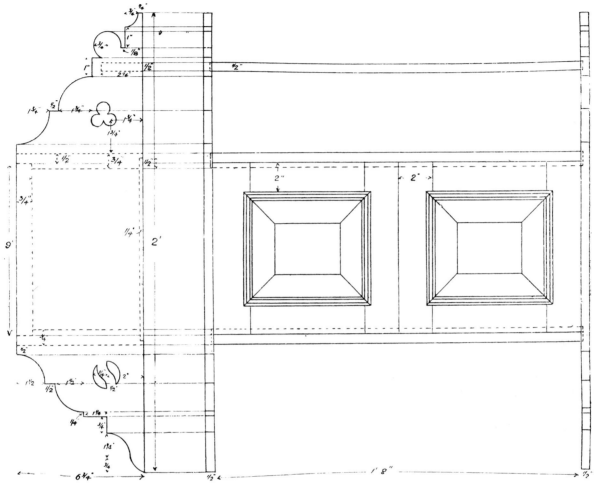

FIG. 1.—FRONT AND SIDE ELEVATION.

5. With bow saw, spokeshave, brace and bit, shape the sides. (N.B.—The edges should be kept square.)

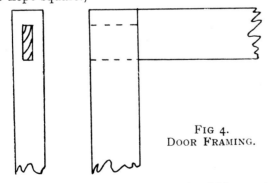

FIG 4.
DOOR FRAMING.

6. If a partition is required, it should be made and fitted now. It should be housed into the shelves, and need not be more than 5-16ths in. thick.

7. Glue the shelves and sides together, taking care to have the glue quite hot and not too thick.

joint together. The rails may be tenoned right through the stiles (Fig. 4).

10. Glue the door frames, and when dry,

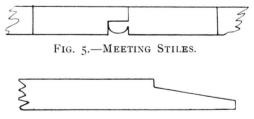

FIG. 5.—MEETING STILES.

FIG. 6.—EDGE OF RAISED PANEL.

clean off. A strip of moulding ($\frac{3}{8}$ in.) should be glued and bradded (use needle points) as shown, to form a rebate for the panels. (NOTE.— It is usual to make the two meeting stiles rather wider than the other pieces of framing. This is shown in Fig. 5.)

11. Fit in the back, which should be $\frac{1}{4}$ in. thick, and fix with small brads.

12. Two pairs of brass butt hinges and two small knobs may be required for the doors, and a lock and key may be fitted.

13. Plane up, make and fit the door panels. Those shown in the illustrations are raised panels (see also Fig. 6). These are kept in position by small pieces of beading glued in from the back.

heart is cut through it would show a pine instead of an oak ground under the heart.

The bead, which is the bottom member of the cornice, is of oak 2½ ins. wide and ⅜ in. thick ; it is rounded on the front edge and mitred round the frame, the bead showing a nice projection. The constructional sketch, Fig. 5, shows also the large ogee moulding, which is mitred round and screwed from the inside, and it is as well to notice the section which shows the method of cutting in the blocks so as to strengthen the cornice generally. The pediment P is cut out of ⅞-in. oak, and can be screwed on the cornice. This pediment being above the eye, the screws, of which the heads are countersunk, do not show.

We give below a list of the names of the various portions, which are lettered for purposes of identification.

P is the pediment ; L is the cornice ; M and R show the edge of the framed back, the edge of which is faced with oak ; N is the end of the top carcase, and is ⅞ in. thick ; S is the end of the bottom carcase ; O is the parting mould, which is mitred and screwed round the bottom carcase ; T is the foot.

The dowels used throughout this wardrobe are all ⅜ in. diameter.

A Child's Easel

MOST of us, in our juvenile days, have inclined to some sort of artistic expression with slate and pencil, and, however crude the effort, the imitative spirit has yet shown well to the fore. Thinking so, one's practical notions turn towards the youngsters in the home circle—those whose horizon is just merging from the wonderland of simple toys, and who then become almost as quickly appreciative as their elders of any really good thing to their liking. To come to the point, why not encourage the young idea to shoot—or, rather, draw, by allowing it to pose as a full-fledged R.A., with easel and board complete ? Properly introduced and sustained, this notion could not but have a beneficial effect upon the youngster, and, in fact, little imagination is necessary to depict him at work before the subject of the little sketch seen in Fig. 1.

The interested reader seeking for a suitable present for a forthcoming birthday might, therefore, do worse than accept our suggestion as the *motif* for his next handiwork at the bench, being, as it is, of the simplest construction, useful and trifling in outlay.

The detail sketches attached will make everything plain at a glance. Dimensions can, of course, vary as preferred, but it is proposed to put the length at 3 ft. 6 ins. as being a suitable size for the average child of about three to four years, an extra 6 ins. being allowed if the youngster should happen to be tall. Two kinds of easel are indicated, the one as at Fig. 1 to have a fixed splay-frame, with strut only to fold flat. This we will take

first. Fig. 2 shows the upper part—say, 7 ins. wide—with the uprights A 3 ft. 6 ins. by 2 ins. by ⅞ in. net, rounded at top for finish, and mortised right through to receive tenons on B, 7½ ins. by 2 ins. by ⅞ in., which may also be pinned in anticipation of a little rough usage. The strut C, 3 ft. 1½ ins. by 2 ins. by ⅞ in., will require a stout hinge for the same reason, and may also be tied to frame by a length of whipcord passing through a screw eye in strut, and knotted to a screw-eye behind

FIG. 1.
A CHILD'S EASEL.

each upright as shown, which will relieve the hinge of much of the strain it would certainly get. The lower rail D (Fig. 3), 15 ins. by 2 ins. by ⅞ in., is tenoned right through as before, and would be fixed at a height of, say, 12 ins. from ground, so as to allow the necessary knee-room for the juvenile artist when sitting. It will be noticed that a tray E is also provided as resting-place for the young gentleman's chalks—though probably it will be the young lady who more often makes use of the same—this being supported on loose pegs, F, in spaced holes. Size for tray, which may be made out of a piece of ordinary ½ in. matching, 18 ins. by 2⅜ ins. by ⅜ in., glued and pinned together as in section shown (E). The pegs should be of hardwood —mahogany, birch, or beech, say, 4 ins. by ½ in.

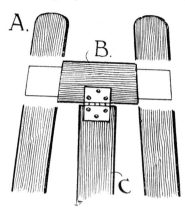

FIG. 2.—DETAILS OF TOP.

diameter, or so, and headed so as to serve as a stop for the tray. The holes might be spaced every three inches.

A word may be said for Fig. 4. which indicates an easel that will pack close or splay out as required. The uprights are cut as for Fig. 1, but when edge to edge with the strut (also 3 ft. 6 ins. long) between, they are bevelled away at top as indicated in Fig. 5, and connected by a round end tongue of 2½ ins. by ¼ in. hardwood fixed at G, but pinned into uprights A, so that these turn when the easel is opened out as at Fig. 4. A stiffening support is obtained by inserting a slip, H, 18 ins. by 1½ ins. by ¼ in., loosely through mortises in the uprights, so that it can be withdrawn when the easel is put aside. This slip is notched where it projects at ends for the convenience of hanging a duster or material satchel. In hingeing the strut for either pattern—Fig. 1 or Fig. 4—the edges immediately behind the hinge will be slightly bevelled away, as hinted at J (end view). The uprights and strut when closed up as at Fig. 5

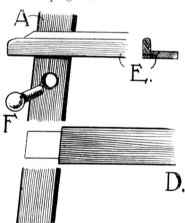

FIG. 3.—LOWER DETAILS.

are sufficiently held together by a tongue in the strut, 4 ins. by 1 in. by ¼ in., in the manner sketched at Fig. 6. The blackboard might be made about 20 ins. by 16 ins. by ¾ in., clamped up with 2-in. clamps, and the corners rounded off to prevent our artist from being unpleasantly reminded of their presence when lifting his board about.

A preparation for the blackboard surface is given as : 3 ozs. finest flour emery, 4 ozs. lampblack, 2 ozs. ultramarine blue ; grind well together ; add ½ lb. shellac in 2 quarts wood spirit ; keep constantly stirred when using.

A summary of parts required is added, net finished sizes for Fig. 1 being given.

2 uprights A, 3 ft. 6 ins. by 2 ins. by ⅞ in.
1 rail B, 7½ ins. by 2 ins. by ⅞ in.
1 strut C, 3 ft. 1½ ins. by 2 ins. by ⅞ in.
1 rail D, 1 ft. 3 ins. by 2 ins. by ⅞ in.
1 tray E, 1 ft. 6 ins. by 2 ins. by ½ in.
1 lipping, 1 ft. 6 ins. by 1 in. by ⅜ in.
2 pegs, 4 ins. by ½ in. diam.
One 1½ ins. brass butt hinge.

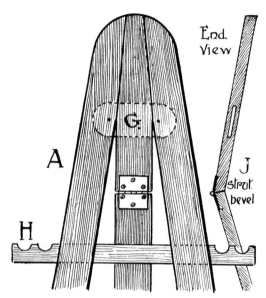

FIG. 4.—ALTERNATIVE DETAILS.

It may be added that, by fixing the lower rail D at a suitable height from the ground Fig. 1 could be used as an easel to go with the child's folding-chair given in issue of December 19th, 1908. or,

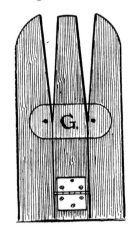

FIG. 5.—TOP CLOSED·

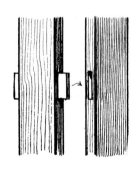

FIG. 6.
TONGUES FOR KEEPING EASEL TOGETHER.

as has been suggested, both could be made to a smaller size as toys, pure and simple, in which case the easel might come out at 1 ft. 9 ins. long, of 1 in. by ½ in. material, with a spread of 4 ins. at top and 10 ins. at ground.

MAHOGANY varies in price according to figure, colour, and texture, from 4d. to 30s. per foot ; the higher-priced logs, of course, being cut into veneers.

GARDEN WHEELBARROW

THE garden wheelbarrow shown at Fig. 1 can be easily made by anyone having a fair command of the ordinary bench tools, such as saw, plane, chisel and brace and bit. The wheel, which is generally a stumbling point with the novice, is easily constructed and when hooped it is quite satisfactory; in fact, a wheel made on the principle shown has already worn out one barrow body part, and is still in good condition and likely to last longer than the second wheelbarrow body.

which engage with the front board, H, by nailing from the front of the barrow.

Fit the piece I, and nail it to the ends H, after which fix the brackets C. Piece D, which steadies the legs, is now nailed in position.

To fit K, take a piece of wood, about 6 ins. longer than you think will be required, and plane its edges so as to bed against the side G and the front board H. When neatly fitted to the required angle, sketch a line with your pencil to what appears to be the correct

FIG. 1.—GARDEN WHEELBARROW: STRONG, USEFUL AND EASILY CONSTRUCTED.

THE STRINES, or handles, should be made out of ash or oak; the mortise holes should be bored out and then cut with the chisel to the sizes shown at Fig. 2.

THE SLOATS, or cross rails, are 3 ins. wide in the centre and taper to 2¾ ins. at the ends. They thus form a wheelwright's self wedging tenon. The sloats may be made of oak, ash, or elm in accordance with any odd pieces of wood that may be handy.

FRAME.—Begin by making the barrow frame, as shown at Fig. 2; after which fix the two legs, F, by securing them with a long ¾ in. or ½ in. bolt, which should run completely through the frame and be secured with a suitable washer and nut at the other side. This bolt and the hoop and axle will be all the metal work you will require to get made at the local smithy, as all other portions are of timber.

Fix in the bottom of the barrow out of ⅝ in. tongued and grooved boarding. This bottom portion is nailed on to the sloats; it hangs over the wheel about ½ in., and over the handle sloat 1 in. Select suitable boarding for the barrow bottom before you set out for the mortise holes. You will then be able to arrange for the sloats to stand down below the top edge of the strines exactly the correct thickness of the bottom boarding and thus save yourself much unnecessary labour of planing off the bottom board flush and level with the top edge of the strines.

THE TWO BRACKETS, B, are now fixed in position by skew-nailing them from the top, as shown in the detail drawing, and putting a good nail or screw from the under side of the strine.

THE FRONT PIECE, H, is planed slightly on the bevel at its bottom edge, and nailed on to the brackets B.

Next, take the sides, G, and bevel the bottom edge so that it beds on the strine, whilst its side leans outwards and beds on the leg F. When the sides are fitted in a satisfactory manner, nail them to the leg F from the inside of the barrow, and nail their ends

angle that will fit the strine. Saw the piece K to the sketched line and, holding it to bed against the barrow side and the front, slide it down and see if it makes a good joint with the strine. It will probably be slightly out, but it will enable you to see the exact part that requires paring off with the chisel.

Repeat this " cut and try " method until the desired joint is obtained; then cut off the portion at the top of piece K, which was left considerably longer than you required, so as to allow for fitting, and nail it in position to the strine, front and the side. Ease off the corners of H and G, as shown at Fig. 1.

WHEEL.—The wood for the wheel should be of ash or oak. Plane up the two cross pieces and halve them as shown at Fig. 3. Find the centre, and mark out the diameter of the wheel; the circumference of the circle will coincide with the angle point on the cross rails. Set out the end of the cross rails and cut the tenons with bevelled shoulders, as shown at Fig. 3. The bevelled shoulders make an angle of 45 degrees with the edges of the cross rails.

Slot mortise the rim rails, A, to fit the tenons, knock them up in their positions, and again mark out the complete circle. Take the rails A off the cross rails and saw and spokeshave them to the required line. Fix the wheel together by smearing the joints with thick paint and put a fine nail or two in the joints, so as to hold all together until the blacksmith hoops the wheel. A square hole is cut through the centre of the wheel after it is hooped, and the axle is driven into this mortise hole and the wheel secured by using a washer and suitable nut.

The small axle brackets, J, are bored only half way through their thickness, and this hole receives the axle. These brackets should be of hard wood, such as ash.

THE BRACKETS, B and J, are held at the front with a ¾ in. bolt and nut, which goes through the strine.

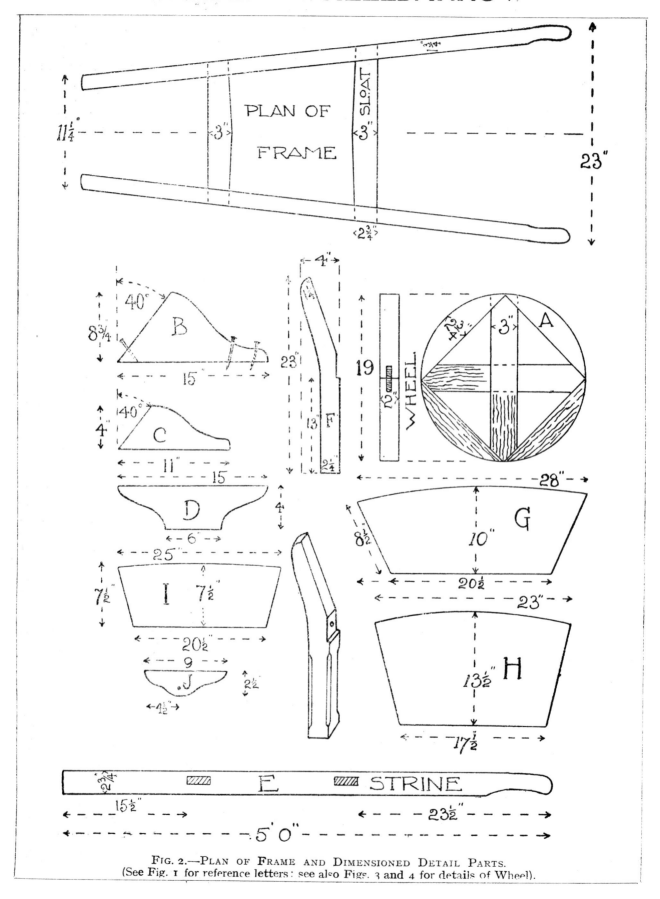

FIG. 2.—PLAN OF FRAME AND DIMENSIONED DETAIL PARTS.
(See Fig. 1 for reference letters : see also Figs. 3 and 4 for details of Wheel).

A NEW Government restriction order in connection with the supply of magazines and periodicals has just come into force. Publishers are now forbidden to supply papers on "Sale or return." This means that newsagents cannot in future return any *unsold* copies of magazines to publishers. Newsagents will thus be able to stock only those magazines and papers for which they have received an order for regular delivery.

This new restriction does not, of course, affect any reader of THE WOODWORKER who has already placed an order with his newsagent. Only, to guard against any possibility of error or delay, it will be wise to confirm this order.

Readers who have not yet taken the precaution to place an order with their newsagent should do so at once, otherwise they will be unable to procure copies. It will be understood that the new restriction bears somewhat hardly on newsagents, who cannot risk ordering magazines on the mere chance of their being sold. So far as readers are concerned, there is no hardship. All they have to do is to ask their newsagent to order THE WOODWORKER for them and they will receive it regularly.

Should any reader experience the least difficulty in obtaining the current issue (or back issues, bound volumes, or handbooks) please write and let the Editor know. Or, to save time, send a letter with postal order to THE WOODWORKER Offices and the books will be forwarded at once, post free. Address : Evans Bros., Ltd., Montague House, Russell Square, London, W.C.1.

Garden Wheelbarrow.—*(Continued from previous page).*

The other end of the bracket, J, is secured with two wrought iron nails. The barrow should be finished with three coats of dark green paint.

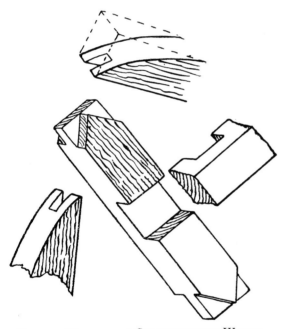

FIG. 3.—METHOD OF CONSTRUCTING WHEEL.

The following particulars will assist the worker :— Wheel, all of ash, 2 ins. thick, or, say, $1\frac{7}{8}$ in. finish ; legs, ash or oak, $2\frac{1}{4}$ ins. square at bottom ; brackets, B, C, and D, English elm, $1\frac{1}{2}$ in. thick ; sides (G), front (H), and back (I), of elm or other wood, such as white deal, 1 in. thick ; brackets (J), English ash, $1\frac{1}{4}$ in. thick ; strines, English ash, size as drawing ; piece K, ash or red deal, $1\frac{3}{4}$ in. by $1\frac{3}{4}$ in. ; barrow bottom, elm, ash, oak, or deal, about $\frac{5}{8}$ in. or $\frac{3}{4}$ in. thick, made in one piece or tongue-and-groove jointed.

Many workers leave the sides, back and front boards roughly sawn with their ends square, until they are fitting their work. The overhanging portions of H and I are afterwards cut off to the required bevel, which will be proved by nailing on the sides. This is probably the easiest method for a beginner to adopt.

How to make Plaster Casts.

Moulds for statuettes, medals, coins, and other objects are generally made of plaster-of-paris, which can be obtained from ony oil and colourman. Mix the plaster with water, working it quite smooth with a stick, and make it of the consistency of thick cream. Pour this into cardboard boxes. Meanwhile, oil the statuette or coin. Press halfway up in the plaster, and allow to remain until set. Then lift out the object, and a perfect mould should be obtained. Repeat the process with the opposite half, so as to obtain a set of moulds, giving an impression of the whole object. Of course, great care must be taken that such mould represents an exact half of the object. When these moulds are quite dry and hard (and plaster-of-paris is very quick to set) they may be oiled and a cast taken as explained below. For coins, medals, and very fine work isinglass moulds are sometimes preferred. The isinglass should be soaked in a little hot water, just sufficient to soften and make it plastic. Place in deep or shallow boxes as required. Oil the coins or medals and press into the isinglass, and dry over a hot plate or lamp.

When the moulds have been prepared, a small groove is filed in the edge so as to reach the depression. The two halves of the mould must be smoothed and adjusted so as to meet perfectly. The moulds are oiled, placed together and tied tight with tapes, but leaving the groove free. Now either prepare an imitation ivory haste, plaster-of-paris, or isinglass diluted in spirits of wine. Whichever preparation is chosen is poured into the mould through the groove very cautiously, shaking it occasionally, so that the mould should be thoroughly filled. If the moulds are large it is well to have two or three filling grooves, so that all parts may be reached, and air bubbles expelled. When the cast has thoroughly set, untie the tapes and take the mould apart. Cut off the projections formed by the groove, smooth away any ridge or unevenness where the moulds meet, and touch up with the finest glass-paper. The casts may be polished, or, if of plaster-of-paris, may be tinted, bronzed, gilded or silvered.

TOY MAKING—A WORKING CRANE

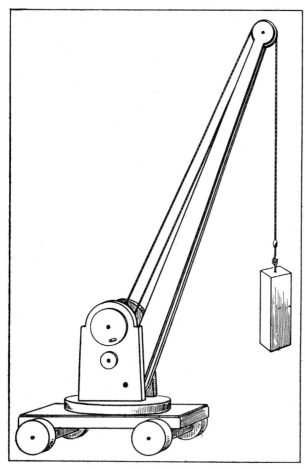

MODEL WORKING CRANE, WITH 24 IN. JIB.

A STRONGLY built model working crane provides not only an acceptable, but an instructive toy for the intelligent youngster. It gives him endless amusement and it also teaches him a lot. The crane we show here is intended primarily as a plaything. It does not profess to be a miniature of any particular type of builder's crane, but it is a correct model in so far as it will lift objects from one corner in the room and deposit them elsewhere.

The model has the four recognised movements : (1) Being on wheels, it is a travelling crane; (2) by means of a revolving disc on the stand it may be turned in any direction; (3) the jib rises from ground level to a vertical position; and (4) the object handled may be raised or lowered. To the boy interested in mechanics—and most boys are—a model of the kind means far more than an ordinary toy.

SIZE.—The model shown has a jib 24 ins. long. The stand (or base) is 10 ins. by 7 ins., and the body of the crane stands about 8½ ins. high, including wheels. This size will be found satisfactory if a really serviceable toy is wanted, and the scale is provided accordingly. Without altering the scale (and simply reading 1 in. as ½ in.) a small model of half the size can be made. In this case the thicknesses given may also be halved. Or, by drawing a new scale, a larger model than that shown, or one of intermediate size, can be built. A crane with a jib of, say, 36 ins., can be made without increasing the thicknesses of wood suggested.

WOOD.—Almost any wood may be used for the model, and—if to be painted afterwards—different woods which may be handy can be utilised. It may be remarked, however, that a heavy wood is desirable for the base—not because strength is required, but in order that the model may lift fairly heavy objects.

STAND (A).—For this we recommend a thickness of ¾ in. or ⅞ in., according to the kind of wood used. To the underside of this stand screw two wheel battens (B), which may be 7½ ins. long to project ¼ in. at each side. The wheels (C), which may be 2 ins. in diameter and ¾ in. thick, are screwed to the ends of the battens, thin metal washers being placed at each side of the wheel. The stand is shown with a simply moulded top edge. Instead of this it may be chamfered or merely rounded. A hole is bored in the centre of the stand to receive a bolt which will afterwards secure the revolving base.

BODY OF CRANE.—The base of this is the revolving disc (D), which is 6½ ins. in diameter and ¾ in. thick. The uprights (E) are screwed to this disc, with a space of 3½ ins. between them. They are 6 ins. high. The width (4 ins.) across the base tapers to 3½ ins., and the semicircle has a diameter of 3 ins. A thickness of ½ in. should be used. It may be added that the uprights will be stronger if tenoned to the base, and if so an extra ¾ in. in length must be allowed.

Each upright has a ¾ in. (full) hole cut at *a* and *b* to take a length of ¾ in. dowel rod. The hole at *a* has the same centre as that of the upright semicircle. The centre of *b* is 2 ins. below this. Holes at *c* are also bored to take the screws which hold the jib spindle.

The revolving base, with its two uprights, is held to the stand by means of a bolt and wing nut (see Fig. 2).

THE JIB (F, Fig. 8) consists of two arms of 5-16 in. stuff, 24 ins. long by 1½ in. wide. These look better if shaped as shown, the straight part tapering from 1½ in. to ⅞ in., and the circle at the top having a diameter of 1¼ in. The width *across* the jib at the base is 3 ins., and at the top only 1¼ in. The arms are joined together by five lengths of dowel rod (as shown at G, Fig. 8). The dowel may be ½ in. (or may vary from ¾ in. at the foot to ½ in. at the top), and is screwed to the arms with round head screws.

The pulley wheel (H) at the top of the jib is 1½ in. diameter, and can be made as shown full size at Figs. 6 and 7. Two 3-16 in. discs are cut as Fig. 6; their edges are chamfered as at Fig. 7, and they are afterwards glued together, the bevelled or chamfered edges providing the groove. If preferred, an iron pulley wheel may be purchased. The pulley may be fitted with a hardwood dowel or an iron pin. To enable it to run freely, washers should be fitted between the wheel and the jib arms.

The jib is fitted to the uprights by means of a length of ½ in. dowel rod (I), which passes through holes cut in the lower end of the jib arms and is screwed to the uprights at *c*, Fig. 3. The dowel should be so adjusted that the jib does not jam on the revolving base.

WORKING THE CRANE.—Two movements of the model have so far been dealt with—it runs on

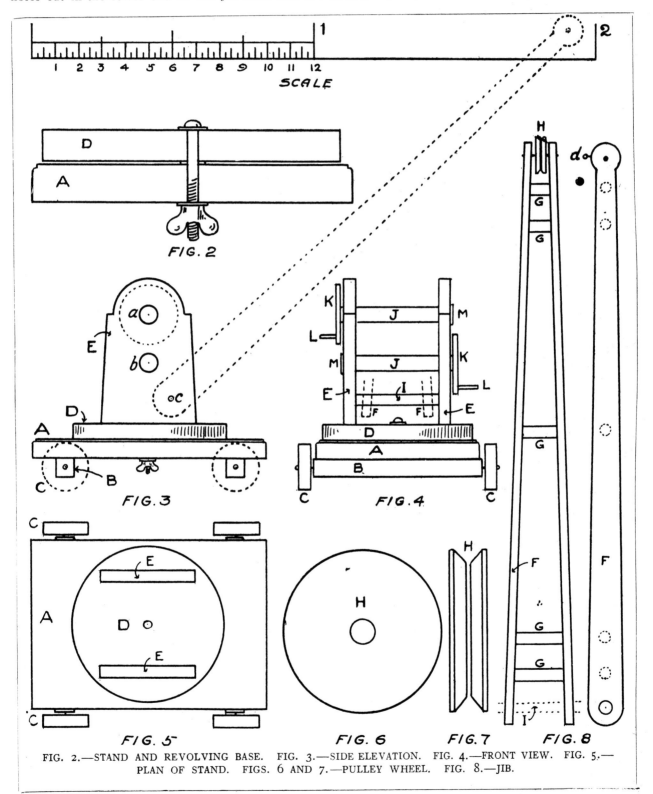

FIG. 2.—STAND AND REVOLVING BASE. FIG. 3.—SIDE ELEVATION. FIG. 4.—FRONT VIEW. FIG. 5.—PLAN OF STAND. FIGS. 6 AND 7.—PULLEY WHEEL. FIG. 8.—JIB.

wheels, and the body (with the jib) turns on the revolving base.

For the other two movements turn to Fig. 4. Take two pieces of ¾ in. dowel rod (J), about 4¾ ins. long each, and pass them through the holes *a* and *b* cut in the uprights. To the right hand end of one roller and to the left-hand end of the other screw wheels (K), which may be 2½ ins. in diameter. To each wheel fit a short piece of dowel to serve for a handle. At the opposite end of each roller screw a wood disc to keep it from slipping.

A chain, fixed to the upper roller and passed over the pulley wheel, has a weight and hook fitted to the extreme end and engages the object to be lifted. Another chain, fixed to the lower roller, is firmly attached to one of the dowel cross bars (G), near the top of the jib. Thus the two wheels (K) operate the two jib movements—the one raising and lowering the jib, whilst the other raises or lowers the object.

If the worker prefers to have both the wheels (K) at the right hand side, all that is necessary is to make the uprights (E) an inch higher, leaving a space of 3 ins. between the centres of holes *a* and *b* (Fig. 3).

Again, if greater leverage is wanted for raising the jib, the upper roller (J) may be allowed to operate this. In this case screw a small picture eye to the top of each arm, as at *d*, Fig. 8. If two chains are used, one attached to each arm at *d*, and both fixed to the upper roller (J), greater strength will be secured; nor will these two chains interfere with the pulley wheel chain which would then be operated from the lower roller.

The finished model may be varnished or painted according to the wood used.

		Long. ins.	Wide. ins.	Thick. ins.
A	Stand	10	7	¾ or ⅞
B	Two Battens	7½	⅞	¾ or ⅞
C	Four Wheels	2	2	¾
D	Revolving Base	6½	6½	¾
E	Two Uprights	6	4	½
F	Two Jib Arms	24	1½	5-16
G & I	Dowel Rod for Jib	12	½	—
H	Two Pulley Wheel Discs	1½	1½	3-16
J	Dowel Rod for Rollers	9½	¾	—
K	Two Wheels	2½	2½	¼
L	Two Wheel Handles...	1	¼ or ⅜	—
M	Two Roller Discs ...	1	1	3-16

Apart from the dowelling, the above sizes are given net. (210)

A POLE PIGEON COTE

PIGEON keeping is a hobby indulged in by many, and a well constructed pole cote is an ornamental feature giving quite an old world touch to the garden.

The cote shown here will accommodate eight pairs of birds. It stands on a pole (A), see Figs. 2 and 3, which should be from 6 ins. to 8 ins. square at the bottom, tapering slightly at the top, and rising from 10 ft. to 12 ft. above the ground. The pole must be sunk a few feet into the ground, and

FIG. 1.—PIGEON COTE.

bedded in concrete, or have a few large stones piled against it when finally erected.

The framework at the top consists of a crossbar (B), 2 ft. 3 ins. long by 3 ins. deep, and equal in width to the end of the pole. This bar is mortised and tenoned to the pole, and carries three bearers (C), 3 ft. 3 ins. long, by 2 ins. square, which are notched about ¼ in. over and screwed to it. The middle bearer is further secured by fitting two brackets (D) between it and the pole. The brackets are cut from 1 in. stuff, and are 1 ft. long on each side, screws being used for fixing. The alighting board (E) is laid over the bearers, and is made up to 3 ft. 3 ins. by 2 ft. 7 ins.

The body of the cote is shown in different stages of construction at Figs. 4 and 5. Boards 1 in. thick or thereabout are used. There are two sides (F), 2 ft. long by 2 ft. 3 ins. wide, between which fits the bottom (G), 2 ft. 1 in. square. The interior is divided by divisions (H) and (I), and supplementary bottoms (J). The division (H) should first be fixed, then the divisions (I), and lastly the bottoms (J), the whole being nailed in position.

The top of the cote is formed with a top board (K), made up to 3 ft. 5 ins. by 2 ft. 9 ins., and nailed over the sides and divisions. Two triangular boards (L), nailed at the ends of the top board, give the slope to the roof, which is formed with weather boards and a ridge roll, as shown at Fig. 6.

The boards which enclose the nests should be made to hinge or button to the cote, to give easy access to the interior for cleaning. The boards

will probably be battened at the top and bottom, and entrance holes are cut, as shown at Fig. 7. It will be necessary to cut notches for the battens in the divisions (H), as shown by the dotted marks in Fig. 4. Alighting boards are fitted at the front for the top nests, as shown at Figs. 2 and 3, the boards being screwed or nailed from the inside, and supported by small brackets.

The body of the cote is fixed over the alighting board (E) at the top of the pole with a few screws. The interior should be lime washed, and the exterior painted. (271)

Light Garden Swing

THE swing shown here is intended for young children, and as it is portable it may be used all the year round. In the summer it may be set up on the lawn, and in the winter in the nursery. The construction is quite a simple affair, while the cost will not run to more than a few shillings.

The following is the quantity of timber required :—A 34 ft. run of 2½ in. by 1¼ in. sound deal for the sides and bottom rails; a 2 ft. 9 in.

FIG. 1.—LIGHT GARDEN SWING.

19

PIGEON COTE AND GARDEN SWING

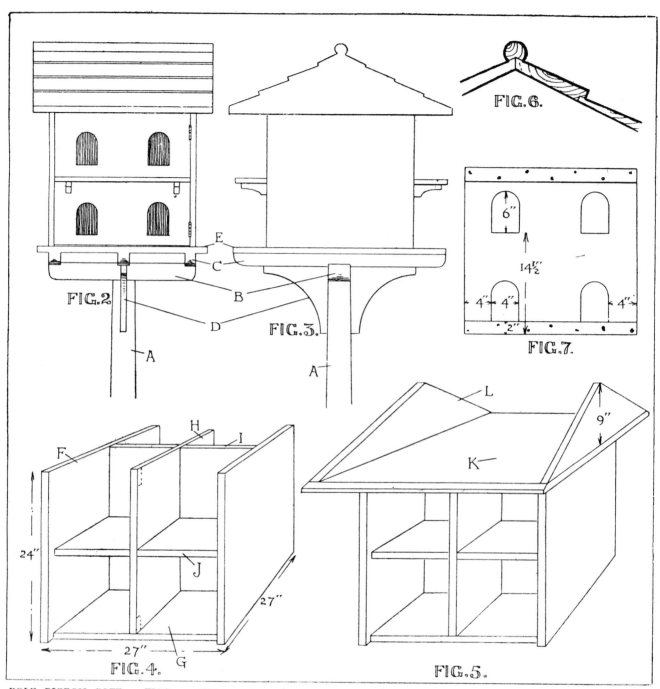

POLE PIGEON COTE :—FIGS. 2 AND 3.—FRONT AND END ELEVATIONS.   FIGS. 4 AND 5.—BODY OF COTE.
FIG. 6.—ROOF SECTION.   FIG. 7.—DETAIL OF SPACING FOR ENTRANCE HOLES.

run of 2 in. by 2 in. for the top rail; and a piece 1 ft. 8 ins. by 9 ins. by 1 in. for the seat.

The sides are framed up in pairs to fit one within the other, and are hinged together at the top.   The main frame to which the top rail is fitted is shown at Fig. 3, and the secondary frame at Fig. 4.   In each frame the bottom rails are tenoned into the sides (see Fig. 5), while in the main frame the top rail is also tenoned into the sides (see Fig. 6), and after it is fitted it should be rounded.   The joints should be glued and either wedged or pinned, and to give additional strength it is a good plan to fix small iron squares, similar

to Fig. 7, in the corners between the top and bottom rails and the sides.

To fix the frames at the top, holes are bored in the sides in the position indicated at Figs. 3 and 4, through which rivets are fixed, as shown at Fig. 8.   Iron washers are required under the heads of the rivets, and washers ¼ in. thick are placed between the frames.

The frames may be held apart (see Fig. 2), with long hooks, or with rule joints.   Hooks are perhaps the safest, but with rule joints the frames may be extended or closed without any bother.

20

LIGHT GARDEN SWING

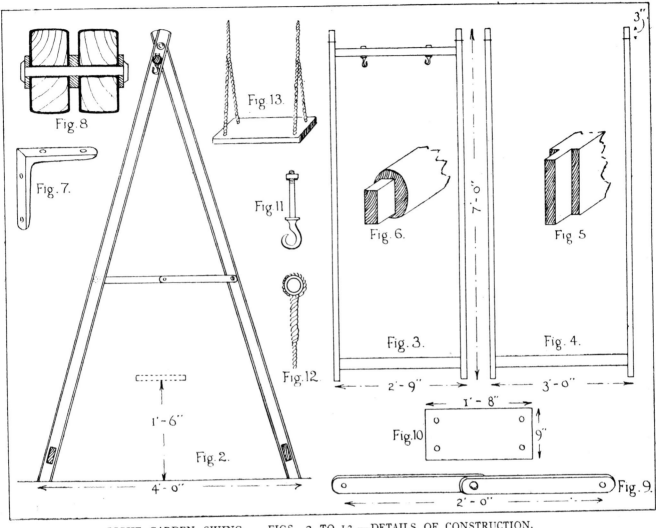

LIGHT GARDEN SWING.   FIGS. 2 TO 13.—DETAILS OF CONSTRUCTION.

Joints should be made as shown at Fig. 9, thin steel about 1 in. wide being used.

There are many ways of fitting the seat, the strongest and most convenient being shown in the illustrations. Four holes are bored in the seat (Fig. 10) for the ropes, which hang from iron hooks (Fig. 11) in the top rail. Thimbles are spliced to the top ends of the ropes (Fig. 12), and the bottom ends are passed through the seat and spliced as shown at Fig. 3.

The swing should be varnished or painted on completion.

(252)

Jarrah Wood.

JARRAH WOOD—sometimes called everlasting wood or Australian mahogany—is reddish brown in colour when freshly cut, but darkens with age to a deep rich mahogany colour. Very hard and dense and generally straight in the grain, with moderately interlocking fibres, it shows very little sapwood. The wood is hard, but very easily worked and polishes well; it resists the teredo pest. Practically proof against white ant, and not liable to attack by dry rot, it is unusually resistent to fire, especially in the case of floors and beams. For durability jarrah is undoubtedly one of the best timbers both in and above ground. For harbour and bridge work it is unique. Specimens have been taken from piles and girders of local works sixty years old, and the timber appeared to be perfectly sound and free from any sign of decay. If anything the wood seemed to be harder, more solid and apparently more durable than freshly cut timber. Its durability is also well known when used for railway sleepers. The tree attains a height of from 90 to 120 feet, with a bole of 50 to 60 ft. and a diameter of 72 ins. and sometimes more.

(217)

readily to fuming, turning an attractive grey tone.

MOUNTAIN ASH. Although having something of the appearance of ash (it is a pale buff colour), this wood is not a true ash. It is suitable for general construction work. It is used extensively for general building construction, railway carriage stock, coach building, motor-body frames, weather boards, casks, tool handles, oars and for cabinet work and high-class joinery. In the United Kingdom its main use is for panelling and interior decorative work.

GREY IRONBARK. There are many varieties of the ironbark in Australia. The grey is generally regarded as the best. It is very hard, and is used for wheels, carriage building and constructional work generally. Some varieties are quite light in colour, whilst others are more of a dark walnut shade.

The timber known as "narrow-leaved" ironbark is of great durability and tensile strength. It is used for outdoor constructional work—girders, posts, sleepers, bridge-work and for wheel-making. Close in grain, it is of a reddish colour.

BLACKBUTT. A hard, close wood used mostly for ship-building, sleepers, docks and general construction. It is highly fire resistant. Unfortunately it is somewhat liable to warp, and the surface often becomes ropey owing to adjoining layers of hard and soft grain. The colour is a yellowish-brown.

There are no true oaks in Australia, but several timbers of quite different botanical families are exploited under this designation, a looseness in the nomenclature being common in regard to the timbers produced in this continent. The principal so-called oak is the silky oak (above mentioned), also red silky oak, sometimes called beef-wood. Then there are the "shee" oaks, passing under the names of shingle oak, he oak, shee oak, river oak and other designations, all these timbers possessing an oak-like figure when quartered.

There are also some excellent woods of the acacia family, such as myall, blackwood and others. These are heavy, dense, hard woods particularly well fitted for fine turnery work, stick making and small articles of cabinet work. The first named, with a notable violet odour, has been utilised for pipe-making. (211)

GARDEN FRAME

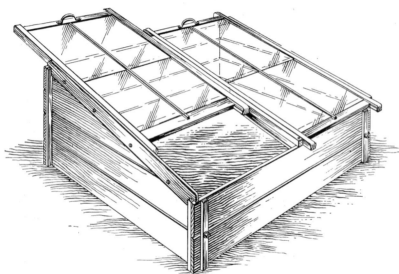

FIG. 1. GARDEN FRAME, SIZE 5 FEET BY 4 FEET
The size may, of course, be adapted to met individual requirements. The frame can be taken apart for storage in the winter.

IN view of the great utility of a garden frame it is well worth while to take some care in its construction so that it will last for several years. The life of a frame can be prolonged by constructing it so that it can be readily taken apart for storage during the winter months.

The frame described is so constructed that it can be easily taken apart and occupy little room in storage. The over all dimensions are approximately 5 ft. by 4 ft., its precise size being determined by the standard size of the materials employed. For example 12 ins. by 24 ins. 21 oz. horticultural glass is used for the lights and the sashes are made to suit this size of glass. The stiles and top rails are made from 2 ins. by 1½ ins. planed quartering. The bottom rails are from 4 ins. by 1 in. board, planed. It will be noticed that the stiles are allowed to project beyond the top and bottom rails, which construction makes for greater strength and simplicity in construction.

SASH CONSTRUCTION.—It is advisable to commence with the sashes. In setting out each sash allow ⅛ in. in excess of the width of the glass; also ½ in. overlap where the panes meet and where the glass overlaps the bottom rails. This is shown in Fig. 2. It will be found more satisfactory to cut the mortises before working the rebates, as the mortising is more easily done by having the full width of the stuff resting on the bench or stool. The joints used in the construction of the sashes are shown in Fig. 4; these should not present any difficulty as they are simple mortise and tenon joints. Care should be taken to see that the shoulders of the joints on the rebated or face side of each sash should project an amount equal to the width of the rebates.

The bottom rails are secured to the stiles by barefaced tenons and wedged in a similar manner to the other joints. One end of each bar rests in a housing formed in each bottom rail. This provides for the weight on each bar to be taken by the full width of each bar. The bottom rails should be ploughed as in Fig. 4 in order to provide a drip. The joints are put together with thick paint and wedged, and the sashes finally cleaned up with a smoothing plane. In glazing each sash, bottom putty only should be used and the glass secured in place by panel pins. Two pins should be driven into each bottom rail to prevent the glass slipping down.

FRAME CONSTRUCTION.—The dimensions of the frame should be such that the sashes overlap the front and back as shown in Fig. 2. The height of the frame at the back is 23 ins. and at the front 11 ins. It is preferable to arrange these sizes to suit the matching so that complete boards are used for the front and back. The matching composing the sides of the frame is held together by 2 ins. by 1 in. battens. These are nailed in place and the projecting end of each nail is clenched. The two ends of the frame are each held in position by 1 in. by 1 in. strips nailed to the front and back. It is helpful to prepare a strip of wood slightly wider than the thickness of the matching composing the ends and use this strip as a gauge when nailing the strips in position. When the 2 ins. by 1 in. battens are nailed in place, the battens at the front and back should be bored for the tie rod shown in Fig. 3. The holes should be bored so that each rod will lie parallel with the lower edge of the frame. Each tie rod is threaded at each end to take a nut and a washer. Care should be taken to see that the rods are threaded sufficiently to enable the front and back to be lightly clamped to the ends. The nut at one end of each rod can be fixed permanently by riveting the end of the rod. If the worker has not the facilities for threading, this can be done at small cost at a local ironmongers.

On each end of the frame is screwed a 4 ins. by ¾ in. batten which serves to retain the sashes in place. The ends of each batten project and rest on the back and front of the frame; thus the ends will be retained in their correct position with respect to the front and back. Centrally of the frame is positioned a runner which comprises a length of 2 ins. by 2 ins. quartering on the under side of which is screwed a 4 ins. by ¾ in. batten. The quartering is screwed to the top edge of the front and back. Sufficient clearance should be allowed so that the sashes slide freely. In order to take the frame apart it is only necessary to remove the two front nuts and remove the two screws securing the runner. On completion, the frame and sashes should be given a coat of white lead paint. A pleasing effect can be obtained by painting the frame green and the sashes white.

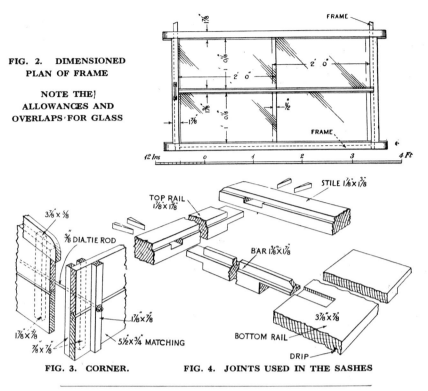

FIG. 2. DIMENSIONED PLAN OF FRAME

NOTE THE] ALLOWANCES AND OVERLAPS FOR GLASS

FIG. 3. CORNER.   FIG. 4. JOINTS USED IN THE SASHES

TIMBER ORDER

Sashes		Long ft. ins.	Wide ins.	Thick ins.
Top Rails (1)	.	5 0	2	1
Bottom rails (1)	.	5 0	,6	1
Stiles (4)	. .	4 9	2	1
Bars (2)	. .	4 3	2	1½

Frame				
Matching Front (2)	.	4 6	5½	¾
,, Back (4)	.	4 6	5½	¾
,, Ends (6)	.	4 3	5½	¾
,, ,, (2)	.	2 3	5½	¾
Battens (1)	.	13 0	2	1
,, (1)	.	13 0	1	1
Runner (1)	.	5 0	2	2
,, (1)	.	5 0	4	¾
Side Battens (2)	.	4 6	4	¾

The widths and thicknesses given are nominal. All lengths are full. (214)

THE WOODWORKER VOLUME for 1937 bound in dark green cloth (size 10½ ins. by 8½ ins.) and with full index, may be had through any bookseller or newsagent, price 6/6 net.

Binding covers alone may be had for 1/- post free direct from the publishers: Evans Bros., Ltd., Montague House, Russell Square, London, W.C.1.

TWIST-BITS and augers are made in two distinct ways. The single-threaded point is used for quick boring; the standard double-threaded point for fine boring. Dowel bits for power feed machines have a square pyramidal point without a thread.

A NEW ELECTRIC DRILL

WE have been interested in a new electrical drill and the uses to which it can be put in woodwork. Normally drills of this kind are usually associated with metal work and with the fixing up of fittings for electrical work and so on. No doubt this will remain its chief use, but, from experiments we have carried out, we have found it to be extremely handy in the woodwork shop.

Perhaps its most obvious use is that of drilling screw holes. It saves a great deal of time and laborious work, but, what is perhaps more important, it can be used in positions which would be awkward, if not impossible, with the ordinary hand brace or drill. The reason for this is that the tool is held still, the drill alone revolving. Care has to be taken in some cases not to take the hole in too deeply, but this is just a matter of judgment. No doubt it would be possible to fit up a depth gauge if a number of holes had to be drilled all to the same depth. Another advantage the tool possesses over the hand drill is that it can be used near the end of a board without danger of splitting the grain. This is chiefly owing to its high speed.

The use which specially appealed to us was that of the preliminary drilling away of the waste when cutting a mortise. A number of holes could be drilled in a very short time close to one another, thus lightening considerably the subsequent chopping out with the chisel. The cutting of other joints could be simplified in the same way.

For blind dowelling the drill is less suitable, there being two difficulties. One is that the drill may drift a trifle when first applied to the wood. The other is the fact that, unlike a twist-bit, the drill has not a point, but a short straight edge. This makes it difficult to judge the exact position in which the drill will start. For through dowelling, however, there is no difficulty.

The electric drill with which we experimented was the Gilbert Junior. It takes drills up to ¼ in. and can be obtained for various voltages. It can be used for wood, metal, tiles, brick, etc., and is distributed by The Rawlplug Co., Ltd., at 35s.   (192)

A DICTIONARY OF WOOD. This is the title of a serviceable handbook prepared by E. H. B. Boulton. It does not profess to be a manual of timbers generally, and its feature is a series of a hundred small photographic reproductions which show the grain of the different woods named. On each opposite page are added brief details as to source, species, sizes, general properties and uses. The plates might perhaps, with advantage, have been larger, but even in their present small size they give an admirable representation of the grain and figure. The book is published at 3/6 net by Nelson and Sons, Ltd., 35 Paternoster Row, E. C. 4.

THE illustrations show a portable shed, easy to take apart and re-erect, often an important consideration. The preparation of a concrete site for a permanent fixture, was described last month but perhaps that type of foundation will be too much trouble when the position is temporary. In this case it will be sufficient to remove the turf and lay three deals, or planks, about 7 ins. by 3 ins. running lengthwise of the shed, at the front, back and middle. The foundation for the deals should be small piers of brick or concrete, three to each deal. It will be advisable to make a portable floor, in

AN ATTRACTIVE DESIGN THAT WOULD ENHANCE A GARDEN.
Length 9 ft. width 7 ft. Height to eaves 6 ft. 6 ins.

PORTABLE
GARDEN SHED

three sections, and the deals form a good seating for the floor joists, which should be 4 ins. by 3 ins. if it is intended for a workshop. Otherwise 3 ins. by 3 ins. will be satisfactory. An alternative is to form a concrete base, about 8 ins. wide, in place of the deals. In this case it should go all round with a strip down the middle to support the joists.

All the framing consists of 3 ins. by 2 ins. redwood with novelty sidings for the boarding, as shown in the illustrations. The span roof is covered with Western red cedar shingles and the whole makes an attractive shed for the garden.

The sections consist of back, two ends, and two front frames ; the roof is in two parts for easy transport. If the shed is made of larger dimensions than those shown, it is better to construct the back in two sections as shown by the alternative in Fig. 3. Also the sashes would be better divided and the middle post of the front frames carried through. The illustrations show working drawings, and consist of elevation, end elevation and plan, with isometric details to a larger scale.

PREPARING THE FRAMING

The end frames are 2 ins. thick and put together with halving joints. They consist of three posts, three horizontal rails, and inclined rails to the pitch of the roof at the top, as shown in Fig. 1. A piece is fixed to the top rails to provide a seating for the ridge, and it also serves as a fixing for the centre post. It should project at least 1 in. on the inside. The sidings are cut flush with the side posts, and 3 ins. by 1 in. strips are planted to cover the ends of the boards both on the ends and sides.

The back framing is 3 ins. thick as shown in Fig. 3,

and presents no difficulties. It consists of four posts and three rails, all halved together where they cross each other. The rails are housed into the corner posts and the posts are housed into the top rail.

FRONT FRAMES

The front consists of two separate frames, 3 ins. thick, one on each side of the door, as shown in Fig. 2. The joints are housed, except for the intersection between the middle post and bottom rail which is a halving joint. it is necessary to secure the feet of the door posts with metal dowels about 2½ ins. by ½ in. These will be let into the

supports whether it is in concrete or wood. If the glass in the sashes is too large to suit the reader a vertical bar may be included, or the middle post run through and four small sashes used instead of the two large ones. Fig. 6 shows the detail for the sill and the arrangement for the bottom rail of the sash. If the rebate on the sill is planted, 1½ in. stuff will be satisfactory. The details for the door post are shown in Fig. 7, which shows a planted stop for the door also serving as a cover for the ends of the sidings. It is also necessary to plant pieces on the posts at the sides of the sashes, between the sill and the siding above the sash. All the vertical framing can be prepared on the ground with the sidings nailed in position, or the frames may be boarded when erected.

ASSEMBLING

The separate pieces of framing should be erected and nailed together temporarily, so that the nails can be easily withdrawn, and the holes bored for the bolts B. It is better to use square-headed bolts. Snap heads have a better appearance, but if corrosion takes place it is a difficult matter to remove the nuts. With square heads spanners can be used on both head and nut. If the heads are considered unsightly they can be sunk into the framing and covered by the sidings, and they are just as effective. Two or three ½ in. bolts should be used at each corner, and it is advisable to use washers, especially under the nuts. The bolt holes should be large enough to allow for easy removal of the bolts.

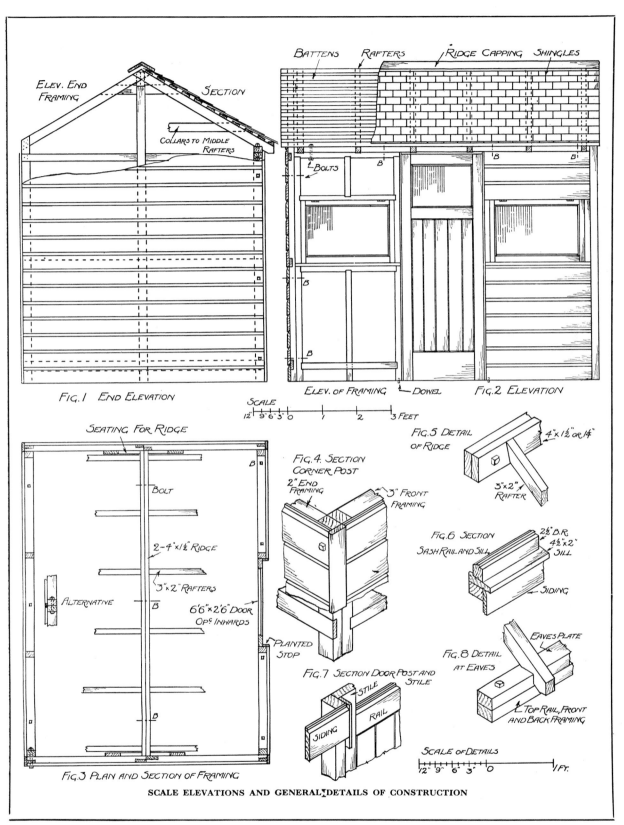

ELEV. END FRAMING

SECTION

COLLARS TO MIDDLE RAFTERS

FIG. 1 END ELEVATION

BATTENS   RAFTERS   RIDGE CAPPING   SHINGLES

BOLTS

B   B   B

B

ELEV. OF FRAMING   DOWEL   FIG. 2 ELEVATION

B

SCALE
12" 9" 6" 3" 0   1   2   3 FEET

SEATING FOR RIDGE

BOLT

B

2-4"x1½" RIDGE

3"x2" RAFTERS

ALTERNATIVE

B

6'6"x2'6" DOOR
OPS INWARDS

B

PLANTED STOP

FIG. 3 PLAN AND SECTION OF FRAMING

FIG. 4. SECTION
CORNER POST

2" END
FRAMING

3" FRONT
FRAMING

FIG. 5 DETAIL
OF RIDGE

4"x1½" OR 14"

3"x2"
RAFTER

FIG. 6 SECTION
SASH RAIL AND SILL

2½" D.R.
4½"x2"
SILL

SIDING

FIG. 8 DETAIL
AT EAVES

EAVES PLATE

TOP RAIL, FRONT
AND BACK FRAMING

FIG. 7 SECTION DOOR POST AND
STILE

STILE

SIDING   RAIL

SCALE OF DETAILS
12" 9" 6" 3" 0   1 FT.

SCALE ELEVATIONS AND GENERAL DETAILS OF CONSTRUCTION

PREPARING THE ROOF

When the framing is erected bolt the eaves plates along the front and back framing, as shown in Fig. 8. The positions of the bolts are shown in the plan, Fig. 3. It is necessary to use two bolts to each of the front frames, but three bolts are sufficient at the back. If the back is made in two sections as shown by the alternative detail in Fig. 3 four bolts should be used. Bolt the two ridge pieces together and place them in position. Then nail the rafters securely to the eaves plate and ridge taking care that the nails do not fix the separate pieces together. If the work is done carefully the rafters, plate, and ridge for each side should be rigid, and easily lifted off when the bolts are removed. The two middle rafters should have collars bolted to them, as shown in Fig. 1, to prevent the door posts from being thrust outwards.

The battens for the shingles should be 3 ins. by 1 in., and fixed as described in a previous article on small span roofs. They should run over the end frames about 2 ins. or 3 ins. The ends may be covered with narrow barge boards to give a more finished appearance. The gauge for the battens should be about 5 ins., as shingles should not have more than 5 ins. margin. The bottom batten should be $1\frac{1}{2}$ in. thick to serve as a tilting fillet.

The shingles can now be nailed to the battens taking care to keep them $\frac{1}{8}$ in. apart to allow for expansion. The nails should be galvanised, and 1 in. from the edges to avoid splitting the shingles. It is necessary to keep the nails 6 ins. from the butts so that they are covered by the shingle next but one above. This provides an attractive and serviceable roof for the garden and is worth the cost and trouble. It requires about 300 random width shingles, 16 ins. long, for the given roof, or 360 for an area of 100 sq. ft., or one square. Small wood gutters may be fixed to the feet of the rafters, but they are not usual for garden sheds.

DOOR AND SASHES

Any type of door may be used, but the example shown has a much better appearance than the usual batten door. It is easily made and is an interesting example of woodworking. The rebate for the glass is continued for the boards below, and the stiles are chamfered through, so there is no difficulty with the shoulders. The boards, or battens, are shown with vee joints. A pair of 4 in. butts are used for hanging the door; an ordinary rim lock is sufficient for securing the door.

The sashes are made from ordinary 2 in. by 2 in. sash stuff with a wider bottom rail, $2\frac{1}{2}$ in. or 3 in. They are hinged at the top with 3 in butts, and require a stay at the bottom for opening. A rebate may be planted round the inside if desired, but it is not necessary. It is advisable to throat the stiles and bottom rail to prevent water working through by capillarity. There is some protection, however, due to their being set back from the face of the sidings.

A shed of this description should be painted on the front and any other portion that is on view from the garden. The back may be creosoted as it is a better protection than paint. The shingles should be left untreated as Western red cedar does not require any protection and weathers to an attractive grey colour.

(316)

———

A THOROUGH KNOWLEDGE of the properties of various kinds of wood is essential to the man who is going to make a success of his woodwork. *Timbers for Woodwork* has been entirely revised and includes all the Empire woods. Published at 3/6 net by Evans Bros., Ltd., Montague House, Russell Square, London, W.C.1.

26

The SEE-SAW BOAT

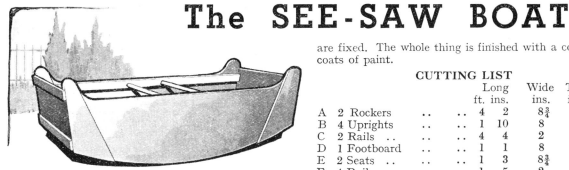

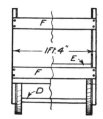

FIG. 1. AN EXCELLENT GARDEN TOY

THIS is a simple toy that will keep the youngsters amused for hours in the garden. It is provided with a pair of rockers and a seat at each end, and a couple of children can rock themselves up and down just as in a real boat. There is no bottom, but just a cross board (D) to form a foot rest. The whole thing is easily made from deal battens and cheap plywood.

The two plywood sides ($\frac{3}{16}$ in.) are 4 ft. 4 ins. long by 1 ft. 8 ins. wide. To mark out the sloping sides measure in a distance of 3 ins. along the bottom edge at both ends and draw in pencil lines to the top corners. The curve is struck by marking up $5\frac{3}{4}$ ins. and bending a lath to run through these points to strike the bottom edge at the centre. The top shape is 4 ins. down. All these details are given in Fig. 2. The shape can be cut out with the bow saw.

The two rockers A are about 4 ft. 1 in. long by $8\frac{3}{4}$ ins. wide by $\frac{7}{8}$ in. thick. They are placed in position against the plywood to enable the shape to be transferred. They are nailed to the inside of the ply. For the uprights B, $\frac{5}{8}$ in. stuff can be used. They can be cut economically from the board by marking a line more or less diagonally. They are nailed to the outside of the ply. Several long stout nails should be driven right through where the uprights B cross the rockers A, and be clenched inside. There are two top rails C and here again nails are driven through and clenched. Before they are put on, however, two holes should be bored in each to hold the handles. After all nails have been driven in the edges can be levelled all round.

The footboard D, the two seats E, and the end rails F are prepared next. Nail the footboard right through the rockers, and place the seats on their top edges. The end rails F are screwed on after the end plywood panels have been nailed on. In Fig. 3 the panels are omitted for clearness. The handles are 1 in. dowel rods, and they must be inserted in their holes before seats or footboard

are fixed. The whole thing is finished with a couple of coats of paint.

CUTTING LIST

					Long ft.	ins.	Wide ins.	Thick ins.
A	2	Rockers	..	..	4	2	$8\frac{3}{4}$	$\frac{7}{8}$
B	4	Uprights	..	..	1	10	8	$\frac{5}{8}$
C	2	Rails ..	..	..	4	4	2	$\frac{5}{8}$
D	1	Footboard	..	..	1	1	8	$\frac{7}{8}$
E	2	Seats ..	..	..	1	3	$8\frac{3}{4}$	$\frac{5}{8}$
F	4	Rails ..	..	..	1	5	2	$\frac{5}{8}$
	2	Panels ..	..	..	4	4	20	$\frac{3}{16}$ ply.
	2	Handles	..	..	1	5	1	dowel rod.

(362)

The whole thing is made easily from deal battens and plywood panels. The sizes given can be taken as a general guide, but need not be followed exactly.

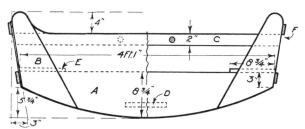

FIG. 2. SIDE AND END ELEVATIONS WITH SIZES

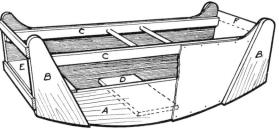

FIG. 3. HOW THE PARTS ARE PUT TOGETHER

COLLECTING A KIT OF TOOLS

WHEN collecting together a kit of tools it is sometimes perplexing to decide what is actually required. There are so many useful gadgets offered that sometimes a real hard working tool is sacrificed to possess one of those gadgets that prove disappointing in use.

Without condemning tools that have been designed for speed and accuracy, it is right that woodworkers should first learn how to handle simple tools. There is art in sharpening and setting a wood hand plane to plane veneers and there is art in sawing an accurate

mitre with a dovetail saw or in smoothing a joint, to fit close, with a chisel. Those things are all done by experienced woodworkers.

It is laid down that woodworkers must serve five years' apprenticeship primarily to become acquainted with tools. It is significant that the first quota of tools supplied to apprentices are simple tools of good quality. And, if experienced men teach beginners to use simple tools, it is advisable for everyone who is interested in woodwork to begin at the beginning and collect a kit that will stand the hard wear and tear of inexperience.

As a suggestion here is the usual list

of tools which are supplied to apprentices :
Jack plane ($2\frac{1}{8}$ in. iron).
Smoothing plane ($2\frac{1}{8}$ in. iron).
4 oz. Hammer.
8 in. Dovetail saw.
12 in. Tenon saw.
Set of bevelled edge chisels ($\frac{1}{8}$ in. to $1\frac{1}{4}$ in.).
Medium bradawl.
6 in. Set-square.
3 ft. Rule.
Ratchet brace.
Set of bits ($\frac{1}{8}$ in. to $\frac{1}{2}$ in.).
Pair of pincers (6 in.).
Wood scraper.
Set-stone.
Oil can.
8 in. Screwdriver.
3 in. Screwdriver.
Glasspapering block (cork).

With this kit of tools it will be found that almost any job can be successfully accomplished. (370)

WOODWORKER

JULY
1940

Vol. 44   No. 560

ECONOMY PIECE FOR THE LIVING ROOM
The DRESSER

ALTHOUGH scarcely suitable for the kitchen owing to the liability for dust to accumulate on the unprotected shelves, the dresser makes an invaluable item in the living room. At the present time it has an added appeal in that, considering its size, it requires a minimum of timber. There are no doors enclosing the upper portion, and, in the present case, there is no timber in the back. Instead, a piece of tapestry is stretched across the whole thing, the plates being supported by laths of wood screwed behind the tapestry. Another point is that, since the dresser is quite small, the thickness of the timber can be cut down considerably.

In design the piece has some unusual features, although in a general way it is founded upon tradition. The lower portion is virtually in the form of a box, fitted with two drawers and mounted upon trestles. The last named are made similarly to the old type of trestle table, having stretchers taken right through and held with wedges. At the bottom of the box the dovetails are taken right through and are allowed to project (see Fig. 3). With a few decorative gouge cuts they make an attractive feature. A similar idea applies to the upper carcase where the ends of the shelves pass through mortises and project outside.

The construction is fairly obvious and calls for little

ECONOMY
POINTS

TAPESTRY
BACK
IN PLACE OF
TIMBER

MINIMUM
THICKNESS
OF WOOD

PANELLED
DRAWER
FRONTS
AND ENDS
INSTEAD OF
SOLID WOOD

BOTTOMS OF
FIBRE BOARD

OPEN
UNDERFRAMING

SMALL SIZE

FIG. 1. IDEAL PIECE FOR THE SMALL MODERN LIVING ROOM
Main sizes are, length 2 ft. 9 ins., height 5 ft. 6 ins., depth 17 ins. There are many features in this dresser that make it economical in the use of timber. It is designed specially for the present circumstances.

explanation. Begin by making the box portion of the lower carcase. The ends are made up first, these consisting of panelled frames with grooved-in panels. Three rails (H and I) are dovetailed to them as in Fig. 3, and, to provide runners, filling blocks are added. These should make a friction fit and be glued in. Skew nails are driven in after the glue has set. After levelling, a guide is added.

Each trestle consists of a slab (O) tenoned into a top cross piece (N) and foot (P). An attractive effect is obtained by taper-chamfering the edges as in Fig. 2. When cutting the mortises in the stretchers to hold the wedges remember to take them a trifle *inside* the mortises in the slabs (O) so that the wedges bear against the last named and so draw up the joints. Screws are driven through pieces (N) into the underside of the box. The top (G) is slot screwed from beneath, the slots allowing for shrinkage, so avoiding splitting.

In the top carcase the top is dovetailed to the ends. The two shelves are tenoned. Bases are fitted beneath the ends to counteract any tendency for the whole to tilt forwards. It is advisable to work rebates in the ends and to screw the rails (F) flush in these. Then, when fitting the tapestry, the latter is tacked to the top, two sides and bottom rail, and the remaining rails

28   B

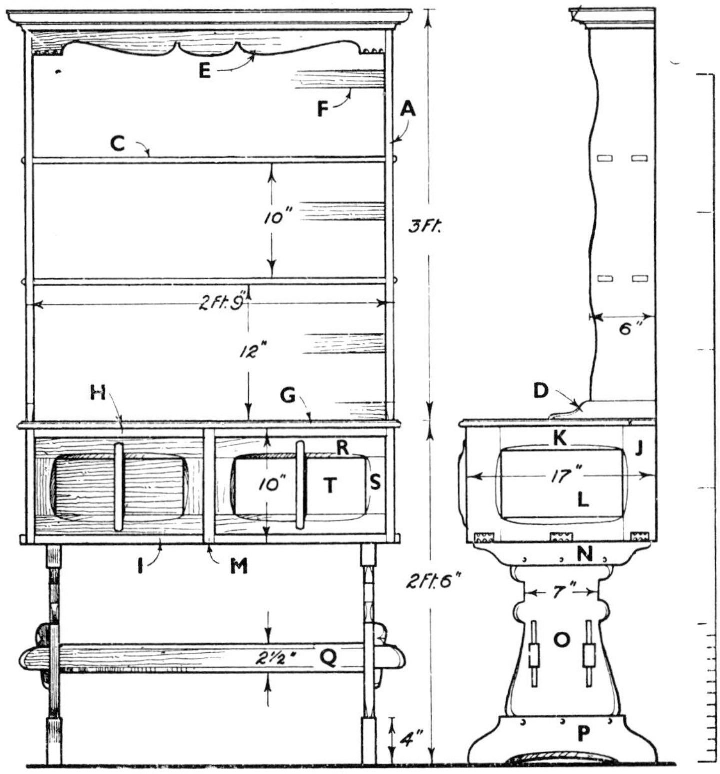

FIG. 2. FRONT AND SIDE ELEVATIONS WITH MAIN SIZES.

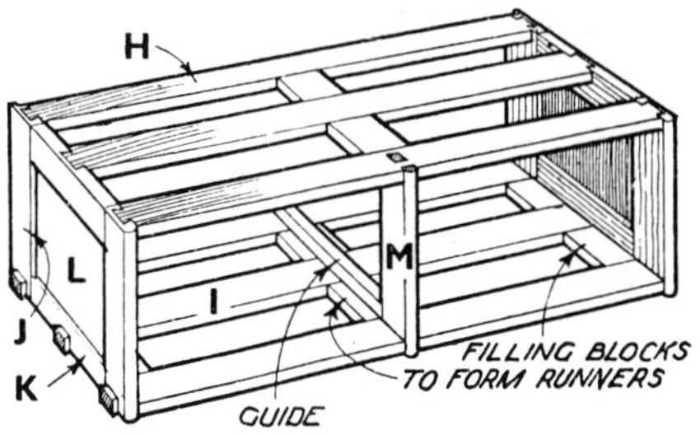

FIG. 3. LOWER CARCASE CONSTRUCTION.

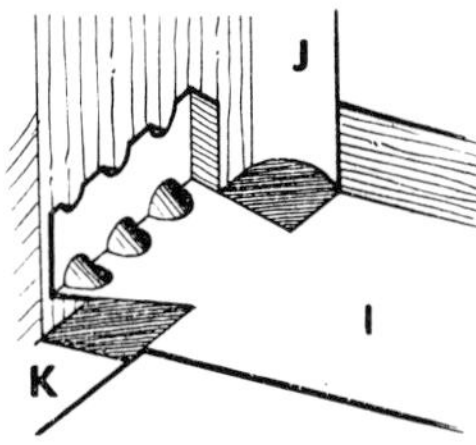

FIG. 4. UNDERSIDE OF JOINT IN CARCASE.

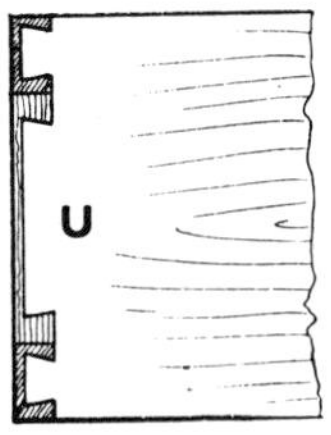

FIG. 5. DRAWER DOVETAILS.

screwed on afterwards. In this way they are concealed. At the top the cornice is mitred round, and the shaped piece (E) screwed behind it. Glue blocks are rubbed in at the ends at the back. Owing to the ends of the top being exactly above those of the box portion, it is impossible to drive screws upwards through the top to fix the upper carcase. The best plan is to drive one screw downwards through the front of the base (D), plugging the hole, and to insert another askew at the back. If preferred the upper carcase can be made to overhang at the back to allow for the wall skirting. (202)

CUTTING LIST

Top Carcase	Long ft.	Long ins.	Wide ins.	Thick ins.
(A) 2 Ends . .	3	0	$6\frac{1}{4}$	$\frac{3}{4}$
(B) 1 Top . . .	2	$9\frac{1}{4}$	$5\frac{3}{4}$	$\frac{1}{2}$
(C) 2 Shelves . .	2	10	$5\frac{3}{4}$	$\frac{1}{2}$
(D) 2 Bases . .		10	$1\frac{3}{4}$	$\frac{3}{4}$
(E) 1 Shaping .	2	8	3	$\frac{1}{4}$
(F) 4 Rails . .	2	9	2	$\frac{3}{8}$

Bottom Carcase	ft.	ins.	ins.	ins.
(G) 1 Top . . .	2	$10\frac{3}{4}$	18	$\frac{1}{2}$ or $\frac{5}{8}$
(H) 3 Rails . .	2	9	$2\frac{1}{2}$	$\frac{3}{4}$
(I) 3 ditto . .	2	$9\frac{3}{4}$	$2\frac{1}{2}$	$\frac{3}{4}$
(J) 4 Uprights .		$10\frac{1}{4}$	$3\frac{1}{8}$	$\frac{3}{4}$
(K) 4 Rails . .	1	4	$2\frac{1}{8}$	$\frac{3}{4}$
(L) 2 Panels . .		$6\frac{3}{4}$	$11\frac{3}{4}$	$\frac{1}{4}$
(M) 1 Upright .		$10\frac{1}{4}$	$3\frac{1}{8}$	$\frac{3}{4}$
(N) 2 Crosspieces .	1	$4\frac{1}{2}$	$2\frac{1}{8}$	$1\frac{1}{4}$
(O) 2 Slabs . .	1	4	$10\frac{1}{2}$	$\frac{7}{8}$
(P) 2 Feet . .	1	$5\frac{1}{2}$	$4\frac{1}{2}$	$1\frac{1}{4}$
(Q) 2 Stretchers .	2	$11\frac{1}{2}$	$2\frac{5}{8}$	$\frac{7}{8}$
Drawers				
(R) 4 Pieces . .	1	$3\frac{1}{2}$	2	$\frac{7}{8}$
(S) 4 ditto . .		$7\frac{1}{2}$	2	$\frac{7}{8}$
(T) 2 ditto . .	1	1	$5\frac{3}{4}$	$\frac{1}{4}$
(U) 4 Sides . .	1	4	$8\frac{3}{4}$	$\frac{3}{8}$
(V) 4 Backs . .	1	$3\frac{1}{2}$	8	$\frac{3}{8}$
(W) 2 Bottoms .	1	$2\frac{1}{2}$	16	$\frac{3}{16}$

Allowance has been made in lengths and widths. Thicknesses are net. Mouldings and small parts are needed in addition.

THE SHARPENING OF GOUGES

IT is by no means an easy matter to sharpen gouges or carving tools. One difficulty is to keep the edge of the tool straight. This requires considerable practice, and it will often be found that neither cabinet makers, carpenters, nor joiners have sufficient practice in sharpening these tools to be able to secure a really serviceable edge.

The proper way is to work the tool on the oilstone in the shape of a figure 8. Meanwhile the tool must be twisted by the action of the wrist so that the metal will be removed evenly. This is easily explained, but it is not an easy matter when it comes to doing it. Gouges and carving tools are of very different shapes, and with many of them to twist the wrist sufficiently is decidedly difficult.

Gouges and carving tools, particularly the latter, require oilstones that will give a keener edge than the oilstones that are recommended for ordinary woodwork. It will be best to rub off the " back " of the tool with the ordinary stone; and, if it is just a gouge that has to be sharpened only occasionally, it will hardly be worth while buying a finer stone for the finishing. If, however, carving is to be done, a good fine stone will be essential for finishing off.

In sharpening all edge tools to a good edge, the difficulty is to remove the burr. The coarser the stone is, and the more the metal is rubbed after the edge is attained, the thicker the burr will be. If a newly ground chisel or plane iron is sharpened well down, the burr will be so big as to be a piece of wire that can be pulled off with the fingers.

When an extra keen edge is essential, as is the case with carving tools (such is also very desirable with gouges), this burr must not be allowed to develop beyond the slightest degree. Fine oilstone slips will be necessary to remove it. One must sharpen on the flat stone a little (in the shape of a figure 8 as already indicated) and then remove the burr with a suitably shaped slip from the hollow side. This double process must be repeated. (843)

CYCLE STAND

SUITABLE FOR SCHOOL OR WORKSHOP

The extent to which pedal cycles are used now a days as a means of arriving at business or school is rapidly growing, and suitable stalls for their housing become necessary so tha. the machines can be safely left.

FIG. 1. ALTHOUGH SHOWN TO HOLD SIX CYCLES THE LENGTH CAN BE INCREASED

THE cycle stand shown in Fig. 1 is sufficiently substantial to withstand the wear and tear that it will be subjected to at school or workshop. Whilst six stalls only are shown the construction would allow of any extension up to a dozen stalls or so where space permits. Dimensions for the six stalls may be length 10 ft. or 2ft.

centre to centre of posts, allowing a trifle for access between. The whole thing may be of common deal, except the projecting arms which hold the wheels. These would be best of ash or other hard straight-grained stuff. Height of posts over-all is 2 ft. 6 ins., and projection of struts 2 ft. 8½ ins.—a 28 in. diameter wheel being shown. For juvenile cycles this projection can be proportionately reduced and some saving of wood can be effected by making each alternate post of 3 ins. by 1½ ins. stuff.

Fig. 2 gives an elevation of the back framework mounted upon blocks clear of ground. The posts are of 3 ins. by 3 ins. stuff, the face being finished to about 2¾ ins. wide. They are capped with blocks of 1 in. stuff nailed on as a

weathering. At the lower end they are halved as in Fig. 3. The top rail shows 3 ins. wide and can be ⅞ in. thick for six stalls or 1⅛ in. net if extended to twelve stalls. It is halved in position 3 ins. below top of posts and screwed or nailed. It is also halved to the intermediate posts as these occur. The second rail is 4½ ins. wide halved in position to agree. The lower rail is of a length to extend 2 ins. beyond each outside post, halved at spaced intervals to receive the posts. The bottom edge is notched in line to receive the struts upon which the posts bed. This rail is of the same width as the top.

Fig. 4 gives an end elevation of the stand showing the sloping arms gripping a 28 in. wheel, and also the arrangement of the forward end of the struts to which the arms are attached (Fig. 5). The struts are of 3 ins. by 2 ins., finished on the upper faces to the same width as the posts, about 2 ft. 10 ins. long. Wedge-shaped pieces of 1 in. stuff 6 ins. long and of the same width as the struts are nailed to their forward extremities above, and blocks of similar size but square nailed under to serve as risers. Corresponding blocks are nailed under each post at back to agree. The front edge of each strut and the blocks above and below are sawn away to give a slope up to the tilting wedge over which the wheel will roll.

The arms are of 3 ins. by 1 in. wood about 3 ft. 6 ins. long and can be screwed to the posts or, as noted in Fig. 3, can be birds'-mouthed to the rails and screwed or nailed to them as well as to the posts. At the front extremity of the struts the arms must be securely screwed on both sides as they will have to withstand a certain amount of impact. The edges of these arms should also be rounded in finishing whilst those who maintain some regard for the new and polished surface of their cycles will prefer to line the inner parts of the arms touched on entry with strips of felt to avoid such scratches as generally make themselves evident in course of repeated stalling.

By way of finish the stand may be given two liberal coats of creosote or it can be painted with good white lead paint. If the stand is likely to be exposed to varied weather conditions, remember to dress all joints with the creosote or paint before assembling, glue being omitted in any case. (380)

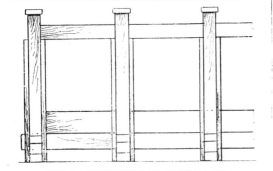

FIG. 2. ELEVATION OF BACK FRAME

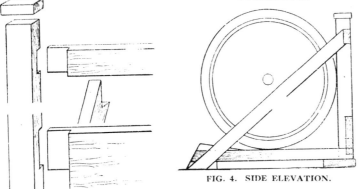

FIG. 4. SIDE ELEVATION.

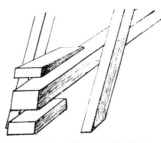

FIG. 3. CONSTRUCTION DETAILS.

FIG. 5. FRONT WEDGES.

DOLL'S HOUSE

DOLL'S HOUSE OF SIMPLE AND INEXPENSIVE CONSTRUCTION

Size over base, 24 ins. by 14½ ins. Height to ridge, 26 ins. (Sizes may, however, be adapted to suit material at hand).

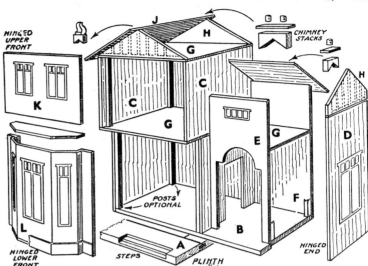

PERSPECTIVE SKETCH, SHOWING CONSTRUCTION OF HOUSE

IN illustrating this attractive yet simple doll's house, the chief object is to give the reader guidance in making a Christmas toy according to the material which he actually has or can readily obtain. Elevations and plans with dimensions are shown, this to suggest suitable proportions; but in the case of a toy it is permissible to make modifications such as the restriction on timber renders imperative. This understood, it is unnecessary to give a cutting list or minute directions as to assembly. If you have the material for making a doll's house of some kind, take the design as a suggestion and follow your own ideas as to size and details.

One or two hints may be offered. Plinth, or base (A) will be a frame of ¾ in. stuff, tongued or half-lapped at corners : front board 5½ in. wide and end and back lengths 2 ins. wide. To this frame the ground floor (B), of ½ in. stuff, will be screwed. Main ends (C) and wing end .(D) might be of ⅜ in. (jointed to width), or of 5/16 in. ply. If, however, corner posts, ½ in. or ⅝ in. square, are used, parts representing walls might all be of plywood. Arched front (E) may be ¼ in. or ⅜ in. ; back (F) 3/16 in. ply ; floors (G) ¼ in. ply ; (H) ⅜ in. ; roof parts (J) 3/16 in. ply. Chimney stacks will be ¾ in. or ⅞ in. (soft wood), with tops of 3/16 in. and pots

of ¾ in. dowel rod.

For upper front (K), which is a hinged door, use ⅜ in. Lower front (L) is built up of ¼ in. or ⅜ in. to form a bay window. Note that a top and bottom are provided to hold all secure. This complete front is hinged to open. Wing end (D) is also hinged to open. All fixing can be done with nails, screws and glue.

Most of the ornamentation can be done by painting. For windows, rectangular openings may be cut as required and fitted with glass. Sills, architraves, etc., are then added by means of 1/16 in. or 1/32 in. narrow plywood strip glued on. Much of the realistic effect will be due to judicious painting.   (926)

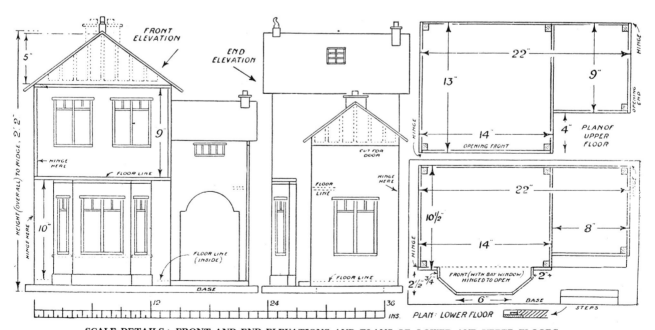

SCALE DETAILS : FRONT AND END ELEVATIONS AND PLANS OF LOWER AND UPPER FLOORS

WOODWORKER

VOL. 48 **DECEMBER, 1944** No. 613

TEN USEFUL BOXES
Ideal Christmas Presents

THE sizes of the various items may be adapted to suit the material available.

(A) Cash Box.—Dovetail together and cut across for caddy lid. Bottom is rebated in and top glued down and neatly beaded. Shaped handles are screwed from inside. An inner tray could be added. 2 sides 10 ins. by $4\frac{1}{4}$ ins. by $\frac{3}{8}$ in.; 2 ends, $5\frac{1}{4}$ ins. by $4\frac{1}{4}$ ins. by $\frac{7}{16}$ in.; bottom, $9\frac{3}{4}$ ins. by 5 ins. by $\frac{5}{16}$ in.; top, $9\frac{3}{4}$ ins. by 5 ins. by $\frac{1}{4}$ in.; for 2 toes, $10\frac{1}{2}$ ins. by $1\frac{1}{2}$ ins. by $\frac{1}{2}$ in.; for 2 handles, $3\frac{1}{4}$ ins. by $2\frac{1}{4}$ ins. by $\frac{7}{8}$ in. Linings from $\frac{1}{8}$ in.

(B) Cutlery Box.—2 ends, 9 ins. by $3\frac{1}{2}$ ins. by $\frac{3}{8}$ in.; 2 sides, 12 ins. by 2 ins. by $\frac{5}{16}$ in.; bottom, $12\frac{1}{2}$ ins. by $9\frac{1}{2}$ ins. by $\frac{3}{8}$ in.; 2 divisions, 12 ins. by $2\frac{1}{8}$ ins. by $\frac{1}{4}$ in.

(C) Tea Caddy.—2 ends, $5\frac{1}{4}$ ins. by $4\frac{3}{4}$ ins. by $\frac{3}{8}$ in.; 2 sides, 8 ins. by $4\frac{3}{4}$ ins. by $\frac{3}{8}$ in.; top, 8 ins. by $4\frac{7}{8}$ ins., by $\frac{5}{8}$ in (shaped to section shown); top lining, $7\frac{1}{2}$ ins. by $4\frac{1}{4}$ ins. by $\frac{3}{16}$ in.; bottom, $7\frac{3}{4}$ ins. by $3\frac{3}{4}$ ins. by $\frac{1}{4}$ in.; for 4 toes, 6 ins. by $1\frac{1}{4}$ ins. by $\frac{1}{4}$ in.

Sides may be rebated (see X) and glue-blocked with a bead. Bottom is rebated in (see Z). Note that toes are glued on anglewise.

(D) Hall Brush or Glove Box.—2 ends, 6 ins. by $4\frac{1}{2}$ ins. by $\frac{7}{16}$ in.; 2 sides, 13 ins. by $4\frac{1}{2}$ ins. by $\frac{7}{16}$ in.; Top, 13 ins. by 6 ins. by $\frac{3}{8}$ in.; bottom, $12\frac{3}{4}$ ins. by $5\frac{3}{4}$ ins. by $\frac{1}{4}$ in.; 2 feet, $6\frac{3}{4}$ ins. by $1\frac{3}{4}$ ins. by $\frac{5}{8}$ in.

(E) Cigarette Box.—As the box is suitable also for playing cards, jewellery, etc., sizes may be adapted as required. On the scale diagram thicknesses are indicated for a box up to, say, 8 ins. by 5 ins. by from $2\frac{1}{2}$ ins. to 5 ins. high. Thicknesses may be slightly reduced for the smaller sizes.

(F) Nail Box.—2 sides, 13 ins. by $2\frac{1}{2}$ ins. by $\frac{1}{2}$ in.; 2 ends, 10 ins. by $2\frac{1}{2}$ ins. by $\frac{1}{2}$ in; mid partition, 13 ins. by $4\frac{1}{2}$ ins. by $\frac{1}{2}$ in. (Note shaping and hand hole). Cross divisions as required will be about $4\frac{1}{2}$ ins. by $2\frac{1}{2}$ ins. by $\frac{5}{16}$ in. Bottom, 14 ins. by 11 ins. by $\frac{1}{2}$ in. Corners will be through-dovetailed and then mid-partition housed to ends. Cross divisions must also be housed, and the bottom is screwed on. It is important to screw the mid-partition from below.

(G) Box (Kitchen) for Household Tools.—Bottom, 19 ins. by 11 ins. by $\frac{5}{8}$ in.; 2 ends, $10\frac{1}{2}$ ins. by $11\frac{1}{2}$ ins. by $\frac{5}{8}$ in.; 2 sides, 18 ins., by $4\frac{1}{2}$ ins. by $\frac{5}{8}$ in.; division, 18 ins. by 5 ins., by $\frac{1}{2}$ in. Handle bar (hardwood), 18 ins. by $1\frac{1}{4}$ ins. by $\frac{7}{8}$ in. Shape the ends as shown. The handle bar is through tenoned and wedged to ends.

The construction of these is so obvious from the diagrams given overleaf that no description is necessary. The cutting lists will prove handy in preparing the material.

Stop-chamfer as indicated and soften the edges with glasspaper. A box of this kind will be left in the white.

(H) Lady's Workbox.—Sides and ends will be dovetailed and afterwards cut across to separate the caddy lid. Bottom is rebated in, a mitred plinth being added below. The piece is suitable for veneering.

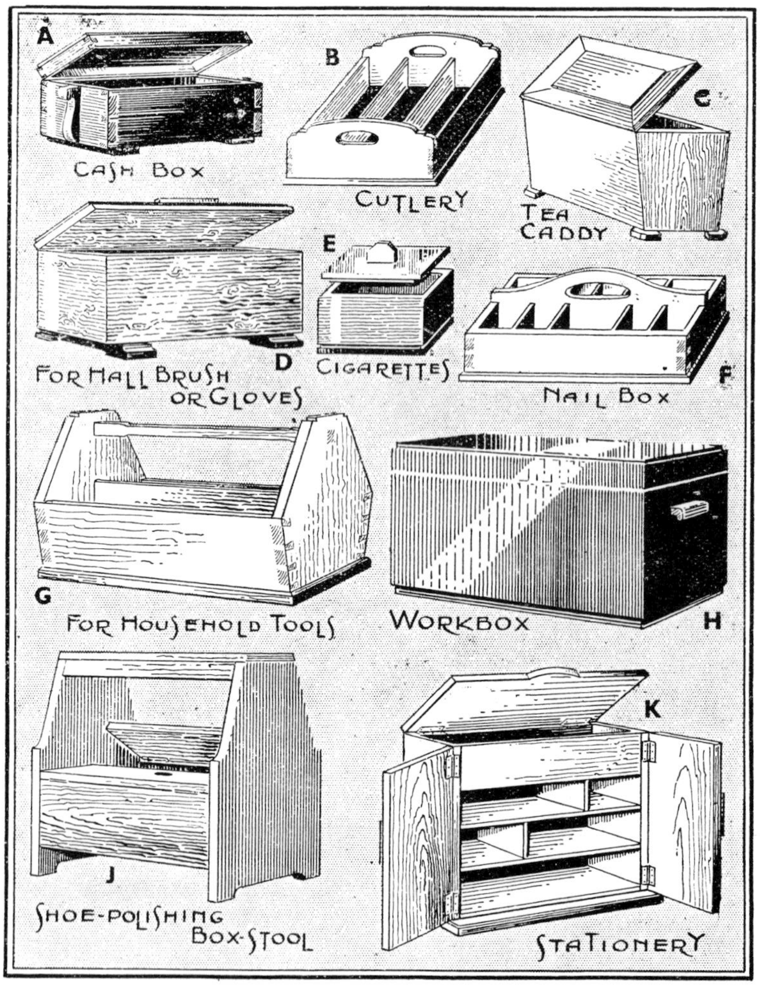

TEN ATTRACTIVE BOXES WHICH CAN BE MADE FROM ODDMENTS

(A) Cash Box, 10 in. by $5\frac{1}{4}$ in. by $4\frac{1}{2}$ in. (B) Cutlery Box, 12 in. by 9 in. (C) Tea Caddy, 8 in. by $4\frac{3}{4}$ in by 6 in. (D) Glove or Brush Box, 13 in by 6 in. (E) Box for Cigarettes or Cards, $5\frac{1}{2}$ in. by 4 in. by 3 in. (F) Nail Box, 13 in. by 10 in. (G) Box for Household Tools, 18 in. by $11\frac{1}{2}$ in. (H) Lady's Workbox, 15 in. by 9 in. by 8 in. (J) Shoe-Polishing Box Stool, 15 in. by $10\frac{1}{2}$ in. by 15 in. high. (K) Stationery Box (with doors), 13 in. by 8 in. by 11 in. high
Scale Diagrams and Details are given on next page.

ELEVATIONS WITH SIZES AND CONSTRUCTION DETAILS

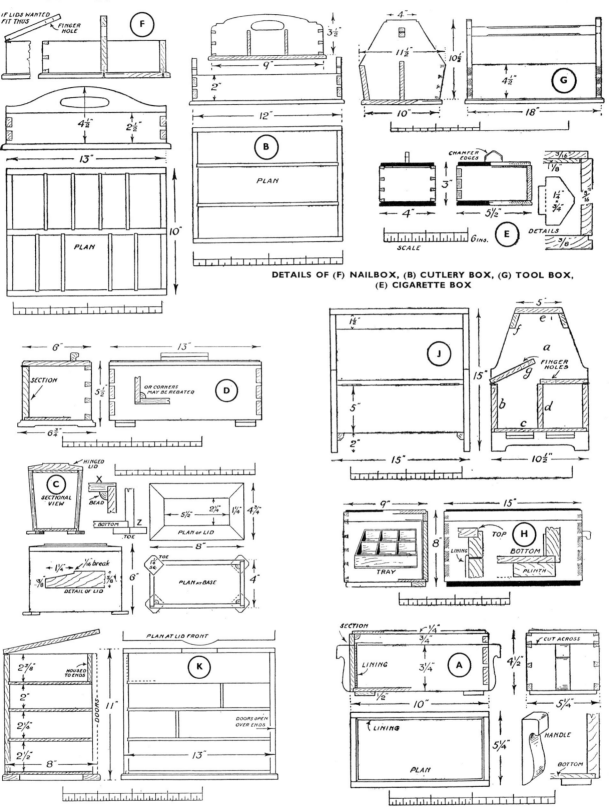

DETAILS OF (F) NAILBOX, (B) CUTLERY BOX, (G) TOOL BOX,
(E) CIGARETTE BOX

DETAILS OF (D) BRUSH BOX, (C) TEA CADDY,
(K) STATIONERY BOX

DETAILS OF (J) SHOE-POLISHING STOOL,
(H) WORK BOX, (A) CASH BOX

ELECTRIC HEATER FOR A GLUE POT

A reader has sent us a description of an electric heater he has made for a glue pot. The construction is very simple and will be of interest to other readers.

AN electric heater for the glue pot which will give good service and form a useful addition to the home work-shop can be made cheaply. A 750 watt porcelain element of suitable voltage can be readily purchased, and this is mounted on a sound wooden block $8\frac{3}{4}$ ins by 6 ins by $1\frac{1}{2}$ ins. The top edges of this are chamfered for neatness. The element is supported from the block, Fig. 1, by two $2\frac{1}{2}$ in. No. 9 countersunk head wood screws a, which are passed through metal tubes b, 1 in. long, the tubes serving as distance pieces. As only two fixing holes are provided on the element, Fig. 2, it is necessary to provide two further supports. These may comprise two 2 in. No. 9 countersunk head wood screws c, Fig.s 1 and 2. A slight space should be left under the heads of the screw to allow for the expansion of the element. The surface of the block below the element is covered with an asbestos cooking-mat cut to size.

For the purpose of wiring up the element and switch, vertical holes $\frac{1}{4}$ in. diameter are drilled through the block opposite the terminals of the element and switch. These holes lead to grooves cut in the base and these in turn communicate with inclined holes as shown by dotted lines in Fig. 2.

This arrangement will simplify the threading through of the wires. It is advisable to use power flex. As there is considerable heat below the element, it is best to make up two brass or copper connecting strips as shown in Fig. 3. The flex is soldered into the loop formed in the bottom of each strip. These strips will avoid having the rubber insulation in close proximity to the element with the resulting scorching of the rubber. Further, better contact will be made with the heater terminals than if the flex is directly connected to the terminals. Connection is made to a lighting or power circuit point by an adaptor or plug according to whether the heater is connected to a lighting or power circuit.

As 750 watts is nearly the maximum load for a lighting circuit, there is the possibility of the fuses of the circuit blowing if lamps and domestic appliances are switched on whilst the heater is in circuit. It is preferable to connect the heater to a power circuit. As a precaution against fire, the heater should be rested on a bracket or shelf well away from the bench or any position where there is danger of shavings accumulating. (404)

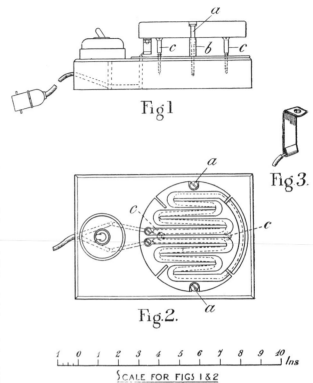

Fig 1

Fig 3.

Fig. 2.

SCALE FOR FIGS 1 & 2

SIDE ELEVATION AND PLAN TO SCALE.
Detail of the copper connecting strip at Fig. 3.

TEN USEFUL BOXES
(Continued)

Sizes are : 2 sides, 15 ins. by $7\frac{1}{2}$ ins. by $\frac{7}{16}$ in. ; 2 ends, 9 ins. by $7\frac{1}{2}$ ins. by $\frac{7}{16}$ in. ; bottom, $14\frac{3}{4}$ ins. by $8\frac{3}{4}$ ins. by $\frac{1}{4}$ in. ; top, $14\frac{3}{4}$ ins. by $8\frac{3}{4}$ ins. by $\frac{3}{8}$ in. ; linings from $\frac{1}{8}$ in. stuff ; 2 plinth lengths, $14\frac{3}{4}$ ins. by $1\frac{1}{2}$ ins. by $\frac{1}{2}$ in. ; 2 ditto, $8\frac{3}{4}$ ins. by $1\frac{1}{2}$ ins. Handles about 4 ins. long can be worked from $\frac{7}{8}$ in. stuff. Preferably they should be tenoned to ends. If a tray is added, this may be about $7\frac{1}{2}$ ins. by 7 ins. by $1\frac{1}{4}$ ins. and $1\frac{1}{2}$ ins. deep. Sides may be $\frac{3}{16}$ in. and bottom and divisions $\frac{1}{8}$ in.

(J) Box Stool for Shoe-Polishing.
—2 ends (a) 15 ins. by $10\frac{1}{2}$ ins. by $\frac{3}{4}$ in. ; 2 sides (b), $14\frac{1}{2}$ ins. by 5 ins. by $\frac{3}{4}$ in. ; bottom (c), $14\frac{1}{2}$ ins. by 10 ins. by $\frac{3}{8}$ in. ; division (d), $14\frac{1}{2}$ ins. by 5 ins. by $\frac{1}{2}$ in. ; top (e), 15 ins. by $5\frac{1}{4}$ ins. by $\frac{3}{4}$ in. ; top strips (f), $14\frac{1}{2}$ ins. by 2 ins. by $\frac{3}{4}$ in. ; 2 lids (g), $13\frac{3}{4}$ ins. by $5\frac{1}{4}$ ins. by $\frac{1}{2}$ in.

(K) Stationery Box or Cabinet.—2 ends, $10\frac{1}{8}$ ins. by $7\frac{5}{8}$ ins. by $\frac{7}{16}$ in. ; back, 13 ins. by $10\frac{1}{8}$ ins. by $\frac{7}{16}$ in. ; bottom, $12\frac{3}{4}$ ins. by $7\frac{1}{2}$ ins. by $\frac{7}{16}$ in. ; Top well front, $12\frac{1}{2}$ ins. by $2\frac{1}{4}$ ins. by $\frac{7}{16}$ in. ; three for well bottom and 2

shelves, $12\frac{1}{2}$ ins. by $7\frac{1}{2}$ ins. by $\frac{1}{4}$ in. ; 2 divisions, $7\frac{1}{2}$ ins. by $2\frac{1}{2}$ ins. by $\frac{1}{4}$ in. ; lid, 13 ins. by $8\frac{1}{2}$ ins. by $\frac{3}{8}$ in. ; 2 doors, $10\frac{1}{2}$ ins. by $6\frac{1}{2}$ ins. by $\frac{3}{8}$ in. ; 2 plinth strips, $13\frac{3}{4}$ ins. by $1\frac{1}{2}$ ins. by $\frac{5}{8}$ in. ; 2 ditto, $8\frac{1}{4}$ ins. by $1\frac{1}{2}$ ins. by $\frac{5}{8}$ in. (399)

Avoid if you can using a plane on a surface which has been glasspapered. The latter process inevitably leaves fine granules of glass in the pores of the wood, and these soon take off the edge of the cutter.

FIELDED PANEL
(Continued from page 192)

gauge line. The direction of the cut must be in accordance with the grain and must be varied to avoid splintering. In the concave portion of the curve it may be an advantage to use a flat gouge, working this outwards from the centre of the panel, though it cannot be started right up against the corner of the rebate. Remove small chips, and work away until the chamfer is nearly down to depth. You can tell when it is right because the mitres form clearly defined lines.

The external mitres will resolve themselves automatically as the waste is removed. They should run exactly from corner to corner without kinks. It is rather more difficult to form the internal mitres, and the best plan is to make a vertical cut with the chisel right along the mitre, marking the position with pencil and straight-edge. Do not cut in unnecessarily deep—just enough to enable the chips to come away cleanly as the waste is removed. This final stage is shown in Fig. 6.

Even with the most careful chiselling a certain lumpiness is inevitable, and a fine file should now be worked around the chamfer to smooth out imperfections. In parts a flat file is used, and a half-round file for the concave portions. Take special care with the mitres, using a file with a safe edge, and working it along the line of the mitre.

A scraper now follows to take out file marks, and finally glasspaper wrapped round a suitably shaped rubber is used. Several rubbers of various shapes may be needed. Finish off with a fine grade of paper, again taking the utmost care not to overrun the mitres. (380)

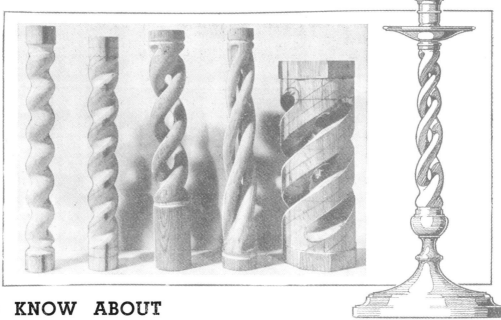

POINTS TO KNOW ABOUT
TWIST TURNINGS

We are all familiar with twist or spiral turning. It is usually associated with Jacobean furniture and was extremely popular a few years back. It was introduced into furniture during the 17th century, and was a combination of lathe work and carving. Today cheap twist legs can be cut entirely by machine, but they have neither a very good finish nor a good design. The best twist legs still require a good deal of carving, especially at the ends. They *can* be made entirely by carving*. It is not always realized however that there are several different kinds of spiral turnings, and here we explain the difference between them.

IT is easy to realise that once a man became interested in making twist turned legs he soon became embarked on many experiments. There is something extraordinarily fascinating about a spiral (who has not been intrigued by a twist bit which "appears" to rise instead of sink when it is driven into the wood?)

One can imagine how it started. A turner in roughing down a plain turned leg knew that as he moved his gouge along the wood it formed a fine spiral groove, but it was so slight that it amounted to little more than rings, and if he halted the tool for a second the spiral did become a true ring. If, however, he moved the gouge rapidly along the length the spiral became more obvious, as shown in Fig. 3. And if only he could move his hands at the same speed every time, if he could work the lathe treadle at the same rate, and if

he could place the gouge in the same cut every time he could so deepen the cut and bring it to a presentable shape.

That was the difficulty, and it was not until the slide rest was invented that the problem was really solved. In this the slide rest was geared up to the lathe so that it moved along the work at a controlled rate. In the meantime, however, the turner had only his pole lathe in which the wood was revolved first one way, then the other, the cut being made on the forward movement only. It did not lend itself to much in the way of experiment, and the result was that in early spiral legs the lathe was used chiefly for the preliminary rounding of the wood. The actual spiral was largely carved out with gouges, though the lathe was a handy means of holding the wood during the process. It was also handy for the final cleaning up with the file in which the latter could easily follow the groove already made and take out all inequalities. The same thing applied to the glasspapering.

Single-Bine Twist.—If you look at Figs. 1 and 2 you will see that this consists of a single bine or bead spiraling its way up the leg. There is only one, and it continues from top to bottom. The pitch may vary within a little, but generally it is arranged to be one in one; that is to say, if you imagine a nut threaded on to the spiral and the latter to be 2 ins. in diameter, it would rise 2 ins. on making one complete turn. It makes a strong leg since there is a good solid centre core of wood running throughout the length.

Double-Bine Twist.—Rather more elaborate if not quite so strong is the double-bine twist given in Figs. 1 and 2. It has a most attractive appearance, and if not cut in too deeply is amply strong enough for most purposes. You will see that there are two bines or beads joined together by a web. There being two of them, the bines are slighter in section, and this gives them a delicate

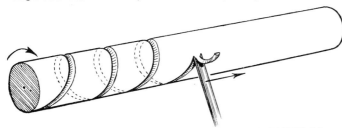

FIG. 2. SECTIONS THROUGH TWIST TURNINGS.
Single bine. Double Bine. Open double Bine. Open Triple Bine.

FIG. 3. HOW TWIST IS FORMED BY LATERAL MOVEMENT OF
GOUGE. AS WOOD IS ROTATED.

---

* *An article on making the open double-bine twist appeared in the* WOODWORKER *for August,* 1944.

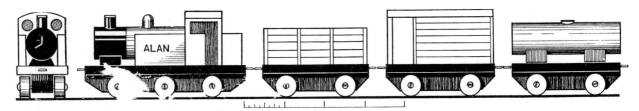

FIG. I. DELIGHTFUL LITTLE TRAIN MADE ENTIRELY FROM SCRAPS. THE ENGINE IS 4 INS. LONG, AND THE TRUCKS 2 INS.
This makes a really strong little toy and its cost is literally nothing since only small oddments of wood are used. The boiler, funnel, and wheels are made from dowel rod. Painting is simple if poster colours are used. These are water colours which dry quickly. They are fixed with varnish.

MINIATURE TOY TRAIN

Compare this with the crude toys offered in the shops at high prices. It has not only a realistic appearance, but is really strong. Purely as a matter of interest, the engine took two evenings only to make, the woodwork being completed in the first and the finishing in the second.

THERE are many additions you could make to this train : carriages, locomotive with tender, station, signal box, and so on. The simplest way is to draw them in full size so that the correct proportions are maintained.

Engine.—The construction is obvious from Fig. 2. Cut out the various parts to the sizes given, trim where necessary with the plane, and rub down any roughness with glasspaper. This latter should on no account be neglected because the toy relies very largely upon the finish for its effect. Rub off any sharp angles and corners. The rounded top to the cab can be chiselled and finished with glasspaper. Use dowels for boiler, wheels, funnel, and dome. To ensure the wheels being all alike in thickness you can fix a stop to a mitre block having a square cut.

To assemble, nail the cab to the boiler, keeping it centred and the right height up from the bottom. Note that glue should be used throughout as well as nails. The strength is thereby increased enormously. Tube glue answers the purpose quite well. The base, which is $\frac{3}{16}$ in. thick, is now nailed to the cab and the saddle prepared to fit beneath the boiler. Its top surface can be hollowed with gouge or file. It is fixed at the same time as the frame block to which the wheels are screwed. Having glued the parts, fix the base with a couple of nails to cab. Drill a hole right through frame block, base, and saddle, and knock a panel pin right through into the boiler. In this way you avoid splitting the saddle piece.

Bore $\frac{1}{4}$ in. holes along the top of the boiler and glue in pieces of dowel to form funnel and dome. The coal bunker is fixed at the rear, and pieces of $\frac{3}{16}$ in. stuff cut to form the side tanks. Glue both bottom edges and sides of the last-named, and nail through into the boiler.

Having cut off the wheels, drill a hole in the centre of each large enough to enable them to revolve freely on the round-head screws to be used. Use $\frac{3}{4}$ in. fine gauge screws and stagger the opposite wheels slightly so that the screws do not foul each other in the thickness of the wood. It will be found that if $\frac{3}{4}$ in. screws are used they will pass nearly through the frame block.

Finishing.—The simplest finish is with poster colours. These are ready for use as they are, but can be mixed with water if necessary. They are obtainable in vivid colours and cover well. They dry quite quickly. Follow with a coat of clear varnish. If spirit varnish is used it will dry rapidly. The same thing applies to shellac varnish. Oil varnish takes much longer to dry but is probably more durable. Details such as the windows, cab door, etc., can be painted in black. Complete all painting before varnishing.

Trucks.—From the instructions given for the engine the trucks can be followed easily. A solid block can be used for the truck portion itself, this being mounted upon a base and frame block similar to that of the engine. For the oil tank a piece of dowel can be used. The guard's van is a solid block and a separate end piece, with a piece of veneer or even card bent around the top and glued down.

(401)

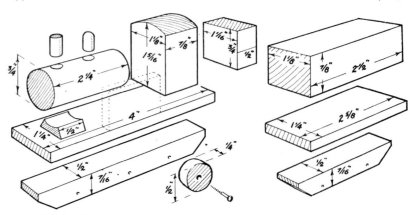

FIG. 2. HOW ENGINE IS MADE.   **FIG. 3. TRUCK DETAILS.**
Chief sizes are suggested here but they can be varied to suit whatever oddments of wood are available.

TWIST TURNINGS
(*Continued*)

appearance though they are far stronger than they look.

Open Double-Bine Twist.—This is really an elaboration of the solid double-bine leg. All that happens is that the grooves between the bines are cut in more deeply until they meet, so entirely separating the two bines except at top and bottom. Naturally a great deal of strength is lost because the centre is cut away entirely and there is no continuous straight grain running from end to end. Matters can be helped somewhat by giving a steep pitch so that the grain is as long as possible at any particular point, but even so the turning is suitable only for light occasional tables, lamp standards, and so on.

Open Triple-bine Twist.—Similar to the double-bine, this is rather more elaborate. It is not used very much, chiefly because it is more awkward to cut. With the double bine the file can be taken straight through between the bines to clean up the inner surfaces, but this can be done to a limited extent only in the triple type. However, it is effective in appearance because the bines are very light. (367)

Articles showing how to make twist turnings without a lathe appeared in the July and August numbers.

Vol. 50   No. 631

WOODWORKER

JUNE, 1946

THE IDEAL TOOL CABINET

A sense of orderliness in woodworking is an important factor contributing to good work. For instance, the bench should be clear of tools, excepting those in immediate use, and when a tool is no longer required it should be replaced in the rack or tool chest. By far the most convenient arrangement is to have a tool cupboard fixed to a wall at the back of the bench and above its level so that shavings are not swept into the cupboard. With such an arrangement, the tools are within easy reach of the worker and, when not required, can be safely stored

IN the tool cabinet shown in Figs. 1 and 2, the tools in frequent use are arranged so as to be close at hand. The heavy tools are accommodated in the cabinet proper, and the relatively light ones in the boxed-in-doors ; thus, no undue strain is placed on the latter. The three drawers are intended for screws, nails, and various small tools. As most workers prefer to use a combination plane instead of separate tools for such operations as ploughing, rebating, etc., a space is provided for the box in which the tool is usually kept. It will be noticed that the saws are placed edge-wise in the cabinet.

Construction.—The carcase, Fig. 5, can be made from $\frac{7}{8}$ in. stuff, finishing $\frac{3}{4}$ in. As the cabinet is divided by shelves and partitions, a good fixing for the back can be obtained ; therefore this may be of $\frac{3}{16}$ in. ply. It is not possible to form the carcase and door frames in one and separate one from the other, as would be done in making a box, since the two doors frames have to fit closely where they meet centrally. If they were made with the carcase, sufficient material would not be available for cleaning off, to obtain a good fit. If possible, it is advisable to true up the stuff for both door

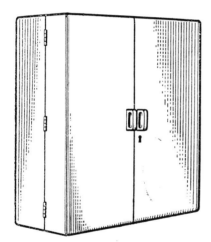

FIG. 1. CABINET WITH CLOSED DOORS

With lightly rounded corners and a painted or lacquered finish, the cabinet makes a most attractive as well as useful item. The closed size is 2 ft. 9½ ins. wide, 3 ft. 7¼ ins. high, and 11 ins. deep. These dimensions can be varied to suit special tools

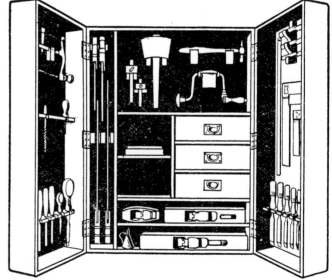

FIG. 2. DOORS OPENED SHOWING TOOL ARRANGEMENT
When doors are opened back flat the position of every tool can be seen at a glance

This effects considerable economy in space as compared with the usual method of laying them flat. Incidentally, the tools shown comprise a useful kit, enabling a variety of work to be done.

As chisels are more in use than gouges, the former are placed on the right hand side of the cabinet and the gouges to the left. It will be seen that the setting-out tools are together on the right hand side, excepting the marking and mortise gauges. All of the tools will be easily recognised, except perhaps the bevel shown at Fig. 3(a).

The tools shown in Fig. 3 are all drawn to scale and the cabinet is dimensioned to suit the layout of the tools.

frames together and rip the stuff down for the sides and ends for each frame. Rebated joints will suffice for the sides and ends of the carcase, and also for those of the door frames. The parts, of course, could be dovetailed.

The partitions (b) and (c) are secured by stop housing ; as also are the shelves (d), (e), (f), and (g). Although this may seem an unnecessary elaboration, it is well worth while since, if the grooves are set out accurately, the shelves will be found to be parallel and no trouble will be found in fitting the drawers. This might not be the case if the parts were nailed together. The plywood back is fixed and pinned in a rebate, as shown in Fig. 6, and it will be necessary to reduce the width

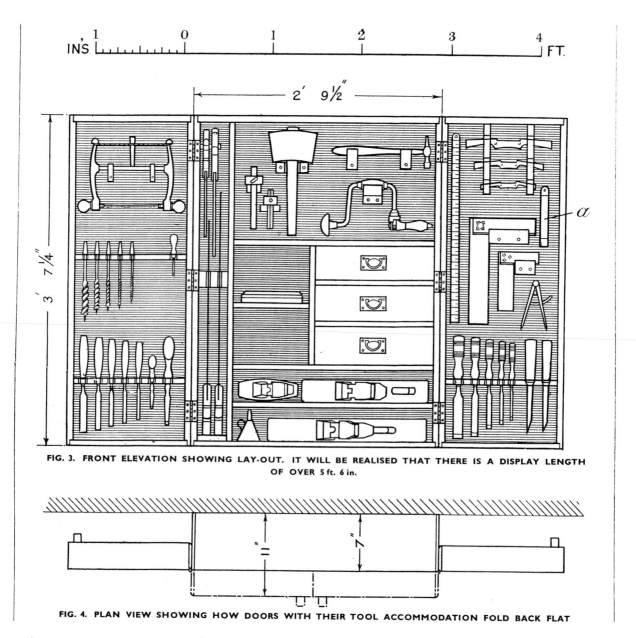

INS 1 0 1 2 3 4 FT.

2' 9½"

3' 7¼"

α

FIG. 3. FRONT ELEVATION SHOWING LAY-OUT. IT WILL BE REALISED THAT THERE IS A DISPLAY LENGTH OF OVER 5 ft. 6 in.

7"

FIG. 4. PLAN VIEW SHOWING HOW DOORS WITH THEIR TOOL ACCOMMODATION FOLD BACK FLAT

of the shelves and partition by an amount equal to the depth of the rebate. The drawer rails which can be 1½ in. by ¾ in. are ploughed on their near edge, as shown in Fig. 7, the ends of the runners being tenoned into the grooves. The rails and runners are glued together and pinned to the side of the cabinet and the partition (c).

Drawers.—The construction of the drawers is shown in Fig. 8. The fronts are made from ¾ in. stuff and the sides ⅜ in., the back being of similar thickness. For the bottom 3/16 in. ply is suitable. This is ploughed into the front and sides and pinned from underneath to the back. If it is desired to have one or more partitions, it is best to stop house them into the front and back, as shown, rather than nail them in position.

If the worker is uncertain of making a success of the lapped dovetails, the fronts could be rebated at the ends and the sides secured in the rebates by gluing and nailing, using 1½ in. oval nails. If possible, ⅜ in. or 5/16 in. ply should be used for the door panels, as ply of the thickness stated will enable the outside edges of the doors to be rounded which will have the effect of improving the appearance of the cabinet.

Tool Supports and Racks.—The profile of one of the spokeshave racks is shown in Fig. 9. In order to avoid short fibres, the grain should run lengthwise. The semi-circular rests can be formed by boring with centre bits according to the size of the spokeshaves, and then cutting to shape with a bowsaw and finishing with scribing gouge and chisel. Fig. 10 shows one of the supports for the hammer. The two are made together by boring a central hole and then cross cutting. In order to position the rip and hand-saws in their pocket a block is positioned centrally, Fig. 3, the blades of the saws resting in saw cuts in the block. The block is shown in Fig. 11. The tenon and dovetail saws are hung on a wooden peg which should be slightly recessed on its upper surface in order to prevent the saws slipping off the end of the peg.

The formation of the other supports and racks will be clear from Figs. 3 and 5. As it will be difficult to obtain a good fixing for the supports and racks from the front, it is a good plan to first glue them in position and then when the glue is set pin or screw each from the back, taking careful measurement in order that the pins or screws will enter each part.

Finishing the Cabinet.—A pleasing form of handle for

38

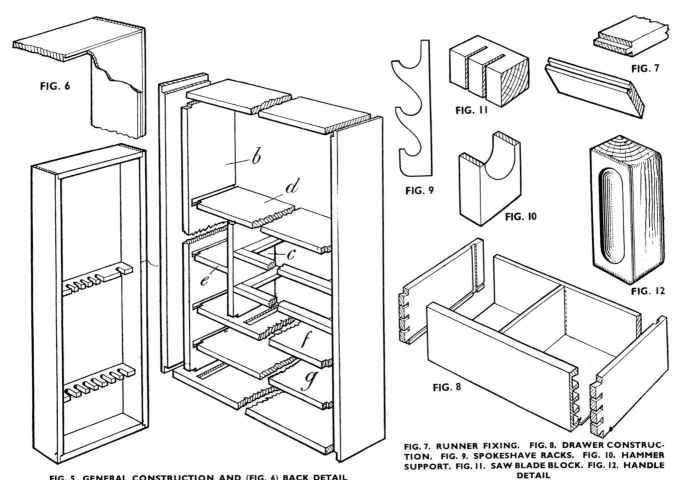

FIG. 5. GENERAL CONSTRUCTION AND (FIG. 6) BACK DETAIL

FIG. 7. RUNNER FIXING. FIG. 8. DRAWER CONSTRUC-
TION. FIG. 9. SPOKESHAVE RACKS. FIG. 10. HAMMER
SUPPORT. FIG. 11. SAW BLADE BLOCK. FIG. 12. HANDLE
DETAIL

each of the doors is shown in Fig. 12. A recess is cut with a gouge on each side and the projecting edges of the handles are rounded. The handles are secured by gluing and screwing from the back. A satisfactory finish to the cabinet can be obtained by sizing and then applying two coats of knotting, or, alternatively, the cabinet can be painted according to the taste of the worker.

As the cabinet with its tools is of considerable weight, it would be as well to support it on two iron brackets, the attachment to the wall being effected by plates positioned towards the top of the cabinet. (677)

39

HOW TO MAKE A
TOBOGGAN

This makes a splendid item for winter sports. It is light in weight so that it is easily carried about, yet thoroughly sturdy

SELECT runners of sound straight-grained birch or ash, or any close-grained hardwood with good bending qualities. Plane up square with a slight taper in thickness towards the front to facilitate bending. They can be ⅝ in. thick at the straight portion to the rear. Next shape side pieces from hardwood of non-splitting texture such as sycamore. Screw and glue runners to these in position shown.

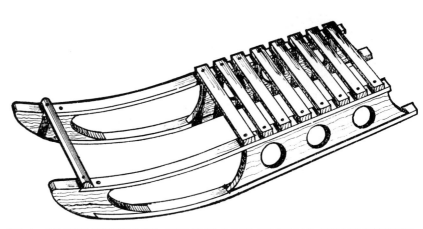

FIG. I. AN ITEM WHICH WILL GIVE YOU A LOT OF FUN IN SNOWY WEATHER
The whole thing should be kept well painted or varnished. Screws should be brass

Nose pieces can be of sycamore too. Shape these to pattern and screw to top runners. Place each side assembly (dealing with left and right independently) in vice in a vertical position at a point just aft of where bend is to begin. Assuming that bottom runner is towards you, force part away over the bench when bottom runner will click into place. The degree of nose tilt is governed by the length of bottom runner, so have this long enough to start with. When satisfied with curve glue and screw runner into nose piece. Length of both bottom runners must obviously be the same. Clean up side assemblies then screw on top battens and foot rest.

If well made, no brackets should be needed, but four or even more could be screwed underneath for any added rigidity. Apart from giving relief to the plain sides, the 4 in. holes are useful hand holes in any emergency.

If desired metal strips can be screwed on runners. Should these be used, tuck them neatly under foot rest, bring right round nose, along runners, then finish at back by bringing over on to top.

This little toboggan looks even better if runners are splayed outwards five or six degrees. (573)

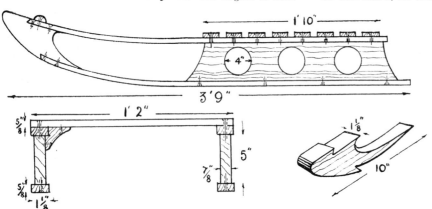

FIG. 2. SIDE AND FRONT ELEVATIONS AND DETAIL OF NOSE PIECE

Treen or Small Woodware, by Edward H. Pinto. In reading this book one's first reaction is that of astonishment at the tremendous variety of things our forefathers used to make in wood. Items that to-day are made as a matter of course in metal, plastics, or china were all fashioned out of wood, often by the laborious process of chipping slowly away with the knife. For such things as boxes, small turned objects, frames, and so on wood seems an obvious choice of material, but when it comes to drinking cups, platters, bowls, and spoons it is difficult to think of conditions which made men turn to wood for making them. No doubt it was often a case of Hobson's choice. Probably the making of many of these items was a rural industry, the tricks of which were handed down in a family. Long experience made men very adept at the craft, and a skilled cabinet maker of to-day with all the modern tools and appliances at his command would be very hard put to if he had to make some of the items that a man of a hundred or more years ago living in a remote village would whittle with his knife.

Mr. Pinto has become well known as a collector of treen, and in his book he illustrates and describes many of the pieces he has gathered together as well as many items from other sources. To anyone who cares for relics of the past it is extremely interesting, and to woodworkers it is specially so because they can appreciate by their own practical experi-ence the craftsmanship the work must have involved. The book contains over 130 excellent photographs, and is extremely well written. It is full of informative notes on the uses to which the items were originally put (this in itself calls for a lot of research plus much experience) and on their manu-facture. Readers who find an appeal in the craftsmanship of a bygone age will find the book most interesting and at the same time very readable. Size about 10 in. by 7½ in. with 120 pages of text and over 60 pages of photographs. Published by B. T. Batsford Ltd., 15 North Audley Street, London, W.1, price 25s. net.

The Art of Woodworking and Furniture Making, by A. Gregory. This is the fifth edition of a successful book. The author is a well-known figure in the world of cabinet making, and is a very capable craftsman. The opening chapter deals with the joints used, and is followed by short chapters on constructional and proportional units. After this are some 45 designs for furniture of all kinds with photographs of the completed items and dimensioned elevations and plans. The book closes with notes on plywood, veneering, and wood finishing. There are 148 pages, size 9¾ in. by 7 in., the whole well printed on good quality paper. Those seeking furniture designs will find it a most useful book. Published by The Dryad Press, Saint Nicholas Street, Leicester. Price 12s. 6d. net

PHOTOGRAPH OF THE COMPLETED BOWL

This particular bowl measures 7¼ in. in diameter by 2¼ in. deep but the sizes could be adapted if preferred

ATTRACTIVE TURNED
FRUIT BOWL

A pleasing fruit bowl turned by a reader. It is built up, brickwork fashion, from segments of mahogany in three layers, sycamore veneer being introduced between the layers and also between the segments. The effect has been enhanced by arranging the grain of the segments diagonally, the result being apparent from the illustration. As we think that this built-up bowl will interest readers who do wood turning, and that the built-up construction gives scopes for individuality in treatment, we describe the methods of our reader in preparing the work prior to turning

FIG. 1 suggests suitable proportions for the bowl and shows the relative thicknesses of the layers. These dimensions need not, of course, be adhered to and the shape can be in accordance with the worker's taste. Also, the number of segments and layers could be varied.

First Stage.—Having decided on the design of the bowl, it is advisable to lay out, full size on a sheet of plywood, a plan and elevation, allowing adequate waste for turning. From the elevation project lines A, B, C, and D to the diameter and scribe the circles E, F, and G. It will now be possible to determine the minimum size of the segments making up the three layers. The three sizes of segments are indicated in Fig. 2 by shading. Templates for the three shapes of segments should now be made, allowing waste for turning and cleaning off.

Second Stage.—Prepare three lengths of stuff, the grain running diagonally. The lengths should be considerably in excess of requirements since a short length of wood is difficult to plane accurately. The size of each cross section can be

ascertained from the drawing, but an allowance of about ¼ in. all round should be allowed for turning. Some care should be taken to get the face sides and edges square with one another. The four segments for each of the three layers are then marked, allowing about 3/16 in. waste between each for the saw cut and cleaning off when glued together.

After cross cutting, each set of segments is marked out with its respective template and the bulk of the waste wood is pared away. The segments will then appear as shown in Fig. 3. At this stage the sycamore veneer for insertion between the layers is marked out and radial lines drawn corresponding to the relative positions of the vertical veneer strips when the layers are assembled. The lines serve to position correctly the layers so that the vertical veneer strips are centrally of the segments below. This stage is completed by cutting out the disc and ring of veneer.

Third Stage.—Corresponding pairs of segments and strips of sycamore veneer inserted between them are now glued and clamped together, Fig. 4. If the gluing is to be done all at the same time, six G clamps will be necessary. If these are not available, the pairs of segments can be glued up on a board, paper being inserted between the work and the board. The clamping can then be effected by folding wedges placed between the work and strips of wood nailed to the board.

Fourth Stage.—When the glue has set, the pairs of segments are removed from the clamps or from the board and the edges to be jointed are shot. The pairs to make up the complete layers are then glued up, sycamore strips being introduced between them, Fig. 5. If it is more convenient, the clamping may be done by folding wedges as before.

When the glue is dry, the faces of the completed layers are faced up, the central layer being reduced to its correct thickness. Care should be taken to see that the mating surfaces are true so that when the layers are glued together close joints are obtained. The next step is to glue the layers together, the veneer disc and ring being placed between the layers in their correct positions (Fig. 6).

If the disc and ring are so positioned that alternate radial lines coincide with the vertical veneer strips of the layer below, the other radial markings will serve to position the vertical veneer strips in the layer above. The vertical joints will thus appear as in brickwork. Finally, a central hole is bored in the layer of smallest diameter to receive the screw of the face plate. This hole is later plugged with a piece of sycamore turned to fit the hole. The grain of the plug should be arranged horizontally.

Alternative Procedure.—The methods described are those

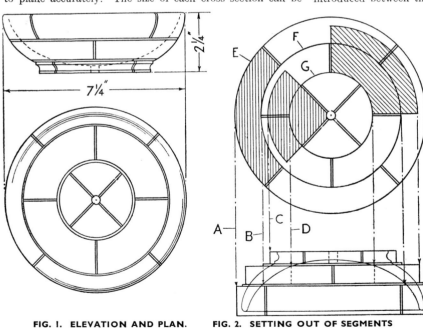

FIG. I. ELEVATION AND PLAN.   FIG. 2. SETTING OUT OF SEGMENTS

In Fig. 2 is shown how the requisite size for the segments and the amount of waste wood that can be removed preparatory to turning is ascertained

employed by the reader who turned up the bowl, but workers may prefer the following methods. Prepare the lengths of stuff for the segments as before but do not cut away any waste wood so that four squares are formed for each layer. These are glued up as previously described, veneer being inserted between the joints. After the faces are cleaned off, a circle is scribed on each according to the required diameter, allowing waste for turning. Two discs of veneer are now cut to size, leaving adequate waste. As before, radial lines are drawn on each for positioning the joints during assembly. The layer of greatest diameter is next glued to a wood facing on the face plate, paper being inserted in between. Since the centre of the layer is marked, the back centre can be brought up to centralise the work.

The other layers are then glued in place, the veneer discs being inserted in the joints. The layers and discs are centred in turn by bringing up the back centre. Finally, the whole assembly is clamped to the face plate by the back centre. This method assures that the parts are concentric before turning is commenced, but it has the disadvantage that more work is involved in hollowing out the bowl since no preliminary cutting away of interior waste wood has been done. This disadvantage assumes a greater importance if the bowl is relatively of large diameter.

After the outside of the bowl has been turned, the work is removed from the chuck. A shallow recess is turned in the wood facing to take the bottom of the bowl which is glued in the recess, paper being inserted as before. The hollowing out can then be done and the bowl finished as required. Care must be taken in removing the work, otherwise the bottom edge will be bruised. As some paper will be found adhering to the bottom of the bowl, this can be removed by glasspapering. If the bottom is to be covered with felt, there is no point in removing the paper.   (312)

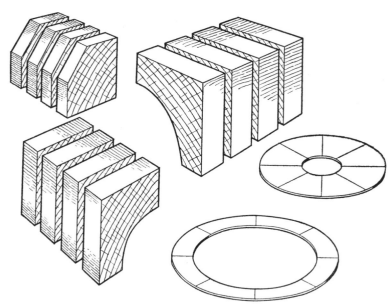

FIG. 3. THE SEGMENTS AND HORIZONTAL VENEER INSERTIONS CUT OUT AND READY FOR GLUING

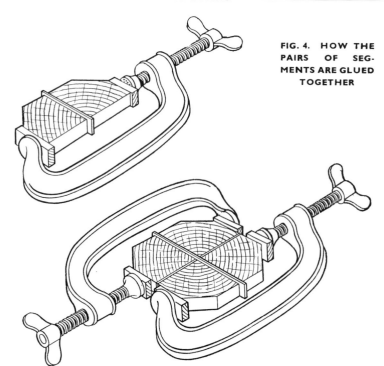

FIG. 4. HOW THE PAIRS OF SEGMENTS ARE GLUED TOGETHER

FIG. 5. GLUING AND CRAMPING THE CORRESPONDING PAIRS OF SEGMENTS

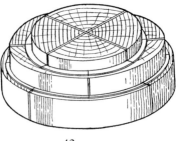

FIG. 6. THE LAYERS ASSEMBLED WITH THE HORIZONTAL VENEERS INSERTED
Note how the radial markings help in positioning the vertical joint centrally of the segments

42

EGG-CUP SET

The distinctive feature of this egg set is that two contrasting woods are used, although it may, of course, be turned entirely from one wood. It may be made up as a set of four, five, or six, this being a matter of adjustment to the base diameter and a little elementary geometry when marking out. The construction of a set of six is described here

CONTRASTING light and dark woods are used, suggestions being apple and black bean, oak and ebony, or, as in the case of this particular set, beech and walnut, which are more easily obtainable.

The Stand.—This needs a piece of the lighter wood 6¼ in. square by approximately ⅞ in. thick. It should be planed down to ¾ in. thickness with both surfaces perfectly flat. The dark wood " cap " should be of similar size and about ¼ in. or more thick to start with, having one surface planed perfectly flat. Mark out the planed surface for the sockets which hold the cups, and using a 1⅜ in. diameter centre bit, drill the 6 holes right through against a piece of waste. Drill a hole through the centre of both pieces to take a suitable small diameter metal peg (an old twist drill of about ⅛ in. diameter is just right for this). To glue, warm the thicker piece well, insert the temporary peg in the centre hole, and apply glue to the planed side of the cap only, taking care not to permit glue to " flood " into the edges of the 1⅜ in. holes. Slip it over the peg, force it *straight down* and cramp. It is important that the cap does not rotate or slip, otherwise the bottoms of " sinkings " will show glue which will be difficult to remove later. The operation is simple if done quickly and confidently. Remove the peg after the glue has set.

Make the assembly roughly round by sawing off the corners and mount on a piece of waste wood, which is screwed to the face plate of lathe. Turn the work d wn to 6 in. diameter, shaping the edge with a round-nosed chisel. Remove from lathe and plane cap down to 3/32 in. thick. Finish off by glasspapering having drilled a ½ in. diameter hole to take the handle.

The Cups.—Dimensions of these are given in Fig. 2. Each cup requires a block of the light coloured wood 2¾ in. long by 2 in. square, each block having its ends " shot " true. (A pair of calipers is useful for testing this). The caps are of the dark coloured wood and are 2 in. square by a full ¼ in. thick. Plane one side of each cap flat, and glue to one end of the block, cramping firmly. If a heat resisting adhesive can be employed, so much the better, since the cups will encounter a certain amount of heat when in use. Reduce the corners in preparation for the lathe, and mount on the face plate using long screws, since they enter end grain. The dead centre can be brought up to steady the work

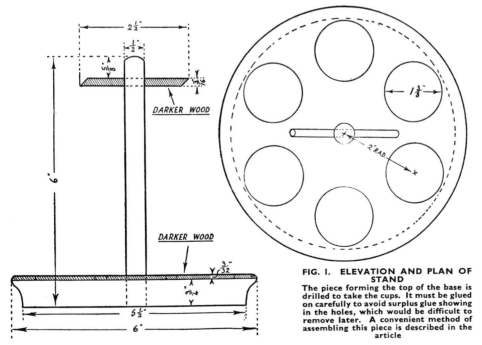

FIG. I. ELEVATION AND PLAN OF STAND
The piece forming the top of the base is drilled to take the cups. It must be glued on carefully to avoid surplus glue showing in the holes, which would be difficult to remove later. A convenient method of assembling this piece is described in the article

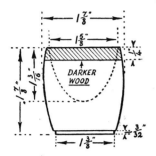

FIG. 2. DETAILS OF CUP

The lighter coloured wood should be about 2¾ in. long before turning, to enable fixing to the face plate and to allow for parting off when finished

until the outside shape has been formed. Turn to a cylinder and "face up" the top to ¼ in. With dividers mark off (a) 1⅞ in. along the length, (b) 1⅝ in. diameter on the end. With a parting tool cut straight down just inside the 1⅞ in. line to a diameter of 1⅜ in., thus forming the rebated base which will sit in the holes in the stand. Next turn the outside shape right up to the buffing stage, then dispense with the dead centre. Cut in from the end, removing the bulk waste, then, using a round-nosed chisel, form the inside shape. A lead pencil marked on its length makes a useful depth gauge. Do not worry too much about the accuracy of the internal shape. Turning all inside surfaces to a similar shape may be left largely to judgment, and a china "sitting egg" from the pet shop will serve as a useful guide. After finishing the inside (taking care not to reduce the top lip whilst papering) part-off at the 1⅞ in. mark, making sure that a convex shape does not develop on the bottom, otherwise the cup will not stand steady.

Pillar and Handle.—The pillar can be formed conveniently out of a length of ½ in. beech dowel, and the handle requires a length of the dark wood turned to 3/16 in. diameter. The handle is glued centrally in a 3/16 in. hole, in the pillar. Should the pillar be a trifle slack in its hole, cut a V slot in the bottom end about ½ in. long and glue in a small wedge. Finally, glue a disc of baize or felt on the bottom.

The job should be left clean if required for use at the table. If intended only as a "Showpiece," however, clear french polish will give quite an attractive finish.

(962)

VANITY TABLE (See pages 174-175)
CUTTING LIST

				Long ft. in.	Wide in.	Thick in.
(A)	4	Legs	.. .. ..	2 5	1½	1½
(B)	1	Front rail	.. ..	2 3	1⅜	1
(C)	1	Front frieze rail	..	1 4⅜	3½	¾
(D)	1	Drawer front	..	8	3½	¾
(E)	1	Back frieze rail	..	2 3	4½	¾
(F)	1	End ditto	.. ..	1 5	4½	¾
(G)	2	End pieces	.. ..	3	4½	¾
(H)	1	Bracket	.. ..	10	3	¾
(J)	1	End rail	.. ..	1 5	4½	⅝
(K)	1	Cross rail	..	1 5⅝	3½	⅝
(L)	1	Clamp	.. ..	4½	1¾	⅝
(M)	1	Top	.. ..	2 4¼	19½	⅝
(N)	1	Clamp	.. ..	2 4½	1½	⅝
(O)	1	Flap	.. ..	1 7¼	10	⅝
(P)	2	Stretchers	.. ..	1 6	⅞	⅝
(Q)	1	Ditto	.. ..	2 3½	⅞	⅝
(R)	1	Block	.. ..	2 1	13/16	⅝
(S)	2	Ditto	.. ..	1 4	13/16	⅝

				Long ft. in.	Wide in.	Thick in.
(T)	2	Drawer kickers	.. ..	1 5¼	⅝	⅜
(U)	2	Drawer sides	.. ..	1 4	3	⅜
(W)	1	Drawer back	..	8	2¼	⅜
(X)	1	Drawer bottom	..	7⅝	16	4mm.
(Y)	1	Carcase bottom	..	2 1⅝	17¼	4mm.

All sizes are net. (M) and (O) in blockboard or laminated board. (X) and (Y) in plywood.

RANDOM REMINDERS

Lubricate the sole of an iron plane occasionally and it will work more easily. Make a pad of cotton wool and soak it in linseed oil. Keep the pad within easy reach for drawing across the sole of the plane when it becomes stiff.

* * * *

A lock can be lubricated by dipping the key in oil before inserting in the lock.

* * * *

Glasspaper is graded by numbers : 2/0 or Flour, 0, 1, 1½, F2, M2, S2, 2½, 3. The lower the number the finer the paper. Usual grades for finer woodwork are M2, 1½ and 1. No. 2/0 is generally used in polishing and when it is necessary to use a rotary movement as when cleaning up woods with no definite direction to the grain as burr walnut.

* * * *

A spot of linseed oil on the polishing rubber assists its movement. Too much oil brings a bright finish, but this will sink, leaving an oily surface.

* * * *

A piece of hacksaw blade, inserted in a slip of wood, can be utilised as a toother in roughing the surface prior to veneering.

* * * *

It generally makes a less unsightly mark if a fine nail is punched right into a moulding or panel than when an attempt is made to extract it.

* * * *

When a lot of taping is to be done it is easier and cleaner to damp the gum with a small brush rather than a cloth.

* * * *

Contrary to the name a scraper is a cutting tool and when set and handled properly should produce shavings.

* * * *

Window and pulley cords will last longer if the rollers and pulley wheels are oiled occasionally.

* * * *

A point ground on the end of a three-cornered file can become a good substitute for a glass cutter.

* * * *

When using a caul for veneering be sure the surface meeting the veneer is clean. Insert a sheet of newspaper between it and the veneer. This saves much trouble and the caul will not stick to the veneer when being removed.

* * * *

Pressure can generally be removed from veneers when the heat has gone out of the caul, but it is safer to leave for an hour or two, especially if the veneer is strong and shows a tendency to spring. (954)

A USEFUL ARTICLE FOR THE YOUNGSTER

CHILD'S DESK

To do their drawings, homework, etc., children require a share of the table, and it often happens that when they are asked to clear the table for meals, it is done with reluctance and, sometimes, not without tears. If the child can have its own desk to work on and in which books and papers can be kept, this is the ideal solution. Further, the child will derive pleasure from possessing a desk of its own. The desk shown here is provided with a strong stool which can be pushed under the desk when not in use, so that little room is taken up. It was designed and made by a reader

A S the desk supports have to be strong and rigid, they are best made from hardwood such as oak, beech or birch. The rear uprights (*a*) are secured to members (*c*) and (*d*) by bridle joints, while uprights (*b*) are through-tenoned into these members (Figs. 2 and 4). It is as well to pin all the joints. To make the supports rigid, brackets (*e*) should be fixed in the angle between each upright (*b*) and its respective member (*c*). Referring to Figs. 2 and 5, it will be seen that wedge-shaped housings are cut for these brackets ; thus, abutments (*f*) are formed which contribute to the rigidity of the supports. It is advisable to cut these brackets so that the grain runs obliquely as in Fig. 5, to avoid short grain. The brackets are glued and pinned in position. At the rear, the two uprights (*a*) are tied together by a rail (*g*) which is stub-tenoned into them. These joints are also pinned.

Desk.—The front sides and back can be secured together by mitred lap joints as shown in Fig. 3 and reinforced with a corner block glued and screwed on the inside. This form of joint has the advantage that no end grain is visible. Secret dovetails could be used if preferred in place of lap joints. The plywood bottom (Fig. 6) is inserted in plough grooves worked in the front, sides and back, but alternatively, the bottom can be pinned to fillets glued and screwed to the surrounding sides of the desk.

As the lid is hinged to the piece (*h*), this piece is likely to become loose if not firmly secured. It is therefore advisable to screw it down on to the desk sides. In order to accommodate pencils and pens, the piece (*h*) has a hollow about 1 in. wide which can be formed with a gauge.

Desk Top.—For the older children it will be well worth while making the top from deal or, better still, pine, if this can be obtained. The use of a soft wood will enable drawing pins for holding paper to be pressed in with greater ease than if plywood were used for the top. If a tee-square is likely to be employed, the left-hand

edge of the top should be made square rather than rounded as shown. A further advantage of using solid stuff for the top is that it can be cleaned off from time to time with a smoothing plane when the top becomes soiled. As solid stuff is very liable to cast, clamps should be tongued and tenoned on to the sides as shown in Fig. 7. If plywood or lamin board is used for the top, it should be lipped as shown in Fig. 8, to hide the edges.

Fixing the Desk to its Supports.—The width of the desk is equal to the length of each member (*c*), therefore the weight will be taken by the front and back of the desk, but in order to obtain a fixing, packing pieces will have to be applied to the upper surfaces of members (*c*) so that they just touch the under side of the bottom. This will permit fixing screws to be inserted through the bottom and packing pieces and into the members (*c*). Three 1 in. No. 6

CUTTING LIST

	Long ft. in.	Wide ft. in.	Thick in.
Desk Supports			
2 Uprights (*a*)	1 8	$1\frac{3}{4}$	$1\frac{1}{4}$
2 Ditto (*b*)	1 8	$1\frac{3}{4}$	$1\frac{1}{4}$
2 Members (*c*)	1 7	$1\frac{3}{4}$	$1\frac{1}{4}$
2 Ditto (*d*)	1 7	$1\frac{3}{4}$	$1\frac{1}{4}$
1 Rail (*g*)	1 $7\frac{1}{2}$	$1\frac{3}{4}$	$1\frac{1}{4}$
2 Brackets (*e*)	4	4	$\frac{3}{4}$
Desk			
1 Front	1 $10\frac{1}{4}$	3	$\frac{5}{8}$
2 Sides	1 7	7	$\frac{5}{8}$
1 Back	1 $10\frac{1}{4}$	7	$\frac{5}{8}$
Bottom (ply)	1 $9\frac{1}{4}$	18	$\frac{1}{4}$
Piece (*h*)	1 $11\frac{3}{4}$	3	$\frac{3}{4}$
Back Piece	1 $11\frac{3}{4}$	$2\frac{1}{2}$	$\frac{5}{8}$
Top			
2 Lengths (for jointing) ..	1 9	$8\frac{1}{2}$	$\frac{3}{4}$
2 Clamps	1 5	3	$\frac{3}{4}$
Alternative ply top	1 11	17	$\frac{3}{8}$
Stool			
1 Seat	1 3	$8\frac{1}{4}$	$\frac{3}{4}$
2 Rails	1 $1\frac{1}{2}$	$3\frac{3}{4}$	$\frac{1}{4}$
2 Legs	1 3	$7\frac{1}{2}$	$\frac{3}{4}$
Alternative legs (splayed in width)	1 6	9	$\frac{3}{4}$

Lengths are full ; widths and thicknesses net, excepting ply, which is full both in length and width.

CHILD'S DESK

countersunk head screws on either side should suffice for the fixing.

Stool.—As this will come in for rough treatment, it should have no weak features in its construction, and the simple but robust design shown is recommended. If the height of the stool has to be increased to suit a child older than seven, it is advisable also to splay the legs in their width as indicated by " dot and dash " lines in Fig. 2. By so doing, the stool will not be easily tilted and upset. On referring to Fig. 9, it will be seen that the legs are housed into the side rails. This is an important feature which makes for greater rigidity. As there are obvious objections to using nails or screws for securing the seat, it is suggested that the fixing be done by buttons as illustrated in Fig. 9. Incidentally, this method of fixing will allow the seat to shrink without splitting. Any tendency for the seat to warp will also be prevented.

Finish.—If the article as a whole, excepting the lid, is made from oak, a pleasing appearance can be obtained by leaving the wood in its natural colour and wax polishing. If, for reasons of economy, deal has to be used, then the supports and desk can be stained and varnished. (112)

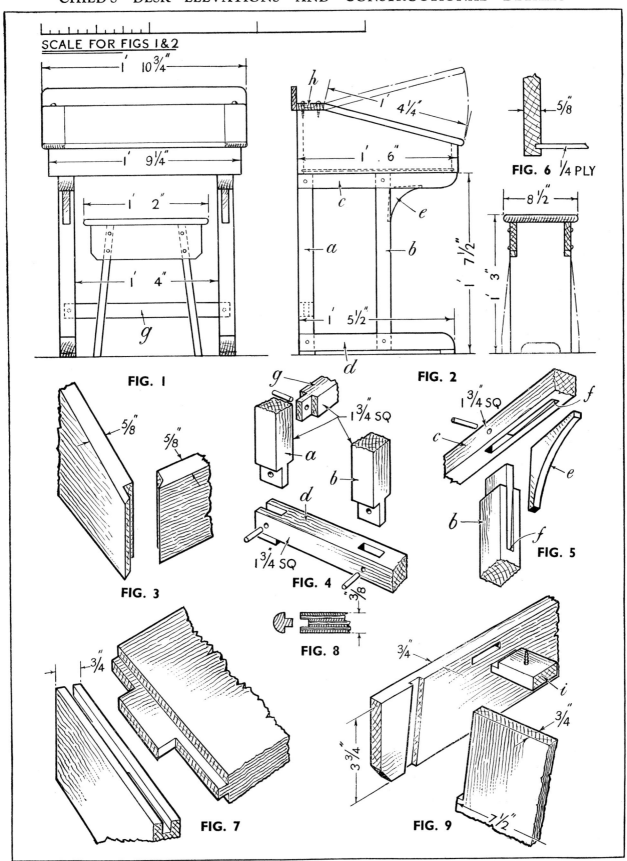

SCALE FOR FIGS 1 & 2

FIG. 1

FIG. 2

FIG. 6 ¼ PLY

FIG. 3

FIG. 4

FIG. 5

FIG. 7

FIG. 8

FIG. 9

ATTRACTIVE ITEM FOR THE GARDEN

PIGEON COTE

This pigeon cote is of simple construction, tongued and grooved boards being employed for the walls and platforms. It may be made up of three separate units so that the whole cote can easily be taken apart for cleaning out. Galvanised screws should be used for assembly to guard against rust. The cote should be kept well away from fences to prevent cats from springing across

AN exploded view of the cote is shown in Fig. 2, the individual units being held together by means of substantial turn-buttons which must be a good fit in their slots to avoid any play. The upper storey could be omitted, in which case the lower one should be made slightly taller to retain reasonable proportions, the roof unit fitting directly on it.

Walls.—The tongued and grooved boarding for the walls is held together by battens nailed or screwed on the inside at top and bottom, the walls being simply butted at the corners and screwed together. Before screwing the walls together, cut out the doorways with a pad saw. The assembled walls are fixed to the platform by screwing up into the battens from below.

Platforms.—These are constructed in the same way, the tongued and grooved boarding being secured together with battens screwed on beneath. Since the battens have to keep the units in position, they must be placed so as to fit flush round the walls of the unit below (see Fig. 2B). Note that the platforms are planed to a slope at their edges to drain off rainwater (Fig. 2A).

Roof.—This consists of a tongued and grooved platform assembled in the same way as the others, a finial post being fixed at the centre, and four triangular pieces being added, to which

FIG. 2 (*left*).
CONSTRUCTIONAL DETAILS

The roof platform is fixed by turn-buttons which engage in slots in the wall, and the upper unit is fixed to the lower one in the same way. Both units are drawn here with a wall missing to show the construction. Metal spring strips could be used, as at B, to prevent the buttons working out of their slots. Details of the supporting post are shown at C and D

FIG. I (*above*). **THE ASSEMBLED PIGEON COTE**

This looks most attractive with a painted finish in two colours, using a light colour for the walls and a darker one for the roof and platforms

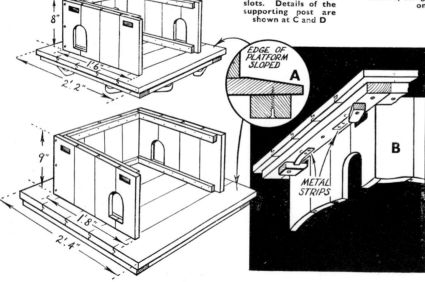

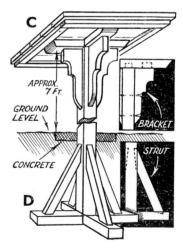

A PAINTED FINISH WILL PRESERVE OUTDOOR WOODWORK

the roof weather-boards (Fig. 3C) are nailed. The central post and triangular pieces can be screwed to the platform from below and at other convenient points on top. Note that the top edge of the roof platform is bevelled off to suit the slope of the roof. This facilitates fixing of the weather-boards, the bottom board projecting well beyond the platform to give the roof sufficient overhang.

Before fixing the roof weather-boards, screw the turn-buttons in position on all platform battens, and assemble the units so that the slot positions for the turn buttons may be marked out on the walls. When cutting the slots, arrange for the buttons to be a tight fit when turned home, thus holding each unit firmly down on the one below. As an additional precaution against buttons working out of their slots owing to movement in a high wind, metal strips may be screwed on as shown at Fig. 2B. These could be recessed into the battens so that, when pressed flat, they allow the button to turn. When the button is turned home in its slot, however, the free end of the metal strip springs downwards to hold the button in position.

Roof Weather-Boards.—It is worth while making a cardboard template for these before cutting. The boards are nailed down to the triangular roof pieces, and the corners of the roof covered with roofing felt to make the joints weatherproof, as in Fig. 3C. Roofing felt should also be used where the boards meet the finial post.

Main Post.—This should be really substantial, say 4 in. square in section. It is stub-tenoned into the cross-members immediately below the bottom platform (Fig. 2C), the cross-members having been halved together and screwed to the platform. Supporting brackets are then added, these being tenoned at the top into the cross-members and screwed to the post.

The best method of fixing the post in the ground is that shown at Fig. 2D, the bracing members giving maximum support. All woodwork below ground level should be treated with some form of preservative. Having been sunk in the ground the supports are packed round with brick rubble, firmly tamped down, concrete being used for the top layer.

Fig. 3 (A & B) shows how the pigeon cote may be divided inside by thin plywood partitions halved together at the centre and held in position between wood fillets at the sides. The partitions could be removable to facilitate cleaning out.

DIMENSIONS

Tongued-and-grooved boards for walls	$\frac{5}{8}$ in. or $\frac{3}{4}$ in. thick
Ditto for two platforms ..	$\frac{3}{4}$ in. thick
Ditto for roof platform ..	$\frac{5}{8}$ in. thick
Battens for walls	$1\frac{1}{2}$ in. wide by $\frac{5}{8}$ in. thick
Battens for two platforms ..	2 in. wide by 1 in. thick
Battens for roof platform ..	$1\frac{1}{2}$ in. wide by 1 in. thick
Triangular roof pieces ..	$\frac{3}{4}$ in. thick
Finial post	$1\frac{1}{2}$ in. square
Cross pieces below lower platform	4 in. wide by 2 in. thick
Brackets	1 ft. 4 in. by 5 in. by $1\frac{1}{2}$ in.
Post	4 in. by 4 in.
Bracing members below ground	4 in. wide by $1\frac{1}{4}$ in. thick
Base cross-members below ground	4 in. wide by $2\frac{1}{2}$ in. thick

(223)

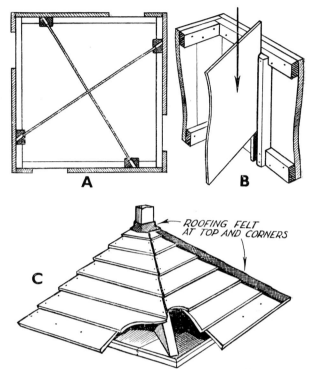

FIG. 3. PARTITIONS AND ROOF DETAIL

A—Each unit could be divided by plywood partitions halved together at the centre and sliding between fillets as at B, so that they can be removed for cleaning out

C—Roof weather-boards are nailed down and the corners covered with roofing felt. Note that the lower boards have a substantial overhang

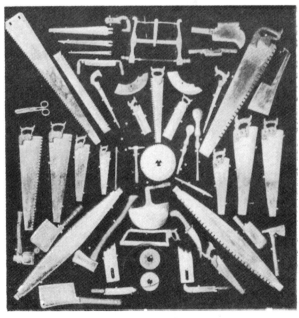

MINIATURE TOOLS MADE BY A READER

The mounting board is 14 in. square. The smallest tenon saw blade is $1\frac{3}{4}$ in. long. All the tools work

Vol. 57   No. 711

WOODWORKER

FEBRUARY, 1953

CARVING SMALL THINGS IN WOOD
SQUIRREL BOOK ENDS

An animal of this kind is essentially decorative, and would look well by itself as an ornament. Alternatively it would make up excellently as one of a pair of book ends as in Fig. 3. A lamp standard is another subject for which it is suitable, the animal being seated in front of the shaft, both fixed to a base

AS in all carving of this kind the work passes through three main stages ; elevation shaping in which the outline is cut through square in first side then front elevation ; the main rounding or bosting in, in which the rough, general shape of the animal is formed ; and the finishing, in which the detail is put in. Make a drawing of the side elevation (Fig. 2) on thin cardboard, drawing 1 in. squares and putting in the outline map fashion.

Preliminary Shaping. A block of wood 6¾ in. by 4¼ in. by 3⅛ in. is needed, though if this should prove awkward to obtain it is simple enough to adapt by making the squares say, ⅞ in. for a smaller carving or 1⅛ in. for a larger one. Do not make it too small, however, for it would be awkward to carve. Square up the block and cut the ends true. Place the card template on one side of the block and draw round the outline. If you have access to a bandsaw the shape can be sawn. Otherwise the outline should be drawn on the opposite face also, the card being reversed, of course, so that the animal faces the same way on both sides. Make a series of saw cuts across the grain in any convenient positions, and chop away the waste with chisel and gouge. A deep cut is made from the front immediately above the ears for instance, another level with the top of the right front leg, and so on. This will enable the whole to be roughly shaped

FIG. I. DELIGHTFUL PIECE OF WORK TO CARVE
This particular animal is in chestnut, but oak or almost any hardwood could be used. Woods with interlocked, twisted grain are best avoided, however, as the carving is difficult

in side elevation. Two cuts in the form of a V will enable the tail to be largely separated from the back.

The front elevation has now to be marked. When a bandsaw is available the front shape is drawn on the flat wood before any sawing is started. Then, when the side elevation has been sawn, the waste pieces can be replaced and the front elevation sawn. This is not practicable when the wasting-away method is used, and the only plan is to mark on the wood certain obvious points and join them with a line put in free hand. For instance, the distance in of the cheek, top of tail, top of back leg can all be measured from the drawing and put in on the block. Joining these lines on the undulating surface is a little awkward, but it can be done—indeed it is the only way.

Once again the saw and chisel can be used to waste away the wood down to the line. Note that in some cases, however, the cut cannot be taken right through. For example the right hand side of the head has the tail behind it, and the cut must be stopped short. This is clear from Fig. 4 which shows the work at this stage.

Bosting - in.— In this stage the main form alone is considered, all detail being left until later. You have to separate the front legs, round the body, give the latter its twist so that it is at a slight angle although the head faces the front (see plan in Fig. 2), cut away the wood at the side of the tail, and generally bring the whole to its approximate general form. No detail whatever is put in. You are concerned only with leaving the main chunks large enough for the detail to be carved in them.

Generally you will find it easier to use the gouge across the grain. Use as large a one as is convenient and keep to it except for places which are too small for it to reach. It is better to obtain mastery over a few tools than to keep passing from one to another. As you proceed look at the wood from all angles, and keep the lines flowing and sweet. The usual fault with beginners is that, starting with a square block, they tend to make the animal itself square in form. Fig. 5

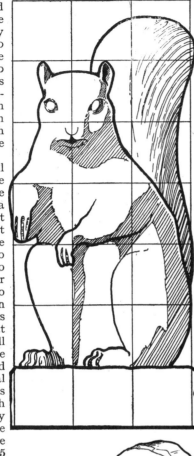

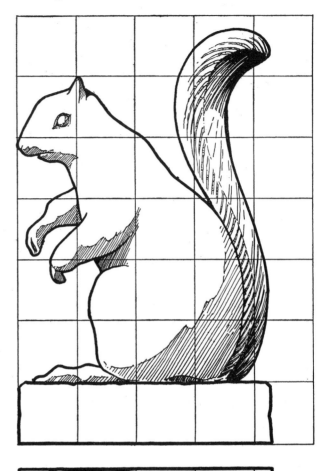

FIG. 2 (above)
DESIGN SET OUT IN SQUARES RE-PRESENTING I IN. EACH

FIG. 3 (right)
APPLICATION AS A BOOK END

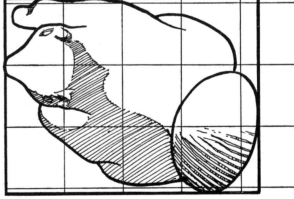

shows the work at this bosting-in stage. That the majority of the cuts are across the grain is obvious from this. Not only is the removal of the chips easier, but any tendency for the wood to splinter out is largely avoided.

Detail.—From this stage on it is a matter of gradually bringing the work to its final form. Remove the wood between the ears and bring the head to its approximate shape. The eyes can then be drawn in and the ears shaped and hollowed. Two small gouges are needed for the eyes. Cut in downwards around the outline, fitting the gouge to as near the line as possible. Slope away the wood to give the roundness of the eye, and ease away or soften the surrounding wood. Razor-sharp tools are needed

for this, and the grain must be followed carefully.

Proceed over the whole body in this way, gradually bringing to the final shape. Large tool marks will be largely taken out, but do not try to get rid of them altogether. Carving should be left from the tool. Glass-paper is never used. To form the hair a small V tool is used. Follow the natural direction and make the deepest cuts towards the lower part. At the neck they die out and are omitted entirely on the head. Cover the whole of the body with these marks so that there are no flat uncut parts left. The base is left with the tooled surface of a flat gouge.

Wax is the best finish for the squirrel. For a light

FIG. 4. FIRST STAGE OF ROUGHING OUT

FIG. 5. PRELIMINARY ROUNDING OR BOSTING-IN

coloured wood use bleached beeswax for the polish. Avoid an undue accumulation of wax in corners as this only clogs the general form.

Fig. 3 shows how a book end is formed. It is simply a plain piece, shaped as shown with the general form finished much as roughly shaped rustic work might appear. It is screwed to the back of the animal and its base. (392)

EFFECTIVE
BACK STEADY
FOR THE LATHE

This is the age of vast strides in mechanical devices for doing this or that job, but sometimes one comes across a piece of apparatus devised many years ago which no modern development seems to improve upon. The curious thing, too, is that it often happens that the thing is often almost completely lost sight of, and might disappear entirely but for the chance of an odd survival. Such a device is shown in Fig. 1 which is a sketch of a back steady used on an old wood turning lathe now standing in the museum at High Wycombe, Bucks.

EVERY man who has done any wood turning knows that when a long, thin piece of wood has to be turned between centres, it is liable to whip badly at the centre and vibrate so that accurate turning becomes impossible. This makes the use of a back steady imperative. One modern device, probably copied from the type used by metal workers is fitted with two wheels which bear at the back of the work. It can be adjusted in any position along the bed, and to suit various diameters of wood. It is effective enough, but consider the advantage of the device in Fig. 1. It is as simple as it can be, is made up of oddments of wood, is very quickly adjusted, and is automatic in adapting itself to the work. It takes up to the diameter of the wood being turned, and it is possible to turn the wood right opposite the steady, the latter automatically adapting itself to the size of the wood as it is reduced.

The sketch in Fig. 1 is almost self explanatory, and could be made up as it is or adapted to suit the particular

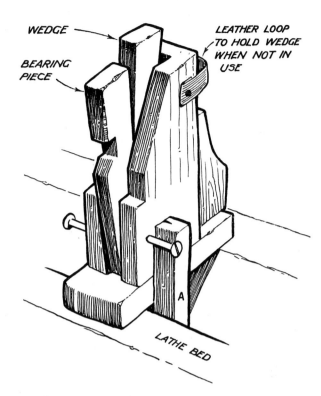

FIG. I. BACK STEADY USED ON AN OLD LATHE
This apparently crude device is most effective in use. It is sketched from an old lathe in the Museum at High Wycombe, Bucks.

form of lathe for which it is required. Fig. 2, for instance, shows the steady as made to suit the *Myford* lathe. In the latter the steady is not fixed to the bed of the lathe, but rather to the stand beneath, the advantage being that it can be moved back and forth without interfering with the tool rest. At the back of the bottom piece screwed to the under-side is a block with a *V* cut at the edge to fit over and grip the edge of the stand. At the front is another similar block with V groove at one edge and tapered at the other, but held by a single screw which is free to move back and forth in a slot in the bottom piece. It is driven up to the stand edge by a wedge which bears against the rebated piece at the front. Thus the whole thing can be adjusted to any position along the lathe, and be held firmly by driving in the wedge.

At the back is a sort of box arrangement in which the bearing piece is freely pivoted at the bottom on a metal rod. At its top is a notch which bears against the work, preventing all vibration. It is held up to the wood by the wedge which drops by gravity. It is not knocked in any way, but just drops by its own weight assisted by the vibration of the revolving machine. Thus, even though the wood is turned right opposite the steady, the latter takes up to the reduced size since the wedge drops down and pushes the bearing piece forward. In use a piece of candle grease is rubbed on the revolving wood opposite the steady to lubricate it.

It will be realized that when a square piece of wood is first put into the lathe it is necessary to turn a round opposite the

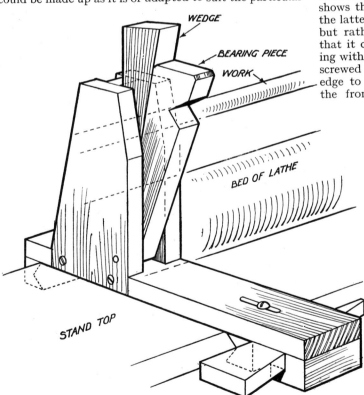

FIG. 2. ADAPTATION OF THE DEVICE TO SUIT A MODERN LATHE
It can be fixed in any position along the lathe, and the bearing piece is automatically pressed up to the work by the wedge, which drops by its own weight

REPLIES TO READERS' QUERIES

STAINING GABOON TO SPANISH MAHOGANY *H.K. (Bradford) has tried bichromate of potash for the purpose, but has succeeded only in slightly darkening the shade.*

Reply.—Either a water or a naphtha stain would be suitable. There is little to choose between them. To make up around a pint of water stain put an ounce of lump vandyke brown in a jar, add a half-pint of very hot water and stir up well. This will give a brown. In another jar put a heaped teaspoonful of bismarck brown, add about a pint of hot water, and stir. This gives a dark blood-red. Let these stand until cool, then pour into fresh jars, leaving all undissolved ingredients. The original jars can be washed easily in water. If you now combine these in the proportion of a quarter brown to three-quarters red and add a tablespoonful of .880 ammonia you will get a stain which, used twice on the gaboon if necessary, will give the rich dark red required. You must try it on scrap first and adjust it by adding more brown or red. This proportion, however, is very near what you want. Bismarck brown is a spirit dye, but it dissolves well in water.

For a naphtha stain the simplest plan would be to get some *Ronuk Mahogany* and some of their *Fumed Oak*. These can be combined and adjusted to give the same effect. (528)

REMOVING PAINT FROM GLASS *J.F. (Chesterfield) has some glass which has had three or four coats of paint. He has tried a special paint remover with limited success.*

Reply.—The only practical way of removing paint from glass is by means of a paint remover, of which there are two varieties—the caustic or alkaline type and the spirituous type. You do not say which kind you have tried, but we assume that you have used a spirituous remover which is very volatile and which has evaporated before it has had time to act on more than a slight thickness of the paint film.

We would suggest that you either try another brand of spirituous remover which keeps "open" and working longer (e.g. "Quickstrip," made by *Quickstryp Chemical Co. Ltd.*, 57 Kingsland High Street, E.8) or else one of the alkaline variety. The latter is much cheaper and quite effective, but the objection to it is that if any alkaline residue is left on a porous surface, such as wood or plaster, it is liable to attack the new paint. It would therefore be necessary to take care that no remover came in contact with the frame or surround of the window, if these are of wood, and that if it did, that thorough washing of the affected surface was carried out before repainting. A spirituous remover which splashed or was otherwise deposited on adjoining paintwork would affect the paint but would leave no potentially harmful matter behind.

In removing the softened paint, you will find a safety razor blade "plane," such as is commonly used for removing posters and other printed matter from shop windows, to be very helpful. If you are anxious to avoid damage to the paintwork of the frame, you should apply the paint remover to the glass, leaving a safety area about ½ in. broad untreated : when the film is removed from the bulk of the work this strip can be tackled, dry, with a razor blade. (79)

WOOD BLOCK FLOOR FINISH *L.G.P. (Bristol) has moved into a new house with beech wood block floor. He would like information on the preparatory treatment and method of polishing. The blocks are marked here and there with splashes of the mastic in which they were laid.*

Reply.—You are fortunate in having a block floor which has not already been coated. These blocks are usually laid in a mixture of boiling pitch and creosote. It is inevitable that here and there some of the mastic goes astray, but experience has shown that the stain is not very penetrating. The fact that these marks exist leads one to believe that the blocks were of the faced, inter-locking type and were left as they were laid.

In normal times such floors are scraped and papered. During this process all signs of mastic disappear and the general effect is much enhanced. If such is the case with your floor it would pay handsomely to scrape it. Floor layers use a scraper blade of about ⅛ in. in thickness, sharpened as a plane iron with the edge further burred with a bradawl or the like. For your purpose, however, a 3 in. Skarsten scraper would be probably the best.

Regarding the question of staining, this depends entirely on individual taste —it would not necessarily spoil the natural beauty of the wood—but it cannot be denied that when the wood under review lends itself to such treatment, a natural finish is desirable. However well staining is done there is always the danger of places where the tread comes wearing bare. This can, of course, be reduced to a minimum—if not altogether avoided—by careful maintenance.

Staining, properly carried out, often helps greatly to bring out the depth and beauty of the markings, but I am not at all sure that this would be the case in all types of beech. The most important thing about staining is that it should penetrate deeply into the wood. Therefore varnish stains should be avoided. They merely lie on the surface. If you stain at all let it be a light medium one, applied as will be described later.

A durable and labour saving surface can be obtained by using an oil stain (if the work *is* to be stained) and applying two or more coats of polishing varnish or lacquer. Over a period of four years the writer has experienced the value of this treatment given to a kitchen block floor.

After treatment it was wax polished in the usual way and periodically given a wash.

The scheme is this :

(1) Swab over with half linseed oil and half *Universal Medium* (made by *Walpamur Co.*) suitably stained—in your case say burnt umber and a little raw sienna (both in oil). Wipe off surplus and leave a day to dry.

(2) Lightly paper and apply a coat of *Universal Medium* with a brush.

(3) After about eight hours flat down with abrasive paper in water with little soap as lubricant. Rinse off.

(4) Apply second coat and flat down as before.

If desired the second coat can be left in its bright state. Normal wax polishing can follow.

If the work is not to be stained omit the colour from the penetrating first coats. *Valspar* clear lacquer is also suitable for the work, particularly if you wish to preserve the light tone of the wood. (99)

BACK STEADY

steady upon which the latter can bear. Generally the wood in the early stages is stout enough to be free of vibration, but if there is difficulty it is generally possible to hold the left hand at the back on the revolving wood once the corners have been taken off to support it whilst light cuts are taken. This enables the wood to be rounded locally so that the steady can operate.

GARDEN CHAISE-LONGUE

This interesting piece of garden furniture can easily be wheeled to fresh positions, and is designed to give maximum comfort. It can be finished with clear varnish, so that the natural colour of the timber is preserved, or painted in a one- or two-colour scheme. If finished in a two-colour scheme it is recommended that one colour accentuates the main shape and the second applied to the surface of the seat and back laths (not edges or ends), the arms, and arm rests

IN order to minimize waste it is best to cut the curved shapes from prepared boards as in Fig. 3. Mark the shapes for the sides (A) and back (B), also the wheel struts (F) (Fig. 4).

It is advisable to plot the shapes on a graph, full size on stiff card or thin plywood, as in Fig. 3. As sections (A) are rather long and thin this could be difficult, but if the card is pinned onto the board from which these sections will eventually be cut it will be adequately supported and there will be a square edge to work from. Having drawn the shapes cut them out for use as templates on the appropriate prepared boards. Cutting these by hand with a bow-saw could be a long and tedious business and it is suggested that readers see if a local timber merchant might be prepared to do this on a band-saw.

After the side and back rails have been cut and cleaned, lay them together at approx. 105 degrees (see Fig. 2). When in this position, the angle between the side and back to take the wheel strut should be about 90 degrees. Cut another template to suit this angle and use it to mark the shoulders of the wheel strut joint. This can be either a mortise and tenon, as indicated in Fig. 4, or half-lap (see dotted lines). Mark also the mortise for the front legs. This is 12 in. to the centre from the handle end.

Shape both the legs so that when fitted the over-all length is 1 ft. 5 in. Cut both leg and wheel strut joints and fit together dry as a check. The gluing and cramping of the legs to the sides present no special difficulty, but if the wheel strut is tenoned it is advisable to joint both sides and back to the wheel strut independently. As each joint is made it can be held in place by driving in two or three panel pins so that they pass through the tenon. A similar procedure should be adopted if half-laps are used, except that screws replace panel pins.

Rails.—These items (C), (D), (E), and (G), Fig. 4, are cut to finish 1 ft. 7 in. The cross rail (G) is curved on the bottom edge to blend with the general pattern. This is a free-hand curve but should not be so deep that the rail is weakened. Holes are bored in the ends of all rails to take pieces of $\frac{3}{8}$ in. dowelling as in Fig. 4 to join with similar holes in the side pieces. Items (G) and (E) are dowelled together before fixing to the sides.

Laths.—These are prepared by squaring, and finishing to the exact width of the main frame. All sides and

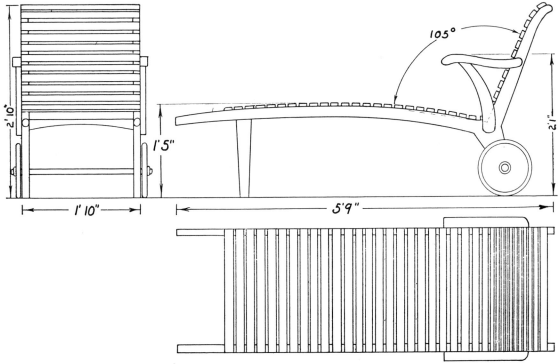

FIG. 2. ELEVATIONS AND PLAN WITH MAIN DIMENSIONS

FIG. I. AN INVITING GARDEN ITEM WHICH WOULD LOOK WELL PAINTED IN GAY COLOURS

edges should be carefully smoothed. Those at the foot and head have their outside corners rounded as indicated in Fig. 2. Each lath is glued and screwed to the side rails, the screws being countersunk and the depressions plugged with a suitable filler. Some slight trimming will be necessary for those situated at the junction of back and side so that each lath is equally spaced from its neighbour.

Arms.—These (J) and supports (I), Fig. 4, are shaped as shown in Fig. 3 (C) and (D) respectively. The meeting angle of the arm and its support can be determined by placing both parts on the side of the main section. The two parts are joined together with glue and dowels. When prepared, each unit is fixed to the sides, again with glue and dowels. Before fixing, see that all surfaces are smooth and edges slightly rounded.

Wheels. — Wooden wheels — 10 in. in diameter could be made, the metal axle, washers and caps being obtained separately. Alternatively, machine made wheels and axle could be fitted.

Finish.—Before varnishing or painting the handle part of the side rails should be tapered and rounded.

Real luxury could be obtained by having a foam rubber cushion or cushions, covered in suitable material, fitted to the whole of the back and seat.

CUTTING LIST

				Long ft. in.	Wide in.	Thick in.
(A)	2	Side rails (1 piece)	..	5 4	8½	1½
(B)	2	Back rails (1 piece)	..	2 5	8½	1½
(C)	1	Middle rail	..	1 7½	6	⅞
(D)	1	Top rail	..	1 7½	1¾	⅞
(E)	1	Front rail	..	1 7½	1¾	⅞
(F)	2	Wheel struts	..	1 0	6	1½
(G)	1	Lower front rail	..	1 7½	2½	⅞
(H)	2	Legs	..	1 4	2½	1½
(I)	2	Arm supports (1 piece)	..	1 4	6½	⅞
(J)	2	Arms (1 piece)	..	1 4	6½	1½
(K)	36	Seat and back laths	..	1 10½	1¼	⅝

Allowance has been made in lengths and widths. Thicknesses are net.

(94)

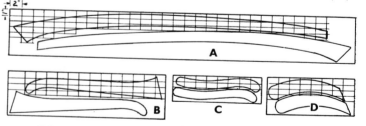

FIG. 3. ECONOMICAL SETTING-OUT FOR CURVED SHAPES
These are plotted on a full-size graph the grid being formed of 2 in. by 1 in. oblongs. Section (A) shows the two main side pieces ; (B) the back ; (C) arm rests, and (D) arm rest supports

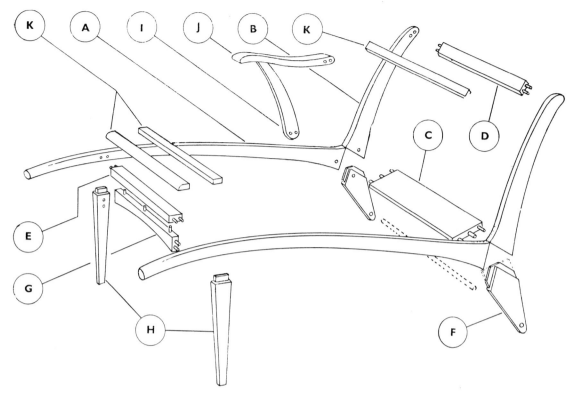

FIG. 4. DETAILS OF CONSTRUCTION

The principal parts are lettered to link with the cutting list. Suitable machine-made wheels and axle can be obtained from the South London Wheel Co. Ltd. (Dept. W), Lion Street, S.E.17. When ordering please give full details of dimensions

MAHOGANY DRESSING CABINET
(See pages 72 and 73.)

CUTTING LIST

					Long ft.	in.	Wide in.	Thick in.
(A)	2	Carcase ends	..	..	4	1	$20\frac{1}{2}$	$\frac{11}{16}$
(B)	3	Top rails	..	..	3	7	3	$\frac{11}{16}$
(C)	1	Bottom	..	..	3	7	$20\frac{1}{2}$	$\frac{11}{16}$
(D)	1	Back	..	..	4	1	42	$\frac{3}{8}$
(E)	1	Plinth rail	..	..	3	6	5	$\frac{7}{8}$
(F)	2	Ditto	..	..	1	9	5	$\frac{7}{8}$
(G)	1	Ditto	..	..	3	6	$5\frac{1}{2}$	$\frac{7}{8}$
(H)	1	Cross rail	..	..	1	8	$5\frac{1}{2}$	$\frac{7}{8}$
(I)	1	Lining	..	..	3	7	3	$\frac{3}{4}$
(J)	2	Linings	..	..	1	10	3	$\frac{3}{4}$
(K)	1	Top	..	..	3	8	22	$\frac{13}{16}$
(L)	4	Door stiles	..	..	4	2	3	$\frac{5}{8}$
(M)	4	Door rails	..	..	1	7	3	$\frac{5}{8}$
(N)	2	End lippings	..	..	4	1	1	$\frac{5}{8}$
(O)	1	Centre lipping	..	..	4	1	1	$\frac{3}{8}$
(P)	2	Door panels	..	..	4	1	21	$\frac{1}{4}$
(Q)	1	Door stop	..	..	4	1	$1\frac{1}{4}$	$\frac{1}{4}$
(R)	3	Shelves	..	..	3	$5\frac{1}{2}$	19	$\frac{5}{8}$
(S)	3	Backs	..	..	3	$5\frac{1}{2}$	$4\frac{1}{2}$	$\frac{3}{8}$
(T)	6	Bearers	..	..	1	7	$1\frac{1}{2}$	$\frac{7}{16}$

As a guide to timber, select figured African mahogany for items (A), (E), (F), and (K). Straight-grained Honduras mahogany is really desirable for (I), (J), (L), (M), (N), (O,) (Q), and (T). Obeche or gaboon is suitable for (B), (C), (R), and (S). Plain gaboon plywood is suggested for the carcase back, (D), and prepared veneered mahogany plywood for the door panels, (P). The inside plinth rails, (G) and (H), can be of deal or whitewood and any odd hardwood at hand may be utilized for tongues.

Sizes are generally full in length and width for trimming up, but thicknesses are net. Scheme the ends, top rails, and bottom to come out of $\frac{3}{4}$ in. stuff to finish as full as possible, say $\frac{11}{16}$ in. (99)

TIMBER IDENTIFICATION, by N. C. E. CLIFFORD

It is only during relatively modern times that anything like scientific identification of timber has been practised. Originally the man who constantly handled or worked in certain timbers, could name them almost by instinct, but the kinds that passed through his hands was extremely restricted, and once he left this group he was quite at sea. Today the range of timbers on the market at one time or another runs into several hundreds, and something more than instinct or intelligent guesswork is needed.

The author of this book claims that it is possible to learn identification from a text book, and in this book he explains the method, and gives the characteristics and features to be examined. It is a well written book and is illustrated with a wide range of photographs of timber, some showing surface markings normally seen, and other highly magnified photographs of end grain, showing the various pore arrangements. Line diagrams are also included, and there are colour plates.

The enlarged photographs of end grain are excellent, but it is extremely difficult to show convincing photographs of timbers as normally seen. Colour is missing, and when timbers have no outstanding characteristics they are often alike.

However, it is a most useful addition to literature on wood; schools, trade training centres, students, and technical people to whom the subject is important in particular will find it useful. Size 10 in. by $7\frac{1}{4}$ in. with 142 pages of text and 32 plates of photographs on art paper. Published by Leonard Hill (Books) Ltd., 9 Eden St., London, N.W.1. Price 37s. 6d. net.

SALT AND
PEPPER SHAKERS

by C. E. BAMPTON

piece, the two outer ones supporting and holding the work. Disc A, 1½ in. thick, should be mounted on the faceplate, trued up, and a ⅞ in. dia. hole bored nearly through. A scrap of felt or similar material is then glued round the inside of the top edge of the hole to prevent damage to the work. Disc B, 2 in. thick, is screwed to the first disc already

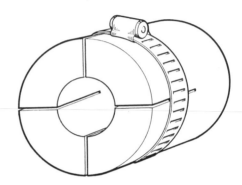

FIG. 2. VIEW OF CHUCK
Note jubilee clip for tightening on work.

on the faceplate (counterbore the screw holes to allow normal size screws to be used) and bore out to 2½ in. diameter. Disc C is ¾ in. thick and is screwed to disc B. A hole, say 1 in. dia., should now be bored, and carefully enlarged with a turning tool until the work rests in the chuck as shown in Fig. 3. This hole should also be felt lined.

Next take the chuck and faceplate together from the lathe, hold them in a vice with disc C uppermost and make 2 in. deep sawcuts with a fairly coarse saw as shown in Fig. 2. A 4 in. dia. jubilee clip can now be used to encircle the jaws thus formed which when tightened holds the work securely for boring out.

ALMOST ANY DARK hardwood is suitable for this salt and pepper pair. Prepare two 6 in. lengths of the selected wood and turn each to the outside dimensions shown in Fig. 1, finishing off by cutting accurately to length with a tenon saw. They can be partly cut through while still in the lathe.

A special chuck must now be made to hold the pieces for interior borings from the tailstock end. The chuck is shown in Figs. 2 and 3 and is made up from three 4 in. diameter discs, the centre one of which is simply a spacing

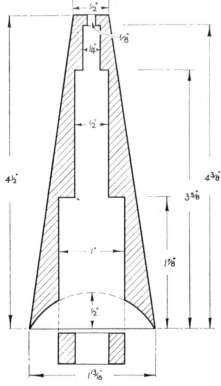

FIG. 1. DIMENSIONS FOR TURNING

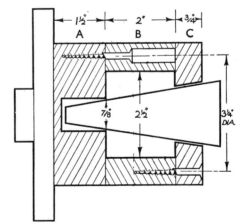

FIG. 3. DIMENSIONS OF CHUCK

58

The faceplate, chuck, and work should now be replaced on the lathe, making sure that the work revolves truly, and with the lathe running at moderate speed, use a round-nosed chisel to form the ½ in. deep cupping in the base of the work, Fig. 1. This of course may be of any convenient profile.

Next bore a ½ in. dia. hole 3⅝ in. deep and beyond this a ¼ in. dia. hole to a total depth of 4⅜ in. (see Fig. 1). This latter should leave ⅛ in. thickness of wood at the top. The ½ in. hole should be enlarged to 1 in. dia. to a depth of 1⅞ in. from the true base of the work, and be careful not to take this too deep or it will break through or weaken the sides of the work.

A plug has now to be turned to fit into the base of the shaker to take the cork. To make the plug prepare a short length of dowelling a reasonable push fit in the 1 in. hole of the base, cut off a ½ in. plug and glue into position. If required the plug may be turned to the concave contour of the cupped base before drilling a ½ in. dia. hole for the cork.

Finishing

Mount a 4 in. piece of ½ in. dowel in a chuck so that the work is a push-on fit for glasspapering and polishing. Afterwards the salt shaker will need a ⅛ in. dia. hole in the top, with five 1⁄16 in. holes arranged in a circle for the pepper piece. Arrange these five holes to splay out slightly from the centre.   (206-110)

Fruit trough

Young ideas

J. Wilson

Fig. I. The completed trough.
It should be taken apart prior to finishing with cellulose or french polish.

Ends. These are made from one piece of wood 6½ in. square by ⅝ in. thick. Before screwing to the face-plate for turning, the wood is marked to an octagonal shape. Diagonals are drawn to obtain the centre, and using this centre, a maximum size circle is drawn. A line is drawn through the centre parallel to the grain of the wood. The waste corners are then sawn off.

Fix the wood to the face-plate by means of two screws, which must be screwed into the wood exactly on this centre line. (The screw holes will be removed later when the wood is sawn in half.) The wood is now turned on the lathe to 6 in. dia., care being taken to ensure that the edge is made perfectly square.

Unscrew the wood from the face-plate, put a face-mark on both halves, and saw carefully down the centre line. The top edges planed square.

Slats. One end of each slat is first squared on a shooting-board, then they are placed together in the tray, the squared ends against the closed end. The positions of the screw holes and the length of the slats are now marked off. Remove the slats from the tray and saw to length, trimming up the ends on the shooting-board. The screw holes are now drilled with a ⅛ in. drill and slightly countersunk to take ½ in. raised head screws. The trough can now be assembled.

Legs. Cut out the shape with a coping saw, and spoke-shave to fit. It may be found necessary to plane slightly the slats to obtain a perfect fit. Mark where the outside edge of the outer slats meet the legs; from these points measure out 3/16 in. and mark. Measure out 2⅞ in. each side of the centre line and join the points to make the slope. Draw a small round on the top corners. The bottom curve can be drawn with the aid of a french curve. (136-355)

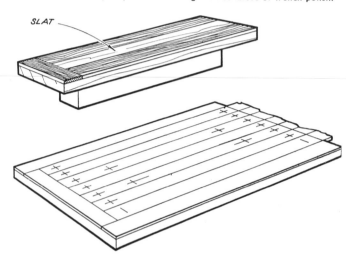

Fig. 2. Planing to size and marking out are easier in trays like these.
The ends should be shot square before marking out.

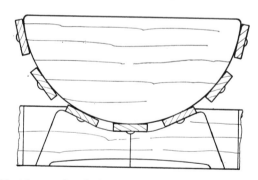

Fig 3. Marking out for the legs.
The taper should be planed before cutting out.

Fig. 4. Side and front elevation.

Cutting List

						Long ft. in.	Wide in.	Thick in.
Ends from	..	..	..	..	..	6½	6½	⅝
7 Slats	..	..	..	..	..	1 1¼	1⅛	3/16
Legs from	..	..	..	..	..	11	1¾	¾

1½ doz. ½ in. brass or NP. raised head screws.

Allowances have been made in lengths and widths; thicknesses are net.

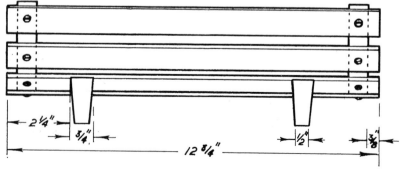

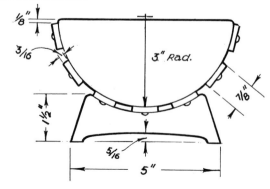

Wall secretaire

A. Yarwood

A wall secretaire will provide a writing surface and a place where writing material is readily available, in a room where floor space is limited. Imitation leather has been fitted to the writing flap to provide a firm, yet resilient writing surface, and box lines and escutcheon have been worked on to the flap to enhance the grain on the front surface.

Carcase. In order to obtain a matching grain it is advisable to cut the writing flap sides from the carcase sides. Thus boards at least 11 in. wide are needed for the carcase sides. The $\frac{3}{4}$ in. extra in width is necessary to allow accurate fitting between the shaped edges of the flap and carcase sides. The timber should be planed accurately to thickness, bearing in mind that the shelf under the top drawers is only $\frac{1}{2}$ in. thick whereas the remainder of the carcase pieces are $\frac{5}{8}$ in. thick (Fig. 1). These pieces are then planed to length. The sides should now be marked out, the writing flap edge pieces cut out with a bow saw and the sawn edges fitted by planing and spoke-shaving. It will be found that the flap side pieces are too wide. This is necessary as will be seen later. The carcase can now be jointed with double lap dovetails on the two top corners and stopped housings elsewhere (Fig. 5). It will be seen from Figs. 1, 2 and 5 that the two top drawers do not run on the drawer shelf but on prepared runners, $\frac{1}{2}$ in. thick, screwed and glued $\frac{3}{8}$ in. back from the front edge and slot screwed across the grain, the slot screwing being necessary to allow movement across the shelf. These drawer runners must be screwed in position before glueing up the carcase. When jointing is completed, work the sloping rebates on the back of the top and of the sides, noting that the rebates on the sides are stopped at the lower edge of the bottom shelf.

Clean up the carcase interior with scraper and glasspaper, and glue up.

Back. This is a frame with panels flush on its front side. This provides a flat surface against which the "pigeon holes" rest. The outer frame is made up from $1\frac{3}{4}$ in. by $\frac{5}{8}$ in. material and jointed with haunch mortice and tenons. The muntins, made from $1\frac{1}{4}$ in. by $\frac{5}{8}$ in. stuff are morticed and tenoned to the top and bottom rails. When the jointing is complete grooves $\frac{3}{16}$ in. wide by $\frac{1}{4}$ in. deep should be cut in all the inside edges and the frame cramped together dry. The panels, either from $\frac{3}{8}$ in. ply or $\frac{3}{8}$ in. "solid", are then sawn and planed to fit in the frame spaces with a bare $\frac{1}{4}$ in. overlap all around each panel. A rebate is next worked all round each panel edge to form tongues which will fit into the frame grooves (Fig. 3). The panels can then be fitted and the frame glued and cramped. When the glue has set, plane the flush face flat and fit the back into its rebates on the carcase. It can then be screwed in position using $1\frac{1}{4}$ in. by 8 screws set in screw caps.

Top drawers. These are made up with false fronts, the front proper being shaped and glued on after the drawer box has been made and fitted.

Being wall mounted, this attractive secretaire saves a lot of space in a small room

The drawers are made up from $\frac{3}{8}$ in. material. The sides are first planed to a tight sliding fit in their respective positions, and their front ends planed to the slope of the drawer fronts. The fronts are then planed to be a tight fit lengthways, but their widths left unplaned. When the drawers are made up and glued, the excess waste on top and bottom of the fronts can be planed off. Drawer slips and bottoms are fitted in a conventional manner.

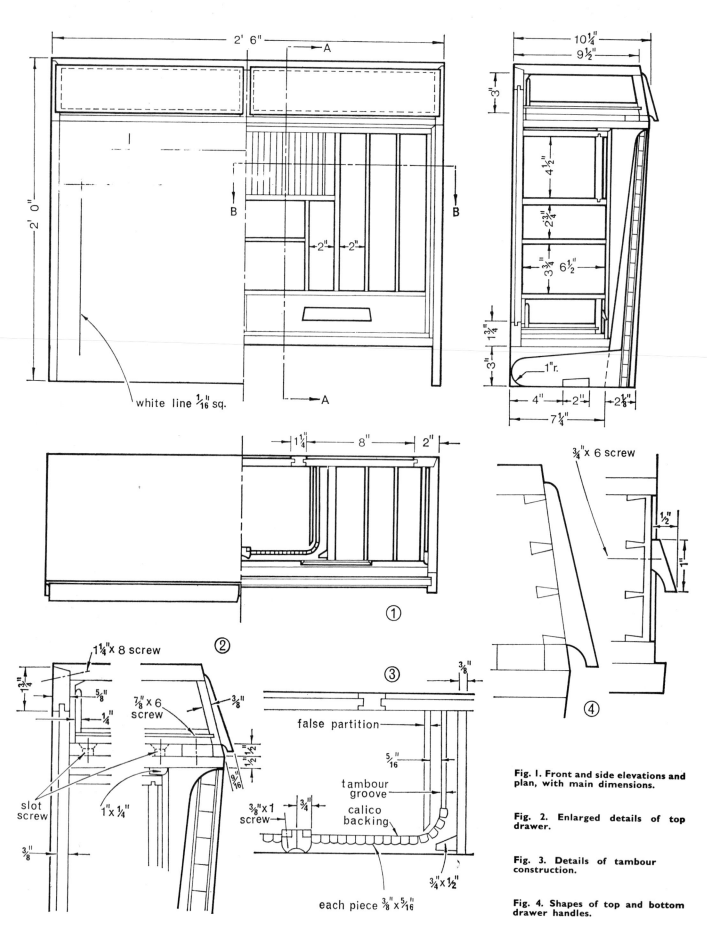

2' 6"

A

2' 0"

white line ⅟₁₆" sq.

B

B

2" 2"

A

10¼"

9½"

3"

4½"

2¾"

3¾" 6½"

1¾"

3"

1"r.

4" 2" 2⅛"

7¼"

1¼" 8" 2"

①

②

¾"x 6 screw

½"

1"

④

1¼"x 8 screw

1¾"

⅝"

¼"

⅞"x 6
screw

3/8"

1½"
1½"
9/16"

slot
screw

1"x ¼"

3/8"

③

3/8"

false partition

5/16"

tambour
groove

3/8"x 1 ¾"
screw

calico
backing

¾"x ½"

each piece 3/8"x 5/16"

Fig. I. Front and side elevations and
plan, with main dimensions.

Fig. 2. Enlarged details of top
drawer.

Fig. 3. Details of tambour
construction.

Fig. 4. Shapes of top and bottom
drawer handles.

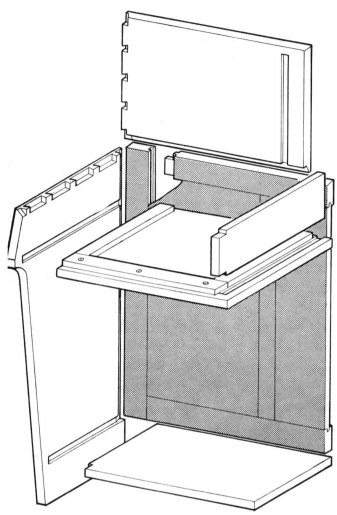

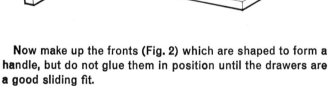

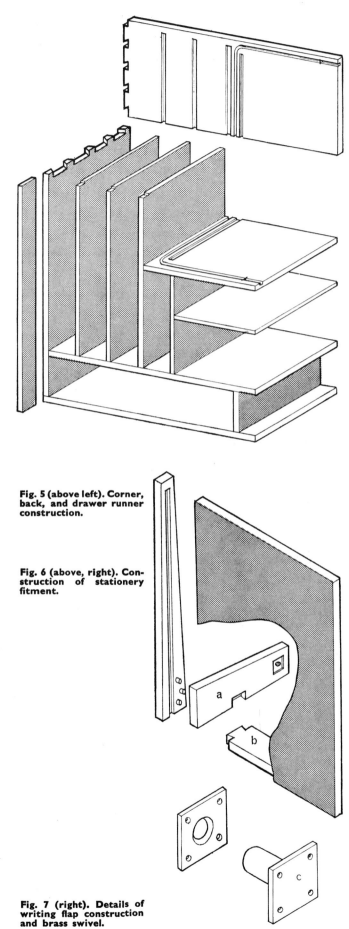

Now make up the fronts (Fig. 2) which are shaped to form a handle, but do not glue them in position until the drawers are a good sliding fit.

Stationery Fitment. This is made with through dovetails on the corners and stopped housings elsewhere (Fig. 6). It is made $\frac{1}{2}$ in. shorter and $\frac{1}{4}$ in. narrower than the space in which it is fitted. A close fit is later obtained by using wedge shaped strips each 1 in. wide by $\frac{1}{4}$ in. thick with front edges rounded and ends mitred at the corners. After cutting all the joints, the tambour grooves must be worked. These are $\frac{3}{16}$ in. deep and $\frac{3}{16}$ in. wide. The parts of these grooves crossing the grain are cut with saw, chisel and router; the parts with the grain can be cut using a scratch stock fitted with a $\frac{3}{16}$ in. wide blade; the curved parts of the grooves are cut using gouges and a thin chisel. It should be noted that the rounded part of the grooves must be slightly wider than $\frac{3}{16}$ in. to allow the tambour strips to run smoothly along them. Stops consisting of insets of small strips of brass, about $\frac{5}{16}$ in. by $\frac{3}{16}$ in. and $\frac{1}{32}$ in. thick, are fitted centrally on the front tambour grooves to prevent the doors sliding past the central position. Note the grooves for the false partitions. False partitions are necessary to prevent articles in the cupboard compartment jamming against the tambours and so preventing them from working.

When all the jointing is complete, the inside surfaces of the fitment members should be cleaned up and the assembly

Fig. 5 (above left). Corner, back, and drawer runner construction.

Fig. 6 (above, right). Construction of stationery fitment.

Fig. 7 (right). Details of writing flap construction and brass swivel.

63

can be glued. It is advisable to make use of strips of Sellotape along all joint surrounds to prevent glue sticking to wood near joints. When the fitment has been glued, it can be cleaned up externally and placed in its position in the carcase. The wedge shaped holding strips are then fitted and their positions marked. Now take off the carcase back and remove the fitment. The holding strips can then be screwed in position against the inside carcase walls and the fitment pushed against them from the rear. Do not at this stage screw the back on again.

In making the small drawers, sides and back need be only a bare $\frac{1}{4}$ in. thick. The handles are made from small strips of mahogany and screwed in position from the rear of the drawer fronts.

Tambours. 32 strips of good, straight grained mahogany, each $4\frac{7}{8}$ in. long by $\frac{3}{8}$ in. wide by $\frac{5}{16}$ in. thick are required. These are all planed to size and one of the $\frac{3}{8}$ in. sides of each piece slightly rounded by planing and glasspapering. To make up each door 16 pieces are placed with the rounded side downwards, side by side, flat on to a piece of thick ply, and then held by thin strips $\frac{1}{4}$ in. thick pinned on the ply on the outside of the assembled 16 pieces. The backs of the 16 strips can then be planed level with a finely set plane. Next glue on to this surface a piece of strong calico cloth 4 in. wide and long enough to overlap each end by about $\frac{1}{2}$ in. A rubber based impact glue, e.g. *Evostick*, is best for this purpose. Shape the handles and glue these to the overlapping calico, fixing with a thin strip of wood in the handle rebate glued and screwed against the back of the cloth. Next work the rebate on the front tops and bottoms of the doors so that a tongue is left which fits in the tambour grooves. The tambours can now be fitted and slid in the grooves from the rear. So that they run easily candle wax should be worked on to the tongue and into the grooves. When satisfied that the tambours are running easily, the false partitions can be glued in and the strips each $\frac{3}{4}$ in. by $\frac{1}{2}$ in. can be shaped and fitted each side of the doors as shown in Fig. 3. The carcase back can now be screwed in position.

Writing flap. The flap sides previously cut from the carcase sides can now be worked. The front edges of these should first be planed so that they are parallel to the groove in which the flap front fits. Then the stopped grooves $\frac{1}{2}$ in. wide by $\frac{1}{4}$ in. deep are cut with plough plane and chisels and the front edges then planed to their finished shape. A slight curve along the length of these edges gives a pleasing finish.

A flat piece of $\frac{5}{8}$ in. lamin or blockboard is selected for the front. It is planed exactly to size and $\frac{1}{2}$ in. by $\frac{1}{4}$ in. tongues worked on the ends by cutting a rebate along the front ends (plan Fig. 1).

The hingeing strips (a, Fig. 7) are shaped and fixed to the ends using $\frac{1}{2}$ in. dowels. The strip (b) in Fig. 7 is then dovetailed into these hingeing strips.

The flap front should now be veneered with afrormosia veneer. It is advocated that this be carried out using an impact glue, the advantage of which is that one need not worry about the warping so often resulting from the use of glues requiring water in their make up. The grooves for the $\frac{1}{16}$ in. line should next be cut using cutting gauge, scratch stock, wide chisel and $\frac{1}{16}$ in. chisel. The line is glued in position and when dry the panel can be thoroughly cleaned up with scraper and glasspaper.

The writing fall can now be glued up and fitted in its position. A purpose-made pair of brass swivels is shown in Fig. 7, the brass plate (c) being let into the inside of the carcase end. Accurate fitting of these is essential. A cut drawer lock must be fitted inside the flap to hold it in position. A piece of imitation leather is now fitted and glued on to the writing surface. Again use an impact glue.

Finish and fitting to wall. The interior is best finished with a brush coat of white French polish rubbed down with wire wool and waxed. The exterior can be treated with two coats of teak oil.

If several $\frac{3}{16}$ in. holes are bored through the frame of the panelled back and screw caps fitted to these holes, the secretaire can be screwed against the wall using $1\frac{1}{2}$ in. No. 8 rawlplugs and 2 in. No. 8 screws. With the writing flap down, its surface should be at about 2 ft. 5 in. from the floor level.

(278-367)

Cutting List	*Long ft.*	*in.*	*Wide in.*	*Thick in.*
Carcase				
2 ends	2	$0\frac{1}{2}$	11	$\frac{5}{8}$
1 top	2	$6\frac{1}{2}$	10	$\frac{5}{8}$
1 bottom	2	6	$7\frac{1}{4}$	$\frac{5}{8}$
1 shelf	2	6	10	$\frac{1}{2}$
1 drawer partition		4	10	$\frac{5}{8}$
2 drawer runners	1	$2\frac{1}{2}$	$1\frac{1}{2}$	$\frac{1}{2}$
4 drawer runners		8	$1\frac{1}{2}$	$\frac{1}{2}$
2 back stiles	1	$9\frac{1}{2}$	2	$\frac{5}{8}$
2 back rails	2	5	2	$\frac{5}{8}$
2 back muntins	1	8	$1\frac{1}{2}$	$\frac{5}{8}$
3 back panels	1	6	$8\frac{3}{4}$	$\frac{3}{8}$
Stationery Fitment				
2 ends	1	4	$6\frac{3}{4}$	$\frac{3}{8}$
3 shelves	2	$4\frac{1}{2}$	$6\frac{3}{4}$	$\frac{3}{8}$
1 drawer partition		$3\frac{1}{2}$	$6\frac{3}{4}$	$\frac{3}{8}$
2 upright partitions	1	$0\frac{1}{2}$	$6\frac{3}{4}$	$\frac{3}{8}$
4 upright partitions	1	$0\frac{1}{2}$	$6\frac{3}{4}$	$\frac{1}{4}$
2 upright partitions		$7\frac{1}{2}$	$6\frac{3}{4}$	$\frac{1}{4}$
1 shelf		5	$6\frac{3}{4}$	$\frac{1}{4}$
32 tambour strips		$5\frac{3}{8}$	$\frac{5}{8}$	$\frac{5}{16}$
2 tambour handles		$5\frac{3}{8}$	1	$\frac{5}{8}$
2 false partitions		$5\frac{1}{2}$	6	$\frac{1}{4}$
2 tambour handle strips		$5\frac{3}{8}$	$\frac{1}{2}$	$\frac{3}{16}$
2 tambour compartment strips ..		5	1	$\frac{1}{2}$
2 drawer fronts	1	2	3	$\frac{1}{2}$
4 drawer sides		$6\frac{1}{2}$	3	$\frac{1}{4}$
2 drawer backs	1	2	$2\frac{1}{4}$	$\frac{1}{4}$
4 drawer slips		6	1	$\frac{1}{4}$
2 drawer bottoms	1	$1\frac{1}{2}$	6	3 mm ply
2 drawer handles		6	$1\frac{1}{4}$	$\frac{1}{2}$
Carcase Drawers				
2 false fronts	1	$2\frac{1}{2}$	$3\frac{1}{2}$	$\frac{3}{8}$
4 sides		10	$3\frac{1}{4}$	$\frac{3}{8}$
2 backs	1	$2\frac{1}{2}$	$2\frac{1}{2}$	$\frac{3}{8}$
4 slips		10	1	$\frac{3}{8}$
2 bottoms	1	2	9	3 mm ply
2 fronts	1	$3\frac{1}{4}$	$3\frac{3}{4}$	$\frac{5}{16}$
Writing Flap				
2 ends—from carcase sides				
1 writing surface	2	$5\frac{3}{4}$	20	$\frac{5}{8}$ blockboard
2 hingeing arms		9	3	$\frac{5}{8}$
1 strip	2	$5\frac{1}{4}$	$2\frac{1}{4}$	$\frac{5}{8}$

Allowances have been made in lengths and widths, thicknesses are net. Small parts extra.

Needlework box

C. J. Colston, D.L.C.

This box, which is made of English walnut and sycamore, was designed to hold patterns, cotton reels and work in progress and not as a store for accumulations of material. The stool is a normal table and as can be seen in Fig. 1, there is provision at the front of the drawer for the storage of knitting needles.

The box. Apart from the sides of the box, which are planed up $\frac{1}{8}$ in. wider than the finished width to allow the top to be sawn off, all the wood is prepared to the finished sizes. Gauge lines are made to mark the positions for the grooves at the top and the bottom of the box and also to mark the position for the cut which is made to remove the top. Now that this has been done, the mitred through-dovetails are marked out and cut, remembering that a large mitred pin is left where the saw cut comes so that, when the top is separated, mitres appear on these surfaces.

The grooves are ploughed in the sides for the top and bottom, and the sycamore bottom is cut to size, rebated all round and fitted, making allowance for shrinkage and expansion.

The top. As can be seen in Fig. 1, this gives the appearance of a fielded panel and it is made as follows.

Four pieces of walnut are carefully selected and matched to give a quartered effect. These pieces are planed square and true to make the oblong centre panel. It is advisable to cut $\frac{1}{8}$ in. grooves in the centre of each edge and fit hardboard tongues in these to give increased glueing area. The panel may now be gouged hollow to relieve it and then glued up. After it has been cleaned up, a groove is cut in the centre of each edge to receive the side rails which are made next. These are mitred on all corners and they are made a loose fit around the centre panel to allow for shrinkage and expansion. Again, each piece is grooved all round and hardboard tongues are fitted into the mitres.

Each part of the top is cleaned up and polished.

All the inside faces of the box are cleaned up and polished and the complete box is glued up taking care that no glue penetrates the grooves. When the glue has set, the lid is sawn from the box, using a fine dovetail saw, and the sawn surfaces are planed to the gauge lines. This ensures a perfectly fitting and matching joint. The lid is then hinged to the carcase and the ebony handle dovetailed into the edge of the lid and finally shaped.

Lining. The sycamore for the lining is rebated on the long sides only and the rebate receives the tray which holds the cotton reels. The lining is made as a mitred box which fits closely inside the walnut one. An alternative method is to fit the lining as a dovetailed box. A sliding stay is made and the locus for its movement is worked out before any attempt is made to fit it. Sufficient wood is removed from the lining to

An elegant design for a needlework box, with a fielded lid panel.

allow this movement to take place without friction and the stay is fitted. The lining is polished, glued up and slid into position.

The tray. Through-dovetails are cut on the corners and the partitions are let into the sides with stopped housings. A bottom is made and grooved into the sides. After checking, the tray is glued up and polished. It should now run smoothly along the rebates in the sides of the lining.

The stool. Fig. 2 shows the construction for this. Double mortice and tenons are used to make the back portion of the stool and the front is made as in the drawing.

When all the joints are cut the sides can be grooved to receive the runners and kickers. It is vital, if the drawer is to fit properly, that these should be parallel and out of

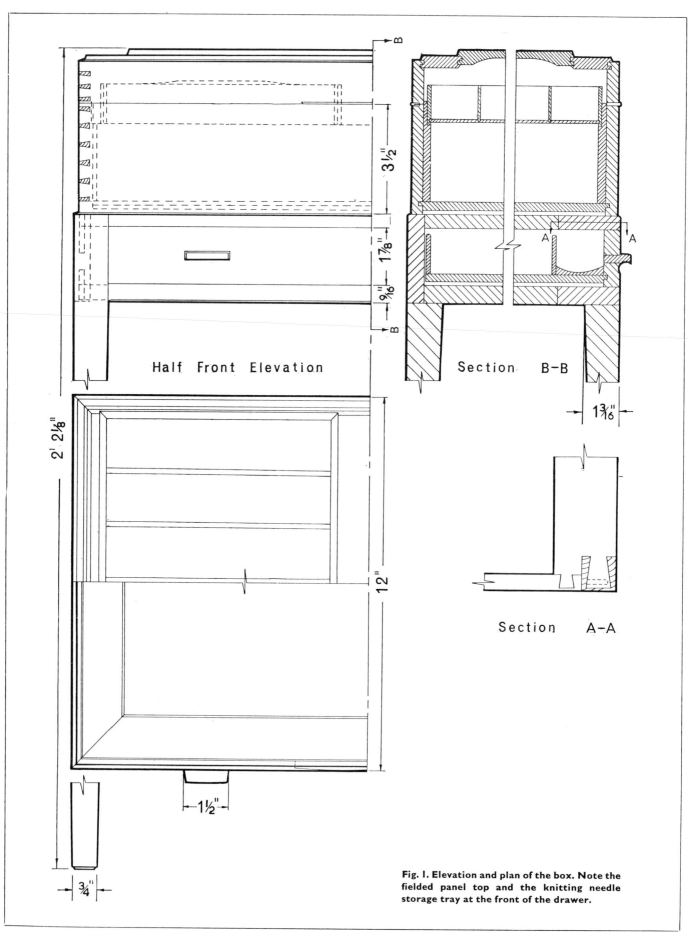

Half Front Elevation

Section B-B

Section A-A

Fig. 1. Elevation and plan of the box. Note the fielded panel top and the knitting needle storage tray at the front of the drawer.

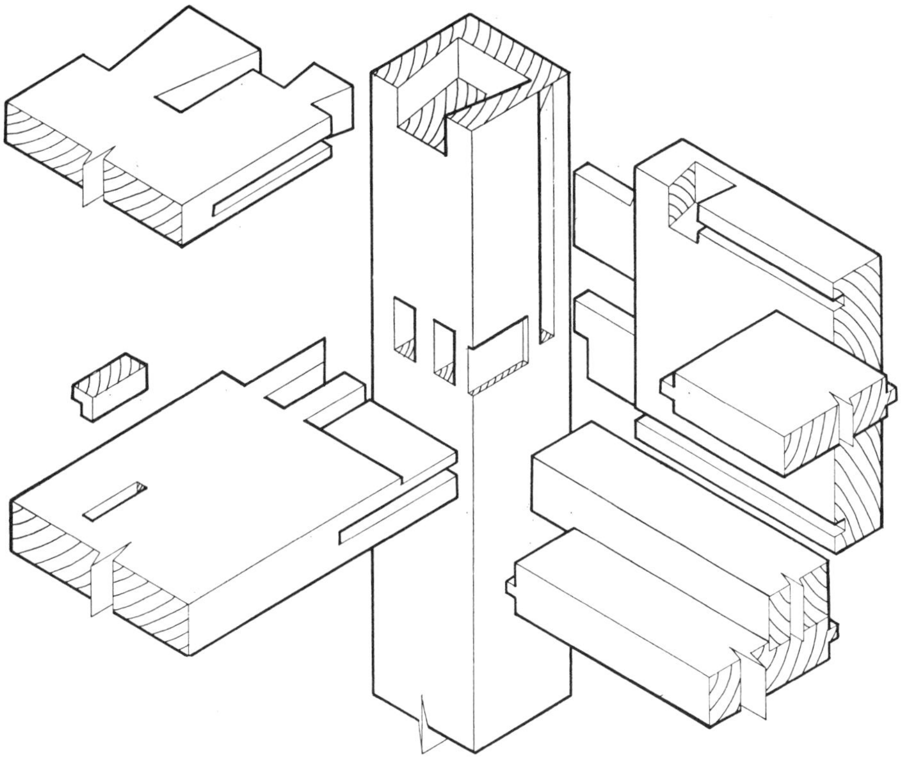

Cutting List	Long		Wide	Thick
Carcase	*ft.*	*in.*	*in.*	*in.*
2 Sides	1	8	5½	⅜
2 Sides	1	0¼	5½	⅜
1 Top panel	1	5	9	⅜
2 Side rails		11¾	1¾	⅜
2 Side rails	1	8	1¾	⅜
1 Bottom	1	7¾	11¾	¼
Underframe				
4 Legs	1	9⅝	—	1 3/16 sq.
2 Side rails	1	0½	3⅛	⅝
1 Back rail	1	8	3⅛	⅝
1 Front rail	1	8	2¼	7/16
1 Front rail	1	8	2¼	9/16
2 Kickers	1	0¼	1¼	7/16
2 Runners	1	0¼	1¼	9/16
1 Button		4	3	⅝
Drawer				
1 Drawer front ..	1	6	2⅛	⅝
2 Sides	1	0	2⅛	⅜
1 Back	1	6	1½	⅜
1 Bottom	1	5½	12	¼
2 Slips	1	0	⅝	⅜
2 Handles		2	1⅛	¼
Tray				
2 Sides		8½	1½	¼
2 Sides		11½	1½	¼
3 Partitions		11½	1½	¼
1 Division		8½	1¾	¼
1 Bottom		11½	8⅛	⅛
1 Lid lift..		5	¾	⅛

Allowances have been made to lengths and widths, thicknesses are net.

wind. When making the runners notice the way a rebate is cut in the top surface to take the drawer guide.

The short sides of the stool are now glued up and the mortices are cut in the front and back rails to receive the tongues on the ends of the runners and kickers. At the same time the mortices are cut for the drawer stops. When all these have been fitted the bottom rail and the back can be glued into place, followed by the top rail. Next, the runners and kickers are glued into place, and finally the drawer guides are glued into their rebates.

After polishing and glueing up, the outside is cleaned up, chamfers cut and all polishing completed. The stool is fastened to the box by screwing through the front rail, slot screwing through the kickers and buttoning at the back.

The drawer. First of all the drawer front is fitted into the opening and the back and sides are cut to length. The lap-dovetails at the front and the through-dovetails at the back are cut and the drawer slips are made. The groove in the front of the drawer is cut to receive the bottom and the bottom is fitted (Fig. 3).

The division at the front of the drawer is now stopped housed into position and the mortices for the drawer pulls are cut. All inside parts of the drawer are polished and the drawer is glued up. Finally the curved piece of wood is made and glued into position. This piece facilitates the removal of the knitting needles.

The drawer stops are now made, ensuring that the grain runs vertically, and glued into position. After the drawer has been fitted the drawer pulls are made from ebony. The grain on these should run from front to back or else they are liable to snap off. The drawer is cleaned up and polished and the handles are glued into position.

A final wax polish is applied and the needlework box is completed.

Fig. 2. (above) An exploded view of the stool corner joints

Fig. 3. (below) Expoded view of the drawer corner joint.

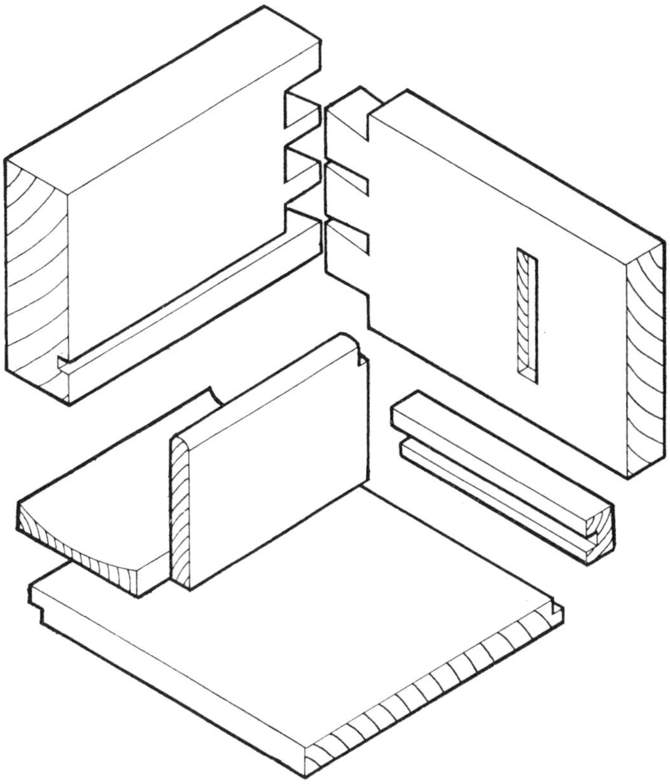

Coffee table: period style

by John L. Ford

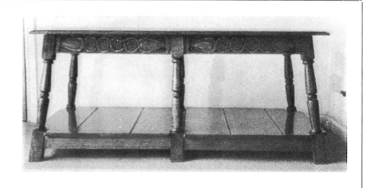

This coffee table, made in English oak, is of generous proportions and can be used for informal meals. Added to this, the lower shelf will accommodate the usual household implements. The top rails, carved with Jacobean-style guilloche pattern, separate the six slightly splayed, turned legs. The construction is fairly straightforward and is carried out in the following sequence.

Legs. As all six legs must be the same shape, a templet must be made. The desired shape is turned from a scrap piece of wood which is then cut in half lengthways so as to lie flat on a piece of plywood. The outline is transferred to the plywood and the shape cut out. This templet is then used to match the six actual legs, each of which can be sanded while still on the lathe.

Carving the upper rails. The outline of the design is first marked in pencil on each rail. As this particular pattern is rather tedious to carve completely by hand, I searched, with little success, for tools which would cut suitable circles. I experimented with tank cutters but as a central hole was left I discarded this idea. The accompanying diagrams show the solution.

The two tools are constructed of hard steel and are of different radii. They are designed to be held in a pillar drill. The smaller one is fitted and the rail to be carved is firmly clamped to the drill platform so that the first of the small circles can be cut. The larger tool is then substituted and will cut the outside semi-circles on the same

centre. In this latter case the drill must be rotated the required distance manually, several times until the required depth of cut is reached. Retaining the larger tool in the drill, the wood is re-positioned such that the next outer semi-circle continues the line of the first cut inner circle. The second inner circle is now cut using this centre. Each new part of the design is started on the larger tool.

Once the basic pattern has been cut as described the central 'floral motif' is easily accomplished with vertical cuts of a suitable U-shaped gouge round the inside of the pre-cut circle. The flower centre is cut using a tool called

a wad punch which I discovered at a local ironmongers. This tool resembles a strong apple corer.

The remainder of the fielding is taken down with suitable tools and frosted, using a repoussing punch.

Frame jointing and assembly. Tenons are cut on the top and bottom rails remembering to allow for the slope of the legs. Careful cutting and checking is required here in order that all joints fit snugly. Having cut the joints all round, the frame is assembled dry to further check that all is well before proceeding. The legs can be cut to

Fig. 1, (above). Showing detail of the guilloche carving.

Fig. 2, (below). Elevations with principal dimensions.

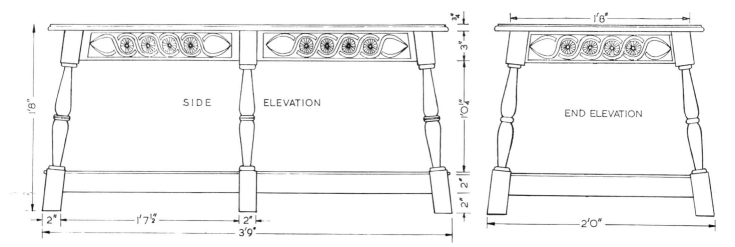

SIDE ELEVATION

END ELEVATION

length at the correct angle after dismantling. On the middle two, this is a sloping cut, using the circular saw with the table set at 90 deg. + angle x (see Fig. 3). The angle is compound on the remaining four and the saw table is kept at the same angle as before but the mitre gauge is also set to 90 deg. + angle x. Make sure that the slope is the correct way for each leg. Both the top and bottom of each leg are cut in the same manner and the cut surfaces should finish parallel. If no circular saw is available the cut can be marked all round the top and bottom of each leg and carefully cut with a handsaw.

In glueing up it is advisable to plane some blocks of wood for the sash cramps so that they pull at right angles when tightened (see Fig. 3). The sides are glued first and, when set, the end rails are glued across.

Top and lower shelf. The top is in two pieces with a rubbed joint down the middle. A simple moulding is worked around the edge in the same manner as that of the oak chest lid (*Woodworker,* October).

The lower shelf consists of a number of boards lying across the lower rails with no attempt made to disguise the edge to edge joints. The edges were, in fact, chamfered slightly, to show them clearly. Two battens are screwed from underneath to hold these in place. No further fixing is required due to the fact that they cannot move either lengthways or sideways when screwed up.

The top is fixed to the frame using brass glass plates as shown.

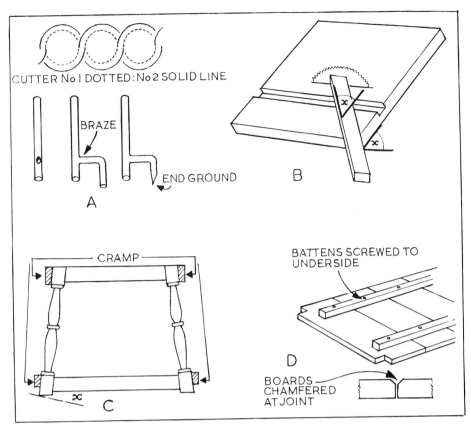

Fig. 3. (A) Details of special bit for guilloche circles. (B) How legs are cut at correct angle. (C) Use of cramping blocks. (D) How undershelf is made up.

Finishing. The table is now ready for cleaning up and, in my case, to be fumed with ammonia, oiled and wax polished as detailed in a previous article.

Parts List

No. req'd	Description	Long ft.	in.	Wide in.	Thick in.
6	Legs	1	8	2	2
2	Top rails (sides)	3	4	3	$\frac{7}{8}$
2	Top rails (ends)	1	7	3	$\frac{7}{8}$
2	Bottom rails (sides)	3	8	2	$\frac{7}{8}$
2	Bottom rails (ends)	1	10	2	$\frac{7}{8}$
1	Top	3	10	22	$\frac{3}{4}$
1	Lower shelf: Sufficient 2 ft. lengths of random widths to make a total width of 3 ft. 9 in.				
2	Battens	3	4	1	1

No allowance has been made for waste. **Also required:** 6 brass glass plates, screws, etc.

These shelves are self-supporting by means of struts which exert a sideways thrust on the sides of the alcove equal to twice the combined weight of the bookcase and the books it holds. The friction between the sides of the bookcase and the wall is thus sufficient to support the bookcase. To ensure that there is adequate friction, either coarse cotton cloth may be affixed to the wall plates or they may be left rough sawn. On no account should any of the parts comprising the bookcase be glued together, unless instructions specify.

(This design is the subject of Provisional Patent No. 06222 dated March 6th, 1971, and must not be produced commercially without the permission of the designer).

by John P. Saunders

SELF-SUPPORTING BOOKSHELVES

The books must be evenly distributed and loading must always commence from the centre outwards. When empty, an even distribution of weight is achieved by the weight of the centre piece being approximately the same as the combined weight of the two wall plates. The centre support is prevented from moving either forward or backward by the shelves fitting closely. This is achieved automatically in the lower shelves by their outer ends resting on sloping ledges—see detail (i) Drg. A. With the top shelves, any looseness is taken up by wedges set in the centre support—see detail (i) Drg. C.

Stage one—The Rod:
Draw up the full scale drawing on hardboard from which all measurements will be taken: See Drg. A.

Method
Measure alcove which is to house the bookcase, accurately; it is preferable to use the same measuring instrument throughout. Set out one line on a sheet of hardboard to represent one wall, and one line to represent the central line so that the distance between the two lines is precisely half the measured length of the alcove. Draw in the wall plate (parts a and b) against the line of the wall. Draw in the centre piece (f)

around the central line and allowing $\frac{3}{16}$in. housing, draw in the top shelf. For the lower shelf allow $\frac{3}{16}$in. housing in (f) and draw the shelf to meet (b)—see detail (i) Drg. A. Draw in the strut (e) inclined at 14 deg. to the horizontal at the wall plate where (e) joins (b), and draw in the notch as shown in detail (ii), Drg. A.

Stage two—Construction:
Wall Plate—Parts (a) and (b)
From material 6in. by 1in., cut two lengths for parts (a) and (b). Set bevel to 30 deg. and mark off the sloped end of (b)—see Fig. 1. Saw the end to an angle of 30 deg.—see Fig. 2. Clean the

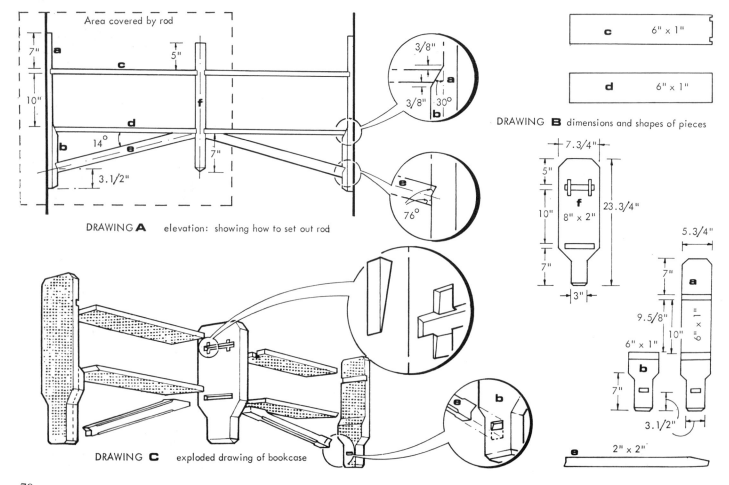

DRAWING **A**   elevation: showing how to set out rod

DRAWING **C**   exploded drawing of bookcase

DRAWING **B** dimensions and shapes of pieces

Fig. 1. Marking off slope on top of part (b)

Fig. 2. Cutting angle on part (b) to 30°.

Fig. 3. Cleaning up slope on part (b).

Fig. 4. Glueing (a) and (b) together to make wall plate.

Fig. 5 Marking out shelf housing in plate.

Fig. 6. Cutting bevels on wall plate with spokeshave.

Fig. 7. Finishing off notch in wall plate.

Fig. 8. Completed wall plate.

Fig. 9. Drilling out housing in centre support.

Fig. 10. Cleaning up bottom of centre support shelf housing with router.

Fig. 11. Cutting wedges.

Fig. 12. Cutting wedge housings.

sawn surface, using a plane: see Fig. 3. Glue (b) to bottom of (a), using cramps (see Fig. 4). Alternatively, screws can be used coming through from the back of (a). Mark and cut the housing for top shelves (c) $\frac{3}{16}$in. deep as in Fig. 5.

The wall plate is now shaped and the edges bevelled, using a spokeshave, or a Surform

shaper; see Fig. 6. From the drawing, mark out the position of the notch which locates the end of strut (e); see detail (ii) Drg. C and chop this out with a chisel, (Fig. 7). Fig. 8 shows the completed wall plate.

Centre Support—Part (f)
This is made from material 8in. by 2in. Mark out the four housings for the shelf ends, two on

each side. Since (f) is wider than part (a) of the wall plates, it is necessary to use a different method when cutting the housings. Using a brace and bit, drill a row of holes $\frac{3}{16}$in. deep within each housing area; see Fig. 9.

Remove waste and clean the edges with a chisel. Finish the bottoms of the housings with

Fig. 13. Completed wedges, one in place.

Fig. 14. Chopping out notches for wedges.

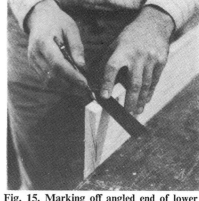

Fig. 15. Marking off angled end of lower shelf.

Fig. 16. Cutting lower shelf to angle of 60°

Fig. 17. Cutting outer ends of struts.

Fig. 18. Shaping inner ends of struts.

a router as in Fig. 10. Cut (f) to shape, and bevel the edges. From ¾in. stuff, cut four wedges 3½in. long by ½in. deep—see Fig. 11. Across each top housing mark out two housings for the wedges 3½in. long by ¾in. wide, set in ½in. from the end of the shelf housing. See detail (i), Drg. C. Cut the wedge housings to slope to ½in. depth, using a chisel, (Fig. 12).

Upper Shelves—Part (c)
The length of the shelves is obtained from the full scale drawing. It is most important that the shelves are cut accurately to length. From material 6in. by 1in. cut the two upper shelves to length, remembering to allow for the ³⁄₁₆in. housing at each end. On the inner end of each shelf chop away two notches to accommodate wedges; these notches are ¾in. wide by ³⁄₁₆in. deep and set in ½in. from the sides. See Fig. 14 and also Drg. B.

Lower Shelves—Part (d)
The outer end of each shelf (d) must be angled to rest on the slope of (b)—see detail (i), Drg. A. Using two pieces of material 6in. by 1in. cut one end of each, square. On your full scale drawing measure the distance from the square end, allowing for the ³⁄₁₆in. housing in (f), to the angled end measuring along the top of the shelf. Transfer this measurement to the edge of the shelf and mark off the angle, using a bevel set to 60 deg.—see Fig. 15, and cut the shelf to this angle: Fig. 16. For a decorative effect, bevel each side of all four shelves.

Struts—Part (e)
On material 2in. by 2in. mark out the outer ends of the struts to fit the notches in the wall plate, using a bevel set to 76 deg.—see detail (ii), Drg. A. Shape the outer ends with two symmetrical saw cuts as in Fig. 17. Cut the length of (e) from the full scale drawing, allowing an extra ¼ in. at the inner end. Cut the inner ends to shape—see Fig. 18.

Bevelling
In general, bevelling should always be stopped short of a joint in order not to interfere with the proper fitting of the latter. The bevelling on the wall plates and the centre support should be heavier than that on the shelves, and the bevelling of the struts should be even deeper than that of the centre piece and wall plates, to give a waisted effect.

ASSEMBLY

Mark the intended positions of the wall plates. You will need two helpers to hold the wall plate in situ. Insert the top shelves into the upper housing of the wall plates at an angle which will allow the centre support to be passed between them. Fit the shelf ends into the upper housings in the centre support, leaving out the wedges. Lower the centre support until shelves are approximately 1in. out of horizontal.

Fit the struts into their notches in the wall plate, and resting on centre support immediately below the lower shelf housings—see Fig. 19. With both struts in position the structure is now self-supporting. The extra ¼in. allowed on the struts will cause the upper shelves in position to rise at the centre support instead of lying in a straight line. Using a straight edge, measure the amount by which the shelves have risen in the middle. The shelves will be brought level by removing one quarter of this distance from each strut. For example: if the distance that the shelves have risen measures 1in., then you will remove ¼in. from the end of each strut. Dismantle the structure and adjust the length of each strut.

Re-assemble as before, but this time before starting, tape the wedges into position. After the struts have been fitted, fit the lower shelves. Untape the wedges and take up any slack in the upper shelves with the wedges. Load the bookcase with books from the centre outwards.

If there should be a tendency for the bookcase

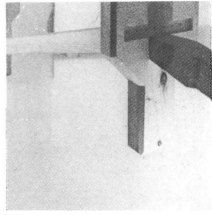

Fig. 19. Position of struts on centre support during assembly.

to slip due to the walls being covered with a slipper-surfaced wallpaper (for example, Vinyl), the wall plates may be coated twice with impact adhesive which must be allowed to dry completely, and this will increase the friction between the wallpaper and the wall plates of the bookcase.

BIRD NESTING BOXES and a TIT FEEDER

Many of us like to do a bit of bird-watching – and here I am alluding to the feathered variety! So why not make a tit nesting box for the garden? Tits are charming little birds to watch, their antics sometimes being fantastic. The box shown here is based on the design used by the Lincolnshire Trust for Nature Conservation on their reserves; they are usually sited in woodlands but are equally suitable for garden use.

by W. L. Rowson

Very few tools are needed to make these boxes; just a saw, hammer, chisel, set-square and a brace with 1⅛-inch bit. 2-inch and 1½-inch wire nails will be needed. Softwood is ideal and off-cuts can come in handy or even old salvaged timber, providing it is sound, can be pressed into service. The wood need not be planed but it is a help if it is of reasonably even thickness throughout.

Tit Box
Little need be said about the construction. It is best to drill the hole before assembly (this need not necessarily be in the side shown) and also to cut the groove in the back to take the top end of the roof. When assembling, nail the back to the two sides and then fit the bottom before nailing on the front. The batten under the roof should be positioned to stop it sliding out of the groove in the back. A good coat of creosote on the outside only will help to preserve the box.

If you want a rustic effect, go to your local timber yard and get some outsides or "slab" to clad the box with – these are the first pieces to come off the saw when they start

converting the log. Pieces about 4 inches wide will be the most useful; they can then be trimmed in width to take two pieces on each face of the box and roof.

Entrance Holes
While a 1⅛-inch hole has been specified in the tit box, a 1-inch hole will allow a blue tit, marsh tit, and coal tit to pass. The 1⅛-inch hole will allow a great tit and tree sparrow as well but will keep out house sparrows.

In practice only blue tits will use the smaller hole, so despite the threat of tree sparrows it seems better to use the 1⅛-inch hole. In woodlands there is always the possibility of a redstart, and these need a 1½-inch hole, so if siting several boxes in woodland it may be a good plan to have, say, one in six boxes with 1½-inch holes.

Tit Feeder
The feeder shown is a useful adjunct to the nest box. It can be hung from a branch of a tree or suspended from a pole in the garden or even on a bracket on a wall. It is very easily made from a "log" about a foot long

and 3 inches to 4 inches diameter. Silver birch logs make particularly attractive feeders. Bore the 1-inch holes about half-way through, not forgetting the one in the bottom. Pack the holes with a mixture of suet or hard fat and peanuts with a few raisins mixed in; hang it up in your chosen site and wait to see the fun when the birds find it!

Owl Box
The owl box you will not be likely to want in your garden or you may be rather unpopular with any near neighbours! It is really a box for woodlands and nature reserves and has proved very successful with tawny owls. A refinement to this type of box is to build in a small inspection door in one of the sides about two-thirds of the way down.

If you are feeling energetic and have time to make boxes to these two designs on a voluntary basis, why not look up your local Conservation Officer; he will most likely be delighted of an offer of help in this way for boxes to place in the reserves under his control. Wood may be a problem; most Conservation Officers are on a tight budget for this purpose, but a little scrounging round builders' and timber yards can sometimes prove fruitful, particularly if the boss is at all nature-minded — more and more people are becoming so these days.

Siting Boxes

In the garden, providing it is reasonably secluded, a box can be sited nearly anywhere if one or two points are born in mind. Cats are probably the biggest nuisance, so if these are about don't nail the box to a tree, or it will have an irresistible attraction for the feline genera. A wall is perhaps as good a position as any; try not to make the box too conspicuous. If you can do this and have it in view of the kitchen window you will be able to do your bird watching behind glass! Height of box — in the garden I would not put a box less than 5 feet from the ground, and probably 6 feet to 7 feet is better. It is best not to have the entrance hole facing south because of strong sunlight but there should be no difficulty in avoiding this.

Boxes in Woodland

With permission, small boxes can go virtually anywhere, such as woodlands, copses, on isolated trees or tall hedges, but again the placing should be discreet. For example, if near a path or ride, site them off the route and on the opposite side of the tree so that casual passers-by will not see them. Do not advertise the location of the boxes as small boys still take eggs!

The owl boxes need to be a little higher, say 8 feet or more, and wired to the underside of a stout branch at an angle of 30 degrees or more from the vertical. If you need advice consult your local Conservation Officer, he will be very pleased to help. Do not use nails in such trees as oak, ash, or beech for fixing the boxes. Nails can be used when erecting on hawthorn, blackthorn or alder and if there is not a choice of trees then use wooden plugs or loosely wire them on.

A charming addition for your garden

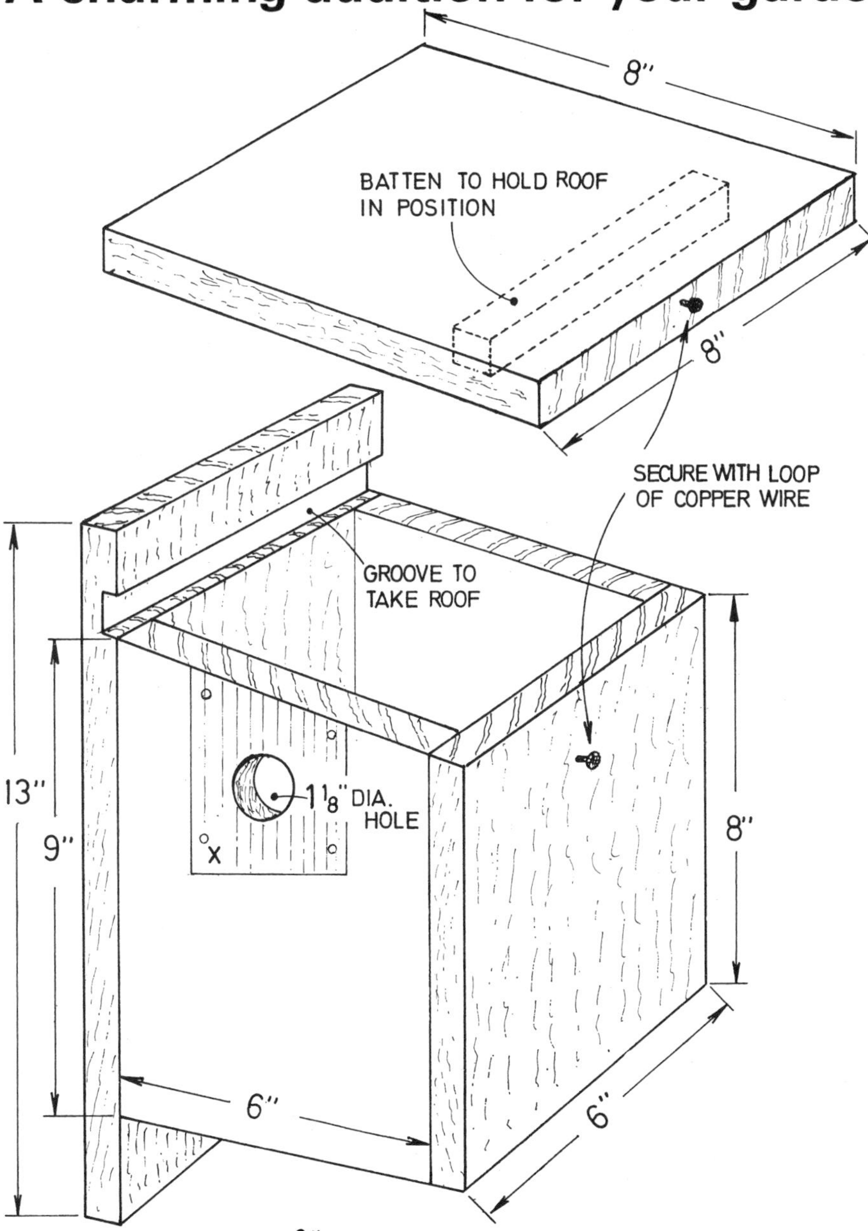

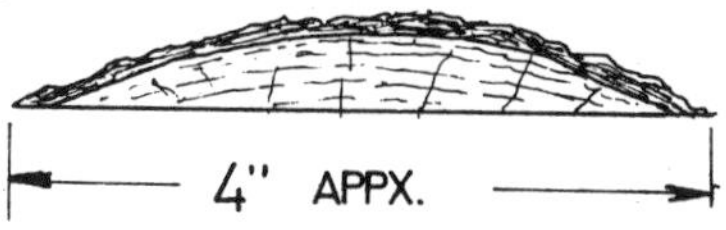

8"

BATTEN TO HOLD ROOF
IN POSITION

8"

4" APPX.

OUTSIDE PIECES WITH BARK ON
FOR CLADDING IF RUSTIC EFFECT
IS WANTED.

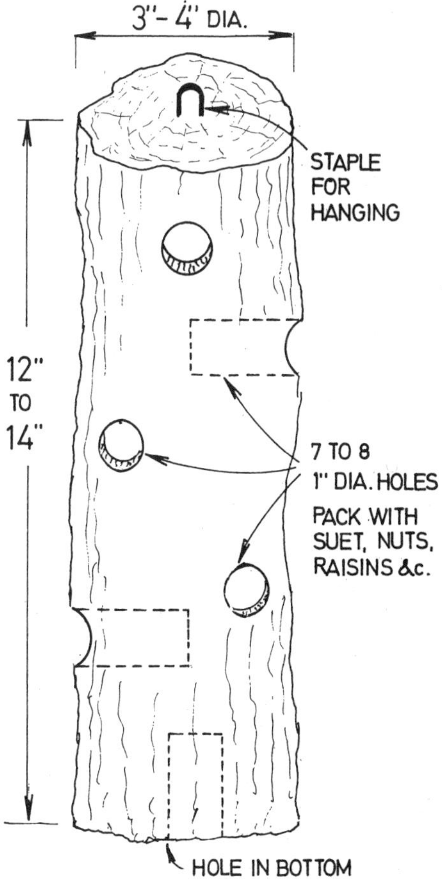

SECURE WITH LOOP
OF COPPER WIRE

GROOVE TO
TAKE ROOF

3"- 4" DIA.

STAPLE
FOR
HANGING

13"

9"

$1\frac{1}{8}$" DIA.
HOLE

8"

X

12"
TO
14"

7 TO 8
1" DIA. HOLES

PACK WITH
SUET, NUTS,
RAISINS &c.

6"

6"

ALL TIMBER $\frac{3}{4}$" THICK

HOLE IN BOTTOM

X = METAL PROTECTION PLATE WHERE GREAT
SPOTTED WOODPECKERS ARE COMMON

TIT & SMALL BIRD NEST BOX

TIT FEEDER

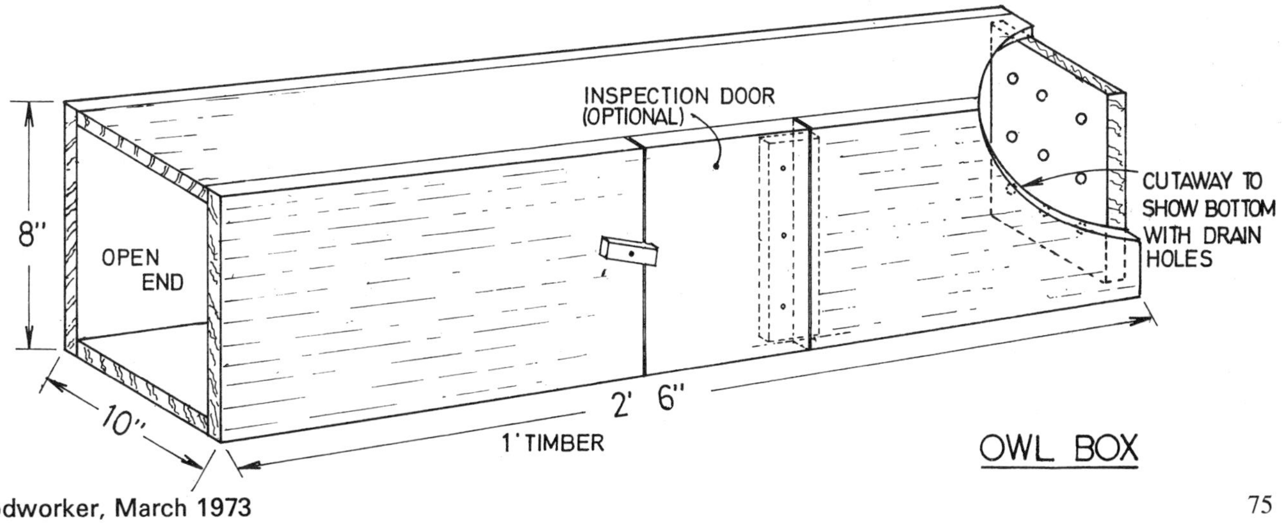

INSPECTION DOOR
(OPTIONAL)

CUTAWAY TO
SHOW BOTTOM
WITH DRAIN
HOLES

8"

OPEN
END

10"

2' 6"

1' TIMBER

OWL BOX

Double Entrance Gates

A handsome design frequently requested by readers

by I. S. Hough

The curved stiles are made up from two pieces which are glued, cut to shape and then screwed together – Fig. 1. We can now set out the stiles and rails as in Fig. 2. The mortices in the stiles should be stopped 1in. from the face of the stiles. The bottom and top rails of the gates were tapered as in Fig. 2, but may be left parallel. On farm gates the top rail is tapered on both faces, and the clapping stile is of a lighter section than the hanging stile, to reduce the weight being cantilevered. The clapping stile is then worked as Fig. 2 – detail 'A'.

Before assembling the gates the internal edges and the faces of the rails should be dressed off. The gates can now be assembled, gluing and cramping the rails to the stiles and

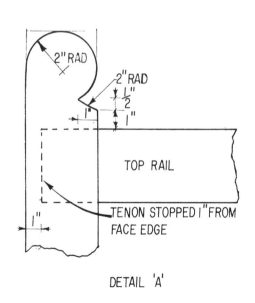

DETAIL 'A'

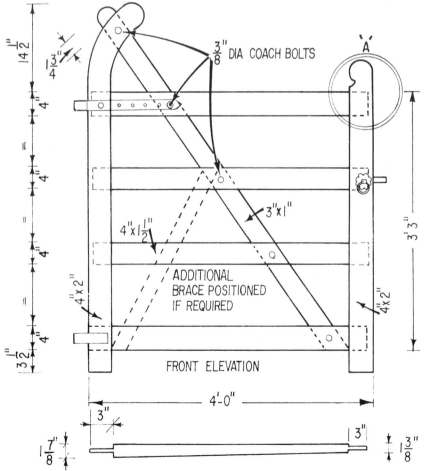

FRONT ELEVATION

PLAN OF TOP AND BOTTOM RAIL

FIG 2

Double Entrance Gates

No. req'd.	Description	Long ft. in.		Wide in.	Thick in.
Parts List					
2	Stiles	4	0	4	2
2	Stiles	4	9	4	2
2	Top rails	4	0	4	2
2	Bottom rails	4	0	4	2
4	Mid. rails	4	0	4	$1\frac{1}{2}$
2	Braces	5	9	3	1
2	Pieces for curved stiles	1	6	5	2

All to be free from shakes, large or dead knots, etc.

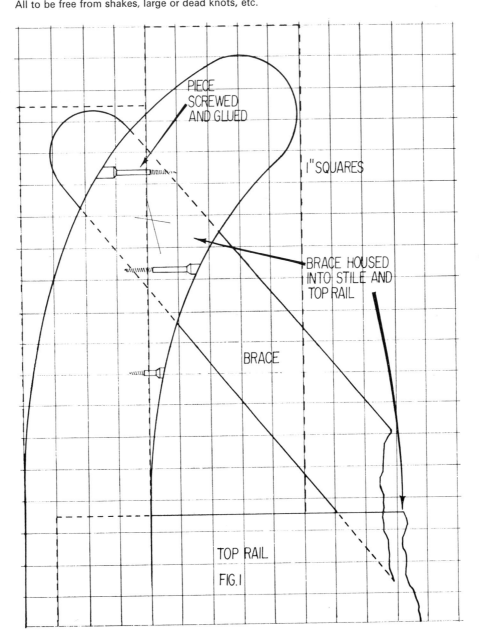

PIECE SCREWED AND GLUED

I" SQUARES

BRACE HOUSED INTO STILE AND TOP RAIL

BRACE

TOP RAIL

FIG. I

squaring-up by measuring diagonally from corner to corner. The brace should then be placed in position and marked for housing into the top rail and stile. When the housing has been cut out of the stile and the top rail, all the mating surfaces of the brace to the gate should be well primed.

The brace is then bolted to the frame with five coach bolts, which are later cut off flush with the nut. A further brace may be added (Fig. 2), but the gates illustrated have been hanging for four years and have not dropped. Also the gate stop was positioned so that the clapping stiles rested on to it, and when not in use the gates are kept closed.

The gates should be well primed and under-coated, and if periodically cleaned and painted should last for years.

When I did the "Techniques of Woodturning" series a year or two ago, it caused quite a lot of interest, and many readers wrote in as a result. Recent correspondence, however, has indicated that numerous people feel I am giving too much design, without enough information on the basic execution. In fairness to new readers, and particularly to youngsters who are taking up the craft as a hobby after leaving school, I will be presenting a number of articles over the coming months which will deal with some basic aspect or technique, and supply a design which features it. Maybe even the more experienced of us could do with a little refresher course occasionally!

by Gordon Stokes

BEAD TURNING AND A BEAD LAMP

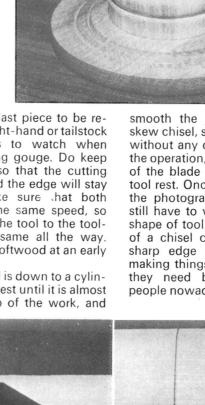

The finished lamp

This month I have taken one of the real basic woodturning cuts, namely the bead, and examined in detail the methods employed in making it. The project I have included is a simple table lamp, which will really test your skill if you cut the shape as it should be cut, and produce identical beads all along. Every do-it-yourself enthusiast knows what half round beading is, and if you look at the section through a piece of this, you have the shape known to the woodturner as a bead. The cutting is not difficult after practice, but the knack of doing it right can take a little time to develop.

My illustrations of the technique are done with the aid of a piece of softwood, which was first run down to a cylinder with the roughing gouge (short bevel and ground straight across at the end) working from left to right in stages of two or three inches at a time, finally removing the last part from right to left. If it feels easier you can reverse the whole pro-

cess, so that the last piece to be removed is at the right-hand or tailstock end. Two points to watch when using the roughing gouge. Do keep the handle low, so that the cutting action is right, and the edge will stay sharp. Also make sure that both hands travel at the same speed, so that the angle of the tool to the tool-rest remains the same all the way. Fig. 1 shows the softwood at an early stage.

When the wood is down to a cylinder, raise the tool rest until it is almost level with the top of the work, and

smooth the job with a very sharp skew chisel, straight from the grinder, without any oilstoning. Fig. 2 shows the operation, and the right-hand side of the blade is raised a little off the tool rest. Once again it is obvious, in the photograph, that manufacturers still have to wake up as regards the shape of tool rests, for the hard steel of a chisel can easily bite into the sharp edge of the soft-steel rest, making things far more difficult than they need be. Incidentally, some people nowadays refer to tool rests as

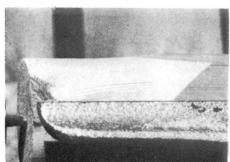

Fig. 1. Beginning the roughing down on a square piece of pine. If the work is done in stages there will be no danger of long splinters flying off.

Fig. 2. Skew chisel positioned for a smoothing cut. Once the angle has been correctly established, care must be taken to maintain it.

Fig. 3. Two marks are made with point of skew chisel to establish position of bead.

Beads and a bead lamp

hand rests. The thing is, of course, both, but while the tool must be on the rest at all times when cutting, this is not true of the hand, so we ought to get our priorities right!

With the skew cut, the shaving should come from the tool between the short corner and the centre, and opposite the point at which the tool contacts the rest. Depth of cut is con-trolled by slight raising or lowering of the handle, and the angle of the tool to the job must be kept the same all the way, which will mean having one's feet positioned to allow the body to lean.

Once the wood is nice and smooth and truly cylindrical, we mark the position of our first practice bead as shown in Fig. 3, using the point of a skew, but not pushing it in too far, or it will receive a nasty friction burn. Something about three eighths of an inch wide will do for a start.

The beginning of the process of cutting the bead is shown in Fig. 4, with the tool rest at little below the centre line. The right-hand side of the blade is lifted just a fraction off the tool rest, and two things are vitally important to getting this technique right. One is that the edge of the chisel should be, and should remain, parallel to the work, and the other is that the point at which the cut starts

Fig. 4. Correct position of chisel to begin cutting of left-hand side of bead. Only the point is used.

Fig. 5. Left-hand side of the cut has started. Note the small amount of wood being removed.

Fig. 6. On a wide bead cuts are made in the corners first, then the bead is completed in the normal way.

Fig. 7. Cutting a bead with "beading and parting tool". Note the rough cut left by the parting tool.

Fig. 8. Large and small bead completed. Sides are being trimmed away at an angle with point of skew.

Fig. 9. The trimming cut partly completed. Note how thumb guides blade.

Fig. 10. Here the right-hand side has been trimmed, left-hand side is left untouched for comparison.

Fig. 11. Rough square of 3-inch ash mounted between centres for making the lamp.

Fig. 12. Stages of cutting from right to left have brought the job to this point. The remainder will be cut the other way.

Fig. 13. Marking out the beads with a pair of dividers.

Fig. 14. The job after the beads have been cut. It will now be sanded and burnished with a handful of shavings.

Fig. 15. A gererous coat of sanding sealer is applied with a cloth. Clear, French polish is as good as anything.

Beads and a bead lamp

is critical as regards height on the work. If the point is too high it will not cut at all, and if it is too low it will cut not merely with the point, as is correct, but well behind it, so producing an inverted 'V' shape. One feels for this correct cutting point, and when it is found, the chisel will be seen to be cutting a fine line on the wood. Half the bead is cut first, and the chisel point must be moved along as it is rolled over, the cut finishing with the chisel completely on its side on the rest. That is easy to say, but will not be found too easy to do until a fair amount of practice has been put in. The second half of the bead is cut in the same way, moving the tool in the opposite direction, and again all the work is done with the actual point of the tool and no more. If you remember that, it will save a lot of trouble. The start of a bead cut is shown in Fig. 5, and you can see that very little wood is being cut away.

With a wider bead, as in Fig. 6, the corners are done first, then the final shape is put in by cutting the whole thing in the same way as for the narrower one. Taking the corners out first gives the tool freedom to move round its arc.

A tool which has its supporters, of whom I am not one, is a sort of hybrid chisel cum parting tool, known (would you believe?) as a beading and parting tool. I see no particular virtue in this tool, but I have shown it in use in Fig. 7, and you can see that the parting tool itself has been taken in each side of the bead, which is sometimes helpful where the design will permit it. The tool is rolled round to produce the curve, cutting only with its corners.

The large and small beads are complete in Fig. 8, and the long corner of the skew is being used to cut away the wood immediately

Fig. 17. Cutting a disc for the lamp base on the Willow 15-inch bandsaw. (right)

Fig. 16. "Speedaneez" polish will give a good shine after the final glass-papering. (below)

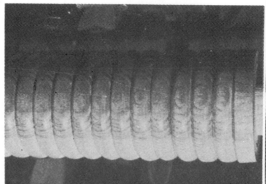

adjacent, so giving a neat appearance. Here, as with the cutting of the beads, only the point of the tool does any work, the rest of the blade being leaned away just a fraction as the cut proceeds. Many people – too many, in fact – do this sort of thing with pointed or diamond-shaped scrapers, but if they only knew what a perfect finish the sharp skew gives they would throw such tools out. Fig. 9 shows the same cut half completed, and Fig. 10 shows a bead with the right-hand side trimmed away, and the left-hand side untouched.

A lamp made with a bead motif can look very nice as the heading photograph shows, and I started with a 3-inch square of ash firmly mounted between centres, Fig. 11, which I quickly roughed down to a cylinder with the $1\frac{1}{4}$-inch roughing gouge, and smoothed off with the skew. In Fig. 12 you can see that most of the wood has been removed, working from right to left, leaving an inch or two to be taken off the opposite way.

A pair of dividers used with the machine running, Fig. 13, set out the markings for the beads, at about $\frac{3}{8}$-inch width. These are then cut with a freshly-sharpened skew, as in

Fig. 14, making sure that the joint between each is clean.

When the beads have been cut and are all alike, a good application of sanding sealer is applied with a cloth while the job is stationary, and when dry the final sanding is given, with very fine paper. Now some Speedaneez friction polish, and the surface should be as in Fig. 16. Note the pin on the left-hand end of the work, which was cut with a parting tool and will fit into the base. Fig. 17 shows a piece of 1-inch wood being cut to a circle for making the base, which was turned on a woodscrew chuck. The gentleman looking so serious about the job is Mr. Terry Green, who also owns the thumbs and things in the other illustrations. Being interested in my activities he kindly offered his services, and I suppose I can say, without fear of contradiction, that "green fingers" can be very useful in the turner's shop!

As a matter of interest to new readers, many of whom write for back numbers – which are not often available – the *Woodworker Annual* is out, and there are still some copies left, price £2.74 post free.

We recently examined the details of bead cutting, and applied them to the making of a table lamp. This month I have a double subject article for you, dealing with the question of cutting coves, which are exactly the opposite of beads, and also showing the processes involved in making bowls from boards, so that they end up deeper than the thickness of the original material. This is considered by some to be a gimmicky business, but it can be a useful technique at times.

Wood Turning
CUTTING COVES

Gordon Stokes

Before we start on all this, Fig. 1 shows a piece of wood which I had kept for quite some time for a specific purpose, but regrettably I had to throw it away after getting as far as the stage in the photograph. There were two very bad shakes in it, and the point is that they were virtually impossible to detect until the turning revealed them. The moral is, of course, that if you have a planer it may well pay to run your turning stock over it when you get it home, so that disappointments like this can be avoided.

Fig. 2 illustrates a technique which a surprising number of people seem to be totally unaware of, yet it is almost essential to the man who wants to produce first class work. I refer to the trimming off of end grain between centres, using the point of a sharp skew chisel. The cut, like everything else, is easy when you know how, but if you don't know it can be awkward to master. One of my oft-repeated maxims about turn-ing, as many readers know, is that with gouges and chisels, if used correctly, only that part of the blade which is receiving support from the tool rest can safely touch the wood. If you look at the illustration, it will be obvious that the point of the tool, which is getting the direct support, can touch the wood with impunity. If the upper part of the edge were to do so, however, there would almost certainly be a dig-in. The cut is made therefore with the point pressing in to the surface of the wood, and the rest of the blade leaned very slightly away from it. If the edge is sharp and the point taken straight to the centre rather than from above or below, the result will be a highly satisfactory marble-like finish. The handle of the tool will need to be raised as the point moves forward, a similar motion, in fact, to the normal parting tool cut.

Coves are cut with a spindle gouge, which is a fairly shallow tool, ground to a finger nail shape at the end. A typical cove is shown in Fig. 3. Basically, the operation is a scooping motion. The gouge starts as shown in Fig. 4, well and truly on its side, and with the handle held horizontal. It is pushed forward into the wood, rolling over on to its back as it goes, and the handle is lowered at the same time. The amount by which the handle is lowered is quite considerable and because of this the cutting edge finishes at the centre of the hollow, too high on the work to cut. This prevents any tendency to cut "uphill", which as we know, is not a good idea at all. That completes one half of the cut, and the other half is done in the same way, again lowering the handle so that the cut finishes at the centre. At this stage it is unlikely that the shape will be perfect, or that the finish will be entirely satisfactory, so the job is trimmed up again with a light cut from each side, Fig. 5. To clarify all that a little, examine Fig. 6, which

Fig. 1. With wood as rough and hairy as this, it is often difficult to detect fine cracks until the surface is removed.

Fig. 2. Trimming end grain with the long corner of a skew chisel. Resulting finish is excellent.

Fig. 3. Typical cove shape cut in a piece of softwood.

Fig. 4. Commencement of left-hand half of a cove, gouge on its side, handle horizontal.

Fig. 5. First two cuts have left surface rough. One or two light slicing cuts with sharp gouge will soon put matters right.

Fig. 6. First half of cove is cut. Note how waste wood curls back.

Fig. 7. Shaping the end of a parting tool, and bringing the edge to a suitable condition for the job.

Fig. 8. Grinding away the sides of the tool behind the cutting edge, so that it will not bind in the cut.

Fig. 9. Faceplate is centred to disc by sighting through central hole at mark left by dividers when circle was scribed.

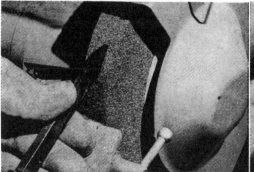

Fig. 10. The disc set up on Myford ML8 in readiness for making the bowl blank. Tool rest has been positioned for trimming outer edge.

Fig. 11. How the parting tool is used to cut off the bevelled rings.

Fig. 12. Two rings have been cut off and pulled forward to show the principle.

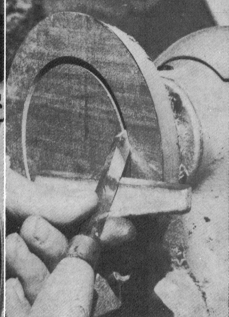

*Woodwork Machinery
(from page 151)*

shows a completed cove, and the tool as it is at the end of the first cut. The same amount of timber will now be taken out on the right-hand side, so removing all the roughness.

The biggest problem which arises in connection with this cut is that the gouge will often skid violently sideways when first presented to the wood. A little thought will make it obvious that the bevel has nothing to rub on until the cut is under way, and as we are well aware, it is the rubbing of the bevel which allows us to control the tool. What, then, is the answer? In fact it is quite a simple one, and all that is required is a small cut made with the point of a skew, or the corner of a parting tool, to provide a notch into which the edge of the gouge can drop.

Another point to note here is that

in this cut the gouge should be peeling off nice twisty shavings, and if such is not the case you may be sure that it is either blunt, wrongly presented, or both. Why not try a table lamp similar to the one we did when we discussed the beads, only this time using coves?

Now, what about this instant, do-it-yourself, collapsible bowl-from-a-board idea? Before we begin on this, I suggest you have a good look at your parting tool, for it must be in first class condition for this work.

Fig. 7 shows the edge of a parting tool being ground, and the end shaped so that it is about the right angle. The angle is far from critical, but if it gets too short in the bevel there is a likelihood of kicking back. I find when grinding parting tools that, as the edge is so small, it is best to grind the extreme edge first, then push the tool up the wheel to grind

Fig. 13. This bowl is in four parts, but it is possible to have more. It will now be glued up before turning.

Cutting Coves

the rest of the bevel. If the job is done the other way round the edge will be reached when the frictional heat has risen, and there is a chance of burning the metal.

For the job we are about to tackle, there is another point to be watched, and that is that the blade must be relieved behind the cutting edge. If this is not done, it will tend to rub and jam in the cut, causing a great deal of heat, which will do the steel no good whatever. In Fig. 8 I am using the corner of the wheel, brushing the tool across in a sweeping motion and stopping just short of the edge. This means that there will be clearance behind the cutting edge and the tool will do its job without getting all hot and bothered.

For my bowl blank made from a board I used the outboard faceplate of the Myford ML8, and the piece of African mahogany was about an inch thick, possibly a fraction more. I screwed this to the faceplate, and

mounted it securely on the machine, Figs. 9 and 10.

What we have to do to make this type of bowl blank is to take the parting tool right through the material, cutting off a series of rings. Fig. 11 shows the idea, and the angle between the side of the tool and the surface of the wood is probably about sixty degrees though this can be varied to some extent to taste.

With the outer ring or two it may be an idea to drop the speed of the lathe down a little from its normal 1,000-1,200 rpm and speed it up again when the work gets smaller.

Those with bad nerves may be a little tense when doing this, but there is little danger really. You will know by the rising pitch of the sound when the tool is nearing the breakthrough, and the severed ring will bob around quite happily. As the rings are cut off they can be secured to the headstock with adhesive tape, but it is better to remove the faceplate and work, take away the ring then put the job back and carry on.

I changed over from a face-plate

to a screw chuck towards the end, so that I could get another cut, for the plate was beginning to get in the way. Fig. 12 shows how the job looked on the machine with two rings cut, and in Fig. 13 you can see it with three, ready to be glued up.

Ordinary Evostik Resin W will do well for this sort of thing. It is very difficult to apply pressure, so we rely on plenty of glue and a good rubbed joint. Most turners like to alternate the grain direction in the rings, which makes the final assembly less likely to twist and warp.

As far as the turning of this kind of blank goes it is pretty straightforward. I always use a ¾ in. deep long and strong gouge, nicely sharpened, and keep it on its side. Some books say that only scrapers should be used, but if the user is capable of handling it properly, a gouge will make a quicker and far cleaner job.

One final word of warning. Before attempting to turn anything like this, do make sure that it has had ample time to dry out and set, and that there are no gaps in the joints.

BOOK REVIEWS

MODERN WOOD TURNING
By Gordon Stokes
Published by Evans at £2.50 net

Contents: types of lathes and their characteristics, advantages and disadvantages; chisels, gouges, oilstones, grindstones, goggles, scrapers, sharpening tools; basic work between centres and on the faceplate; cutting beads and coves; making various kinds of furniture legs including cabriole and club foot; turning spheres; split turning; bowl turning: turning vases and egg cups; long-hole boring; laminated blank turning: turning coopered work; spiral work; making lamps; how to get a professional finish: designs for candle holders, table lamps and match barrels.

Assessment: everyone who has read this magazine during the past three or four years will have read Gordon Stokes's articles on wood turning and will know his inimitable style of writing and workmanlike approach.

As you would expect, he deals with the subject with authority and assurance. When you've answered as many questions and demonstrated turning techniques as often as he

has, you're bound to get a pretty good idea of what worries and confuses learners!

Invaluable as it is to beginners in the craft, the scope is so comprehensive that even old hands will find something they didn't know before.

If you're interested in wood turning, you cannot do better than buy this book.
Size: 8½in. by 7in.; 128pp. with index, hard covers, fully illustrated.

WOODLAND CRAFTS OF BRITAIN
By H. L. Edlin
Published by David & Charles at £3.95 (UK only)
Contents: these encompass a wide range, including the following: tree felling, hauling and conversion; chair bodging; chestnut cutting; elm in traditional timber work; willows in craftwork; woodland carpentry; millwrights, wheelwrights and shipwrights; charcoal burning; herbs, dyes, resins, foliage.
Assessment: this book is a delight and once you've started to read it you'll not want to put it down.

It's a new edition of the original book which was published in 1949.

Note the date: it means that the author was in the privileged position of witnessing the last of the old crafts while being able to appreciate the potentialities of the future.

If you've a relative or a friend who is as keen a woodworker as you are, recommend this book to him and put him in your debt!
Size: 8¾in. by 5¾in.; 182pp with index; illustrated with many photographs.

PRACTICAL WOOD CARVING & GILDING
By W. Wheeler and C. H. Hayward
TOOLS FOR WOODWORK
By C. H. Hayward
Both published by Evans, £2.50 each net.
These are revised editions of the original handbooks, metricated where applicable. Contents include the following:
Practical Woodcarving – tools and equipment: sharpening and handling the tools: drawing and design: tool cuts: carving in the round: gilding tools, materials and methods. Also designs to carve.
Tools for Woodwork – details of and sharpening methods for, saws, planes, chisels and gouges; marking tools, boring tools; spokeshaves, etc.; hammers, punches, pincers; cramps; appliances; powered hand tools.

These books have long since achieved the status of "standard" reference books by virtue of their practical and comprehensive treatment of the subjects.

By Phillip Miles

A Regency Style

Side Table & Desk

This feature covers two separate pieces of furniture, a small side table in English walnut and a desk identical in basic construction but with the addition of a small stationery compartment and top panel in leather. The desk is made in Australian walnut. The drawings cover bothpieces in detail.

The design is based on the elegant, traditional manner of the early nineteenth century, but without the fuss or frills. Although fine and slender in appearance the pieces are perfectly rigid and the desk provides an adequate writing surface. Any first rate cabinet hardwood may of course be used, provided that it is seasoned and dry enough to withstand the hazards of central heating, but if in doubt, cut to working lengths and stack in a warm dry place for a few months. A piece of quality furniture is, in the last analysis, an assembly of quality pieces of timber, each single item made with geometric precision, accurately dimensioned,

free of wind, and all surfaces flat and true. Allow a small margin for hand planing on all show surfaces if machines are used, as nothing is more distressing than to have ripples showing through the polish on a quality hardwood.

If you are using well figured timber, check before preparing to the cutting list so that figure and colour can be used on each piece to the best advantage.

The Leg Frame

All dimensions and details of

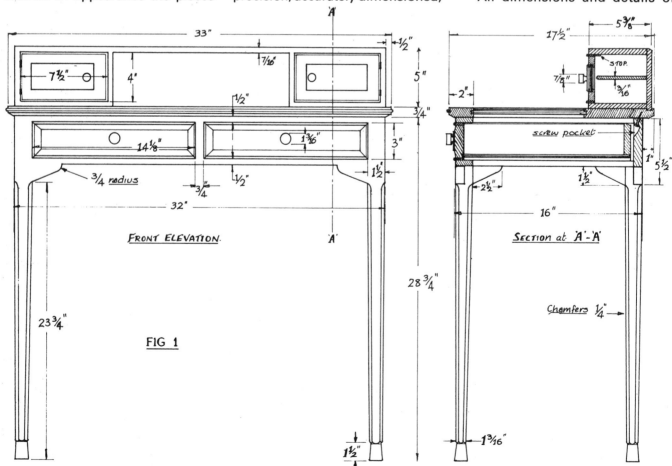

FRONT ELEVATION.

FIG 1

SECTION at 'A'-'A'

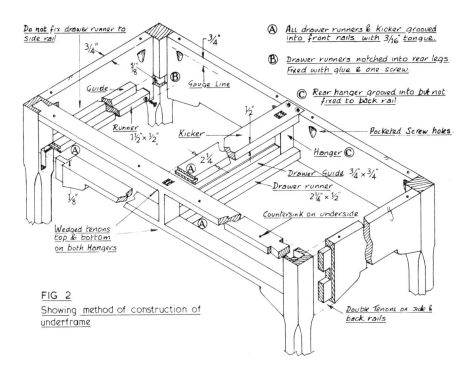

Do not fix drawer runner to side rail

3/4"
3/4"
1/2"
1/8"

Guide

Ⓐ All drawer runners & Kicker grooved into front rails with 3/16" tongue.

Ⓑ Drawer runners notched into rear legs. Fixed with glue & one screw.

Ⓒ Rear hanger grooved into but not fixed to back rail.

Ⓑ
Gauge Line

Runner 1 1/2" × 1/2"

Kicker

1/2"

Pocketed Screw holes.

Ⓐ

2 1/4"

Hanger Ⓒ

Drawer Guide 3/4" × 3/4"

Drawer runner 2 1/4" × 1/2"

1/8"

Ⓐ

Countersink on underside

Wedged tenons top & bottom on both Hangers

Double Tenons on side & back rails

FIG 2
Showing method of construction of underframe

construction are shown in the drawings. Methods are basic and traditional, and present no problems. Cut the rail brackets and glue to the rails as in Fig. 6. before cutting the tenons. If they are cut from adjacent stock, grain and figure will match up. Check the legs for being dead straight and mark the centres of both ends. These marks are vital in the glueing up stage even if the reader omits the bottom turning as shown in Fig. 1. Taper to within 5¾in. from the top and work the chamfers to within 6½in. from the top to allow for the runout to match the line of the brackets at the point of contact with the leg. Complete the legs by cutting all joints and turning the foot if required. This is a terminal feature and also reduces the effect of contact with the vacuum cleaner on the arrisses. Finish the tenons on the side, back, and bottom front rail, and the dovetails on the top front rail. Mark all shoulders in the same register by cramping the pieces together, using a knife, and ensuring that they are dead square to the face edge. It is a good idea to check the trysquare now and again, as we all tend to take it for granted. Make sure the stock face and the blade is free of obstructions such as spots of glue or burrs.

Note that the inner shoulder of the bottom front rail extends ⅛in. beyond the front shoulder, but only for the thickness of the rail, to allow the rail to register into the supporting groove shown in Fig. 2. After checking all joints on a dry run the legs can be glued up to the end rails, using two cramps.

The value of the centre marks will now be evident as pressure on

either of the cramps will vary the distance between the bottom centres, and it is essential that this matches exactly the top centres if the legs are to be parallel. Refer to Fig. 5. In the cramped position, check for wind in the assembly using the winding sticks across the bottom of the legs and the top rail, and if all is well lay to one side to set.

Meanwhile finish the joint cutting in the back and two front rails to accommodate the hangers and

the drawer runners and kicker. A centre kicker is adequate for small drawers but side kickers may be fitted to the top of the side rails if preferred. The tongue to the rails may be worked in the solid, or both rails, runners, and kicker may be grooved 3/16in., and a push fit plywood tongue inserted. Allow the rear hanger to fit into a vertical groove about ⅛in. deep in the back rail.

Glue the front hanger into the bottom front rail and wedge, making sure that it is exactly 90 degrees to the face. On assembly, the top rail then drops over the tenon and into the dovetails. Glue and wedge the rear hanger into the kicker and the centre runner and allow to dry, ensuring that they are exactly parallel. A block 3in. thick placed loosely between the kicker and runner whilst the cramps are on will see to this. Now screw the kicker and the outside runners into the back rail and the leg rebates, and do a dry run of the whole assembly. Note the sequence, take apart, and then reassemble with glue. The last section into position is of course the front top rail.

It is essential when cramping, to repeat the adjustments of the cramps as in the side members, so that the centre marks at the bottom of the legs, measured freely, are exactly 30½in. with all joints close. Sight front legs for wind.

The front rails may "bow" under the cramps, and to prevent this secure a piece of 2in. by 2in.

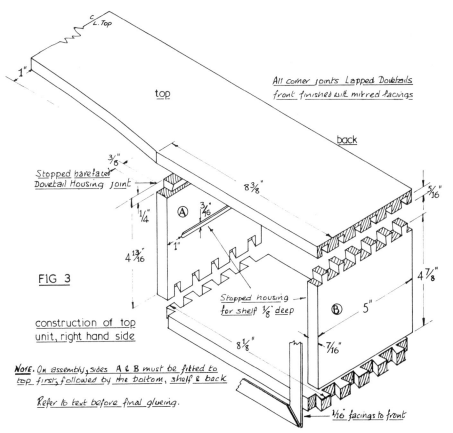

c
L. Top

1"

top

back

All corner joints Lapped Dovetails front finished with mitred facings

Stopped barefaced Dovetail Housing joint

3/8"

8 3/8"

5/16"

1/4"
Ⓐ
3/16"

1"

4 13/16"

Stopped housing for shelf 1/8" deep

Ⓑ 5"

4 7/8"

FIG 3

construction of top unit, right hand side

8 1/8"

7/16"

1/16 facings to front

<u>Note.</u> On assembly, sides A & B must be fitted to top first, followed by the bottom, shelf & back

Refer to text before final glueing.

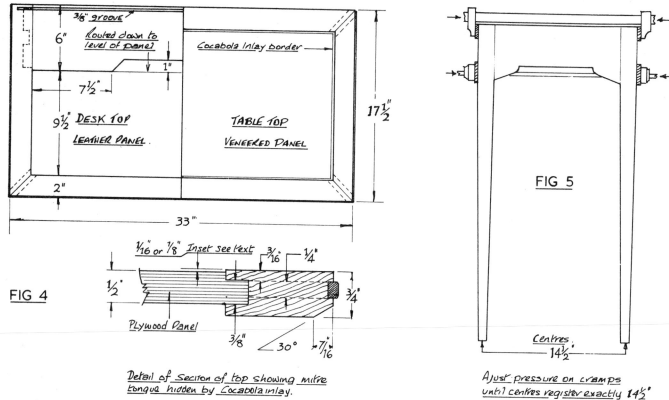

3/8" groove
6"
Routed down to level of panel
Cocabola Inlay border
1"
7½"
9½" DESK TOP LEATHER PANEL.
TABLE TOP VENEERED PANEL
17½"
2"
33"

FIG 4

1/16" or ⅛" Inset see text
3/16" 1/4"
½"
3/4"
Plywood Panel
3/8"   30°   7/16"

Detail of Section of top showing mitre tongue hidden by Cocabola inlay.

PLAN & DETAIL of TOPS

FIG 5

Centres. 14½"

Ajust pressure on cramps until centres register exactly 14½" freely, with joint closed.

softwood to the front rails before the pressure is on. Avoid too much pressure however and with the cramps in position and the leg centres checked, measure the whole assembly for being exactly square in plan.

When all checks prove positive, allow to dry on a level surface. During all cramping operations do not forget the soft blocks on the cramp faces.

The Top

This is simply a framed panel of ½in. ply of good quality. The plan and details of the tops are shown in Fig. 4., the desk back edge being 6in. wide and double tenoned. The top for the side table differs, in that all frame members are identical at 2in. width, and all corners are tongued mitres. The panel inset for the desk is 1/16in. to accommodate the leather, and the panel inset for the table is ⅛in. to accommodate saw cut veneer. In the originals both tops were inlaid on the edge with Cocabola to the dimensions in Fig. 4, which is also the position of the mitre tongue. The inlay was completed on the back edge on the side table.

The veneer in the original was cut from a piece of highly figured walnut, a full ⅜in. thick after planing, then cut down the centre edge to produce, on opening, the sawn faces of adjacent figure which were matched to produce a mirror image pattern. The veneer being a full ⅛in. allowed for planing to a

finish. The top was completed with a Cocobola border to the veneer ⅛in. wide. Saw cut veneer being fairly thick, is easy to handle, but it is necessary to tape the joints and cramp down firmly when glueing into position. Allow a week or two for the panel to dry out before fitting the border inlay. Clean up and sand to a finish, and fit to the table frame when the drawers have been made and fitted.

The Drawers

These can be made up whilst the top is cramped and drying. The fronts are cut from ¾in. stuff, fielded as shown in Fig. 1, and fitted with a cock bead. The drawer sides are ⅜in. stuff, and the bot-

toms good quality veneered ply. Construction is traditional with dovetails fore and aft. Make the drawer fronts a push fit into the front frame before rebating for the bead. Do not allow the bead to extend more than 1/16in. or the effect will seem gross and overdone. Glue the guides into position on the runners, and fit the drawers, which must just brush the guides along the whole length. Allow a very slight clearance under the kicker, but the front is to be a finger push between the front rails. Small drawers must not be fitted too tightly on light furniture. Cocobola knobs were turned and fitted to the original pieces.

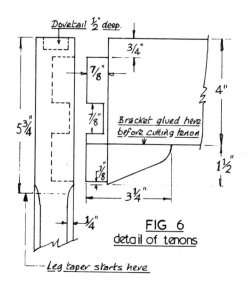

Dovetail ½" deep.
3/4"
7/8"
7/8"
4"
Bracket glued here before cutting tenon
3/8"
1½"
3/4"
5¾"
1/4"
Leg taper starts here
FIG 6
detail of tenons

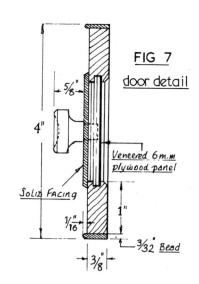

FIG 7
door detail
5/8"
4"
Veneered 6 m.m plywood panel
Solid Facing
1/16"
1"
3/32" Bead
3/8"

Desk Top Unit

The details of construction are shown in Fig. 3 and require no explanation. If possible cut the ends from the top piece to preserve the continuity of figure. Clean up and polish all internal surfaces and shelves and cut the hinge recesses before final assembly. The back piece is very dry solid timber a full ⅜in. thick, glued and screwed to the back face of the unit and projecting ⅛in. below to register with the groove in the desk top. Use ⅝in. brass screws countersunk ³⁄₁₆in. below the surface and cover with plugs. When the plugs are dry chamfer the top edges and the ends of the back 30 degrees, to the glue line. Fit the leather to the desk top and polish the wood surfaces. Polish the unit and fix to the top with screws from underneath into the bottom edges of the sides of the boxes. Now make and fit the doors. These are framed up with tongued mitres corners and the section is shown in Fig. 7. Turn the knobs to match those of the drawers and glue into the front panel. Chose a nicely figured piece for the facing to the front panel. Do not forget the very slight "lead" angle on the closing edge. I used a ¼in. cylinder type ball catch to retain the doors. Round over the ends of the ¾in. solid drawn butts and polish them inside and out.

Final Assembly

Before fitting either top to the underframe check the legs for tears and clean arrisses. I use a well worn very sharp 1in. B.E. chisel held vertically to scrape chamfers, and very careful sanding is required so as not to dub the edges. Check the length of each screw above the frame top through the pockets and the front rail and position and fit the top after polishing, not forgetting the insides of the drawers.

CUTTING LISTS

Underframe

4	Legs	28¾in. by 1½in. by 1½in.
2	Drawer Fronts	14⅛in. by 3in. by ¾in.
4	Drawer sides	14⅝in. by 3in. by ⅜in.
2	Drawer bottoms	14¾in. by 13⅛in. by 4mm ply
2	Drawer backs	14⅛in. by 3in. by ½in.
1	Back rail	30¾in. by 4in. by ¾in.
2	Side rails	14¾in. by 4in. by ¾in.
2	Front rails	30¾in. by 1½in. by ½in.
2	Runners	13⅞in. by 1½in. by ½in.
1	Runner	13⅞in. by 2¼in. by ½in.
1	Kicker	14⅝in. by 2¼in. by ½in.
2	Hangers	4in. by 1½in. by ¾in.
2	Outer guides	13in. by ¾in. by ¾in.
1	Centre guide	11⅝in. by ¾in. by ¾in.
8	Brackets	3¼in. by 1½in. by ¾in.

Tops

Table

2	Rails	33in. by 2in. by ¾in.
2	Rails	17½in. by 2in. by ¾in.
1	Panel	29¾in. by 14¼in. by 12mm ply

Desk

1	Rail	33in. by 2in. by ¾in.
2	Rails	17½in. by 2in. by ¾in.
1	Rail	30¾in. by 6in. by ¾in.
1	Panel	29¾in. by 14¼in. by 12mm ply

Top Unit of Desk

1	Top	32in. by 5in. by ⁷⁄₁₆in.
1	Back	32in. by 5⅛in. by ⅜in.
2	Bottoms	8⅛in. by 5in. by ⁷⁄₁₆in.
2	Sides	4¹³⁄₁₆in. by 5in. by ⁷⁄₁₆in.
2	Ends	4⅞in. by 5in. by ⁷⁄₁₆in.
2	Shelves	7¾in. by 4¼in. by ³⁄₁₆in.
	Facings	5ft. by ⁷⁄₁₆in. by ¹⁄₁₆in.

A present for Grandma

BY FRED (FRANK) PAIN

The children will know if they have a grandma – and grandmas deserve a present now and again. If there is a lathe in the home, any kind of lathe, and someone to do the turning then the idea is complete. This little job is well within the capacity of even an electric drill lathe and with three turning tools, a gouge, a skew chisel and a parting tool that really completes the set-up.

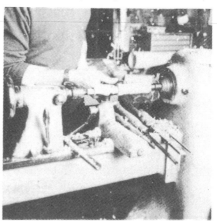

Grandma would really like to have such a present especially made by someone in the family and it is not a difficult job of turning. The hardest part may be in finding the wood but if you keep your eyes wide open you might find a broomstick or something that you might use – "it will never be missed". The three tools mentioned are ample to do the job and, having made this little item, it may lead you to turn other things and so while-away time that may otherwise have gone stale.

I've taught blind men to do woodturning, men who went on to earn their living and enjoy using the lathe. One I taught has sold table lamps for use in Buckingham Palace and another won prizes at the Olympia 'Hobbies and Handicrafts Exhibition'. So don't say 'I cannot do it', for if you only get started you will discover a world of joy and satisfaction in woodturning.

Now for a few tips that you may well find useful. I once had a lathe GIVEN to me just because I showed a man that good woodturning is a paring action. The bevel of the tool rubs the work and you increase the cut by lifting the handle end of the tool. When you sharpen a pencil the tool rests on the pencil and you sharpen with a paring action. You operate the knife so that it is at an angle to the centre-line of the job, this presents the tool to the work at a fine angle and so cuts more easily. If you place the blade at right-angles to the centre-line you cannot cut, only scrape. Try using the gouge and look to see if the bevel of the tool is resting on the work.

One blind man I know turned a shaving the whole length of his house for he knew it would please me. The Council had paid my hotel expenses to teach this man and they provided him with a brand-new lathe that cost over £100, and that was back in 1965. This man would say "It's lovely being blind for you get such a kick out of doing a job". So why not you? (Getting a kick I mean.)

If you must use a scraping action then the handle of the tool is held upwards. A scraping action is used in faceplate work but "cutting wood as it prefers to be cut" is used in work between centres.

I wrote a book called *The Practical Wood-turner* and I read that, so I know what to do! My hobby has been doing turned wooden crosses and I have now given away over two thousand but I've sold my lathe now so please don't ask for one!

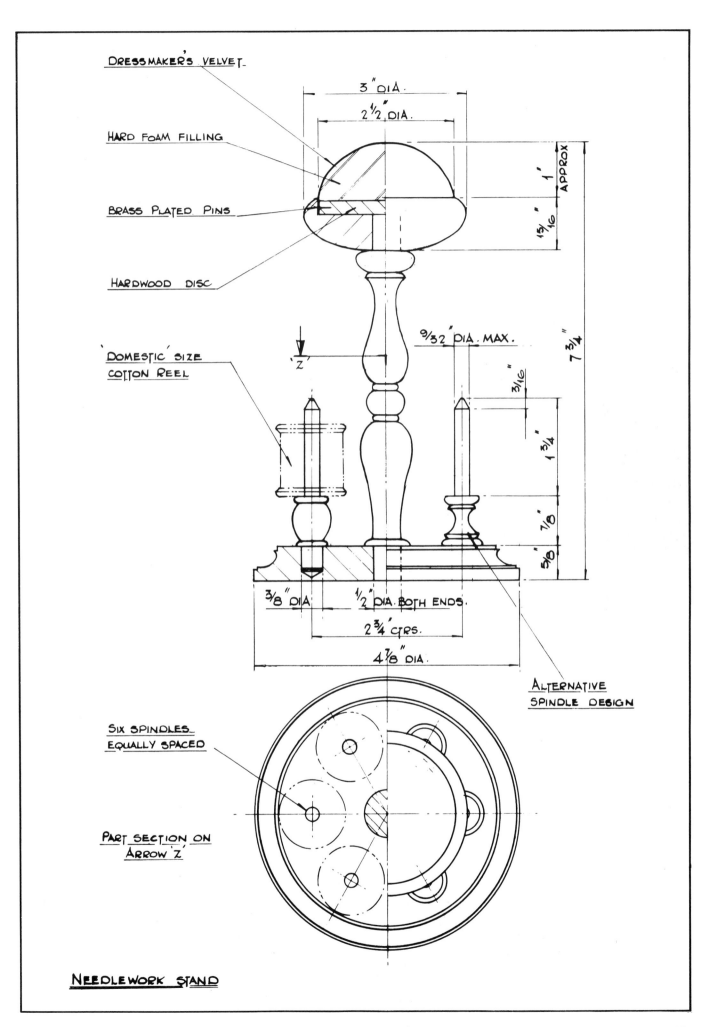

DRESSMAKER'S VELVET.

HARD FOAM FILLING

BRASS PLATED. PINS

HARDWOOD DISC

'DOMESTIC' SIZE COTTON REEL

3" DIA.

2½" DIA.

1" APPROX

¹⁵⁄₁₆"

9/32" DIA. MAX.

7¾"

3/16"

1¾"

1/8"

5/8"

ALTERNATIVE SPINDLE DESIGN

3/8" DIA.

½" DIA. BOTH ENDS.

2¾" CTRS.

4⅞" DIA.

SIX SPINDLES EQUALLY SPACED

PART SECTION ON ARROW 'Z'

NEEDLEWORK STAND

PINE DRESSER TO

C. J. Colston DLC explains how he made a pine dresser. For easier
fitting into an alcove the piece was constructed in two parts

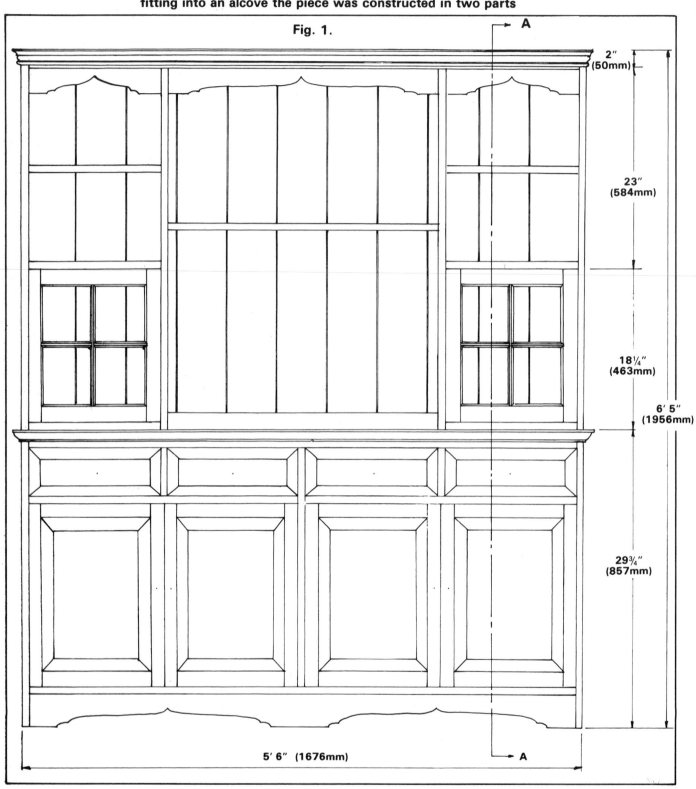

Fig. 1.

A

2"
(50mm)

23"
(584mm)

18¼"
(463mm)

6' 5"
(1956mm)

29¾"
(857mm)

5' 6" (1676mm)

A

This dresser was designed to fit into an alcove so the size of the alcove was an important factor in determining the dimensions of the piece. To make it easier to put in I built it in two parts. This also had the advantage of dispensing with some difficult fitting of the top and allowed the top of the base to project so that the edge could be moulded. The high position of the centre shelf was chosen so that a large vase of flowers could be displayed without masking the shelf behind.

In making the bottom section the first thing was to rub-joint the timbers together to produce the sides, bottom, top and centre division. This was done using 6in. wide boards for all but the top where 7in. boards were used. This allowed ample for the jointing and after the glue had set they were planed to size. The timber was bought planed to 21mm thick but after rub-jointing this was reduced to 19mm.

Having planed the timber to size it was

marked out and the joints for the bottom and sides cut. These are stopped, housed, twin mortise and tenon joints. After they were cut and fitted the grooves for the back panels were ploughed as were those for the plinth. The sides were cut 32½in. long and all the other timbers were planed to size. They are all 19mm thick. Fig. 2 shows the constructions that I used.

Lap dovetails for the top rails were cut and

FIT AN ALCOVE

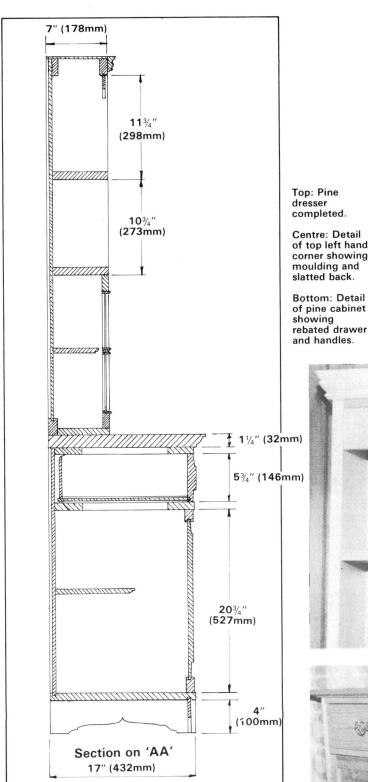

7" (178mm)

11¾" (298mm)

10¾" (273mm)

1¼" (32mm)

5¾" (146mm)

20¾" (527mm)

4" (100mm)

Section on 'AA'
17" (432mm)

Top: Pine dresser completed.

Centre: Detail of top left hand corner showing moulding and slatted back.

Bottom: Detail of pine cabinet showing rebated drawer and handles.

fitted using stopped, housed, twin mortise and tenon joints. The centre division, together with the drawer rails, was fitted next. The basic cabinet was now almost complete with just the division for the drawers and the centre drawer runner to fit. These were fitted with mortise and tenon joints. The mortises for the drawer stops were cut next; if they are not cut before the cabinet is glued together it is difficult to cut them. Indeed, they could not be cut without a drawer-lock chisel and these

PINE DRESSER

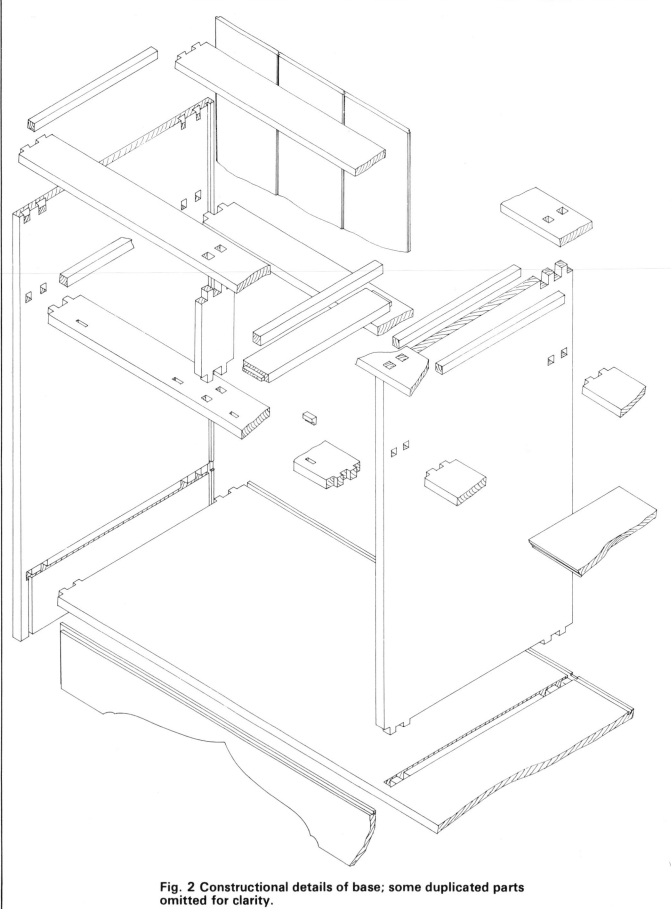

Fig. 2 Constructional details of base; some duplicated parts omitted for clarity.

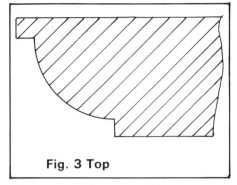

Fig. 3 Top

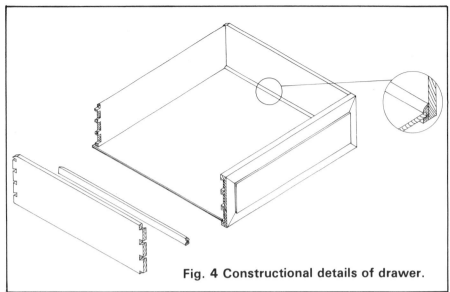

Fig. 4 Constructional details of drawer.

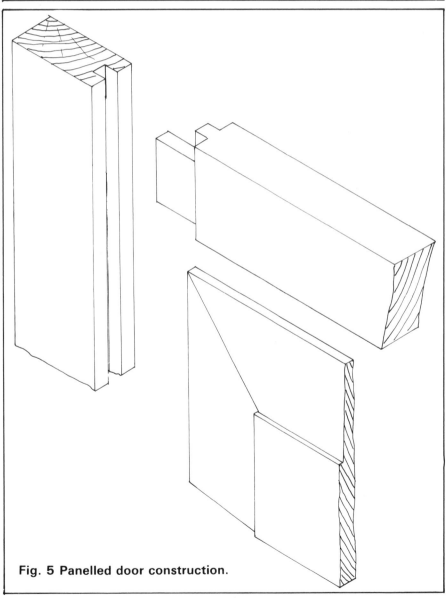

Fig. 5 Panelled door construction.

(text continued from page 441)

are difficult to buy. These mortises are cut with their front edge 25mm back from the front edge of the drawer rail.

The shaping on the two ends (Fig. 1) was cut. At this stage all the inside surfaces were cleaned-up and sealed with polyurethane gloss varnish diluted with 10% white spirit. After this had dried I flatted the surface and glued-up the cabinet. When the glue had set the plinth, drawer runners, kickers and the back panels were fitted. The latter are rebated on each long edge and the bottom edge with a small chamfer cut on the edges to give a relief effect. The top edges are secured with ¾ in. No. 6 screws.

The top was planed to size and the mouldings on the edges were cut. Fig. 3 shows the details of this moulding. The top was screwed to the cabinet making the back edge tight to the rail. I used slot screws to hold the sides and front edge in place to allow the top to expand or contract.

The top was fitted before making the doors and drawers. Fitting it afterwards can disturb the fit and hang of these. All the materials for the drawers were prepared and the lap dovetails at the front, together with the through dovetails at the back, of the drawers were cut and fitted. Fig. 4 shows details of the construction I used.

I prefer to use drawer slips to hold the bottom in place as this allows the bottom to move and in addition it allowed me to use 9mm timber for the sides. The drawer bottoms are 4mm plywood and they are slid into grooves in the slips, which are glued to the inside of the sides and the front before being held into place by two screws in the back rail. The drawer fronts were fielded before gluing-up and after the drawers had set and the bottoms were fitted, they were cleaned-up and fitted into the openings.

Construction of the doors is shown in Fig. 5 and these were made next and fitted. The grooves were fitted with a 9mm panel fielded to match the drawer fronts. The sides and top of the door frames are 1½ in. wide but the bottom rail is 1¾ in. wide. The doors were cut square and hinged from the sides. I set the hinges into the doors so that the line of the cabinet side was unbroken. A rebated overlap could be worked on the door but I decided to fit the doors side-by-side and screw a retaining strip down the inside of the left-hand door to form a dust seal. Two flat bolts hold these doors square and the right-hand doors are held with magnetic catches.

Shelf studs of ¼ in. were used to support the shelves as this enables them to be moved if necessary. The front edge of the shelves is moulded (Fig. 9) and, as for all the mouldings on this cabinet, a Victorian moulding plane was used. Alternatively, a series of scratch stocks could have been used.

Handles and fittings for the drawers and the doors (bought from Martin Bros, Camden Street, Birmingham, which has an excellent selection of architectural ironmongery) were fitted. The drawer stops were fitted, the shapes on the plinth were cut and this was glued in position and the cabinet cleaned-up. Three coats of polyurethane varnish produced a good finish. The first gloss coat was thinned while the last coat was an eggshell finish. Having finished the bottom half of the cabinet, the top part was made. All timber was prepared to size with the two end uprights ½ in. wider than the other uprights to allow them to be grooved for the back panels.

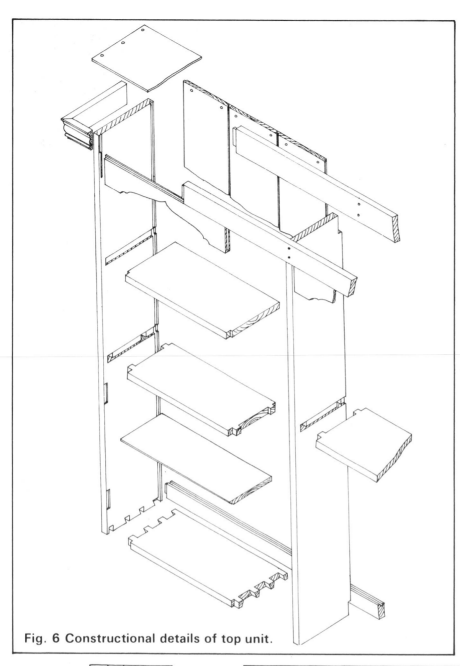

The uprights are lap-dovetailed to the bottom pieces. Fig. 6 shows that the pins are on these bottom pieces and not on the uprights to allow for easy cramping. The bottom is 18mm narrower than the end uprights to allow the back bottom rails to pass.

Once these dovetails were cut the two top rails were mortised and tenoned into the uprights and the shelves were cut into position. Fig. 6 shows the construction used. The top back rail is set-in 12mm to allow the back to be screwed to it and this amount of set-in has to be allowed on both the shelves and the centre uprights. The grooves for the back panels were cut into the end uprights and into the top of the bottom rail.

The frieze was fitted next. This was rebated and fitted into grooves ploughed in the underside of the front top rail, with the ends of the frieze locking into shallow mortises in the sides. Templates were cut in paper for the shaping of this frieze and the shapes were cut with a fine chamfer on the front edge. The inside surfaces were cleaned-up and finished and the carcase was glued-up. The back panels were then cut to size and fitted in the same way as for the bottom of the cabinet and the top board was screwed into place on top of the two rails. The top moulding was cut to the shape shown in Fig. 7, mitred and pinned into place.

The top carcase was now screwed through its bottom shelf into the top of the base before the doors were made. Fig. 8 shows the construction for the doors. I chose this method to avoid cutting long and short shouldered mortise and tenons, which would have been necessary had I worked rebates to accept the glass. I also wanted a moulding to protrude on the face of the doors and by planting the moulding I achieved both requirements. The doors were glued-up and then fitted in place. They were hinged with solid drawn brass butt hinges 2in. long and as on the lower cabinet the hinges were set into the door edge. The glass was 3mm held against the moulding with a bead.

Shelves were fitted on shelf studs so that they lined up behind the horizontal bar in the door and the handles were fitted. Fig. 9 shows the shape of the moulding on the edge of these shelves. Finally, the cabinet was cleaned-up and varnished to match the base.

Fig. 6 Constructional details of top unit.

Fig. 7 Frieze moulding.

Fig. 9 Shelf.

CUTTING

Bottom cabinet

2	Sides	2ft 8½in. (825mm) × 17in. (432mm) × 19mm
1	Division	28½in. (725mm) × 16½in. (420mm) × 19mm
1	Bottom	5ft 5½in. (1665mm) × 17in. (432mm) × 19mm
1	Top	5ft 9in. (1755mm) × 18in. (460mm) × 32mm
2	Top rails	5ft 5½in. (1665mm) × 3in. (75mm) × 19mm
1	Plinth	5ft 5in. (1650mm) × 4in. (100mm) × 9mm
2	Centre drawer runners	10½in. (267mm) × 3in. (75mm) × 19mm
6	Drawer runners	10½in. (267mm) × ¾in. (19mm) × 19mm
2	Drawer uprights	7½in. (190mm) × 3in. (19mm) × 19mm
8	Drawer stops	1in. (25mm) × 1in. (25mm) × 12mm
11	Back panels	28in. (710mm) × 5¾in. (145mm) × 6mm
4	Drawer kickers	10½in. (267mm) × ¾in. (19mm) × 19mm
2	Shelves	29in. (735mm) × 9in. (230mm) × 15mm
8	Door stiles	21½in. (545mm) × 1½in. (38mm) × 19mm
4	Top rails	16in. (406mm) × 1½in. (38mm) × 19mm
4	Bottom rails	16in. (406mm) × 1¾in. (45mm) × 19mm
4	Door panels	18¼in. (465mm) × 13¼in. (335mm) × 9mm
2	Door rebate strips	21½in. (545mm) × 1in. (25mm) × 6mm
4	Drawer fronts	15½in. (395mm) × 5½in. (140mm) × 21mm
8	Drawer sides	15½in. (395mm) × 5½in. (140mm) × 9mm
4	Drawer backs	15½in. (395mm) × 4¾in. (120mm) × 9mm
8	Drawer slips	15½in. (395mm) × ⅝in. (15mm) × 9mm
4	Drawer bottoms	14½in. (370mm) × 15½in. (395mm) × 4mm ply

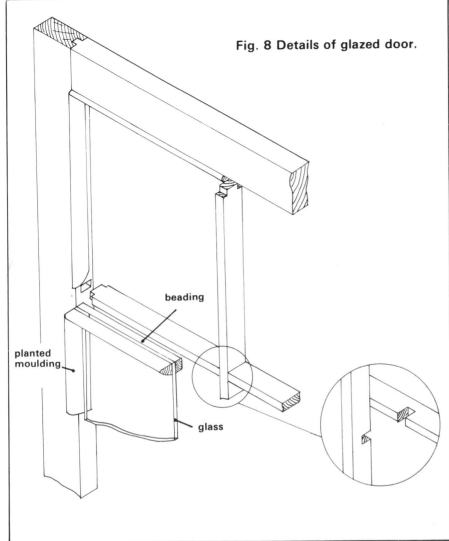

Fig. 8 Details of glazed door.

planted moulding

beading

glass

PINE DRESSER

LIST

Top cabinet

2	Uprights	3ft 6½in. (1080mm) × 7in. (180mm) × 19mm
2	Uprights	3ft 6½in. (1080mm) × 6½in. (165mm) × 19mm
2	Bottom shelves	17in. (432mm) × 6¼in. (160mm) × 19mm
4	Side shelves	17in. (432mm) × 6½in. (165mm) × 19mm
1	Centre shelf	2ft 9in. (840mm) × 6½in. (165mm) × 19mm
2	Top rails	5ft 5½in. (1665mm) × 2¼in. (57mm) × 19mm
1	Bottom rail	5ft 5½in. (1665mm) × 1¾in. (45mm) × 19mm
1	Top	5ft 5½in. (1665mm) × 7in. (180mm) × 9mm
1	Frieze	5ft 5½in. (1665mm) × 3in. (75mm) × 9mm
1	Moulding	5ft 7½in. (1715mm) × 1¾in. (45mm) × 21mm
2	Mouldings	8in. (200mm) × 1¾in. (45mm) × 21mm
11	Back panels	3ft 5in. (1040mm) × 5¾in. (145mm) × 6mm
2	Shelves	15½in. (395mm) × 5½in. (140mm) × 12mm
4	Door stiles	18in. (460mm) × 1½in. (38mm) × 19mm
2	Top stiles	15in. (380mm) × 1½in. (38mm) × 19mm
2	Bottom rails	15in. (380mm) × 1¾in. (45mm) × 19mm
2	Uprights	14½in. (370mm) × ⅞in. (21mm) × 6mm
2	Crossbars	13in. (330mm) × ⅞in. 21mm) × 6mm
1	Moulding	18ft (5.48m) × ½in. (12mm) × 6mm
1	Beading	18ft (5.48m) × ⅜in. (9mm) × 6mm

BOOK REVIEW

60 YEARS OF UPHOLSTERY

On turning the title page of *Practical Upholstery and the Cutting of Loose Covers* (Frederick Palmer) published by Ernest Benn Ltd, 25 New Street Square, London EC4A 3JA, you read 'First edition 1921. Second impression 1980.' This speaks for itself. There are those who would consider such a repeat to be a disregard for the progress of the last 60 years. Others might state convincingly that well-tried and tested methods have a reliability which is lacking in many spheres today.

How often do you hear the remark: 'Things are not made like that these days'? But 'that', of course, can mean almost anything; It can refer to methods or to materials.

Regarding methods, this is a personal aspect and is portrayed by the picture on the jacket of the book. This is of an old-time upholsterer working on a period chair. It tells a story. The man is obviously strong, highly skilled and (less obviously) proud of his work. The methods and the lasting qualities which long tradition engenders create the reason for the writing of the book, stated in the author's preface of 1921: *'Practical Upholstery* was written for the love of the thing.'

I was working on a crossword recently to pass the time on a train journey and one of the clues was 'reviewer'; the solution was 'critic.' (It might have been the other way round. I forget.) Those of us who can remember World War I might look at the advertisements which adorn the front and back endpapers of Palmer's book with a certain nostalgia; and I find myself asking 'Who am I to review (still less criticise) so noble and comprehensive a work?' Are pride in one's skill and love of one's job less in evidence today?

It is not for me to say. But I agree with the publisher; so far as these sentiments are concerned the decision to print a second impression must be a wise one.

Referring to progress over the last 60 years, however, the development of so many new materials makes this a subject much more practical and perhaps less sentimental. Surely we must hand it to the chemists — and others — who have done so much for us all in providing a vast array of new materials which in themselves create new processes and methods of working. One great advantage of man-made products is in the fact that they can be varied by the addition of ingredients to render them fire-proof or rot-proof or insect-proof; and recent calamities have shown the importance of these additives. Palmer's book must be read with this in mind.

Though this is a handsome facsimile of the 1921 production the price — £12.95 — might appear high. But there are 38 chapters on practical upholstery and seven on the cutting of loose covers, each one packed with the knowledge and practical· experience of the author, to say nothing of 413 drawings illustrating the text. When you consider all this you have second thoughts about the price. **C.B.**

PINE DINING TABLE
for
Mrs Markham

Designed and made by R. W. Grant DLC FRSA MSIAD, who also prepared the drawings. Photographs by John Peacock.

Photo 1. 'unobstructed seating at both ends...'

There are times when a client's preferences in the commissioning of a piece of furniture must be followed. Mrs Markham had stipulated that her table was to be 5ft long and 28½in. high with unobstructed seating accommodation at both ends (Photo 1). Pine was wanted to harmonise with other furniture in the room and I therefore spent time in the timber yard selecting clear pieces to suit the job.

The top came from an 18ft length of 1¼ × 9in. stock in order to make up the 27in. width and to ensure continuity of grain and texture. All the timber was cut to rough length and thicknessed, then allowed to stand and settle for a month in the workshop before further work was carried out. Readers wishing to make this piece are advised to select their pine with care although it would look well in any other wood.

Construction is principally straightforward mortise and tenon work and the curves for the members can be obtained by drawing a grid over the scaled elevations shown here, and then enlarging them to full-size in order to make the setting-out templates.

The two end frames were made first, the four curved legs being bandsawn out and cleaned-up with a spokeshave. It is important that the templates for these legs are made to such accuracy that the tenon shoulder lines may be directly scribed onto the legs. This is because no straight reference line will be available for squaring the shoulders. The top and bottom rails were mortised before shaping was worked on them so that when the legs were fitted a smooth blend of the curved lines could be achieved (Photos 2, 3).

To obtain maximum rigidity the legs were tenoned through the top rail and wedged, while the substantial ½in. thick tenons at the feet were dowelled for extra security. Before these end frames were glued-up the edges were polished; sanding sealer and wax was used. The frames were then glued and afterwards flushed-off. A portable router fitted with a ¼in. nosing bit was run round the edges to achieve the distinctive emphasis to the lines of the piece.

The curved tie-bar and two top distance pieces were then prepared and cramped together while marking a common shoulder line. The top distance pieces were lap dovetailed to the end frames and the bottom tie-bar secured by a through mortise and tenon with an overhang housed in above (Photo 3).

The projecting tenon was bevelled-off and rounded as a decorative flourish. The tie-bar was moulded in the same fashion as the end frames. Bar and distance pieces were polished before the whole underframe was glued-up, care being taken to ensure that the assembly was not twisted.

The top boards, which had been cut from one length, were carefully matched and their end grains reversed to minimise any cupping that might ensue. This was also the purpose of adding cleats to the ends. The board edges were shot accurately; and to provide a good register when gluing-up the edges were grooved to take a ½in. wide tongue of hardboard.

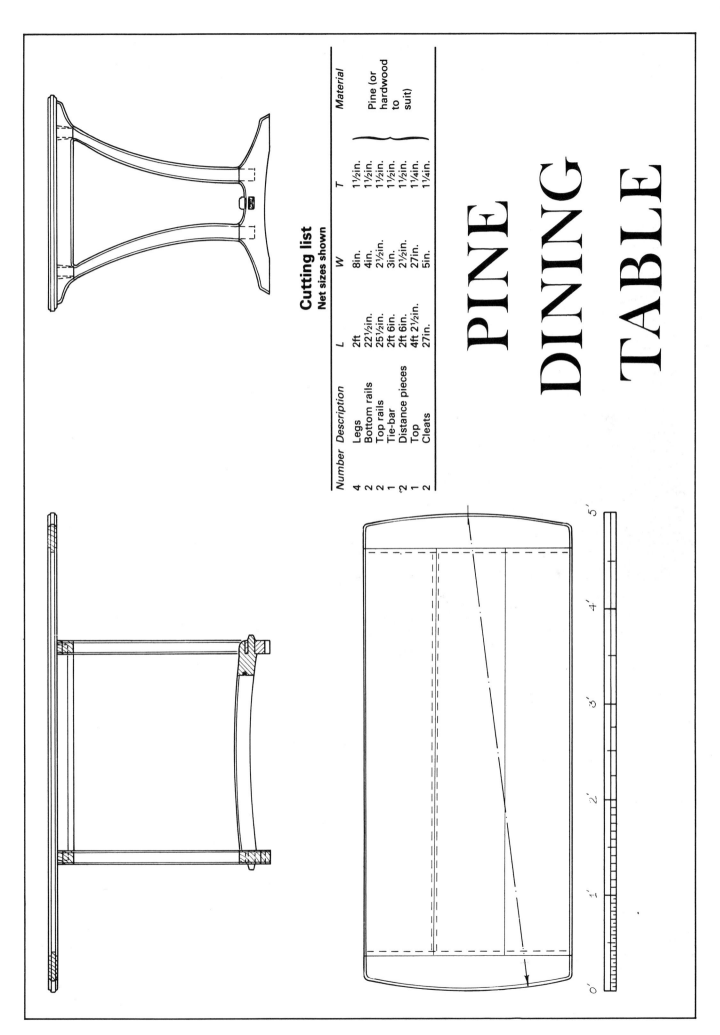

Cutting list
Net sizes shown

Number	Description	L	W	T	Material
4	Legs	2ft	8in.	1½in.	
2	Bottom rails	22½in.	4in.	1½in.	Pine (or hardwood to suit)
2	Top rails	25½in.	2½in.	1½in.	
1	Tie-bar	2ft 6in.	3in.	1½in.	
2	Distance pieces	2ft 6in.	2½in.	1¼in.	
1	Top	4ft 2½in.	27in.	1¼in.	
2	Cleats	27in.	5in.	1¼in.	

PINE DINING TABLE

Photo 2. 'when the legs were fitted a smooth blend of the curved lines could be achieved. . .'

After the boards had been glued the ends were shot square and the router used to take out the groove to receive the cleat tongues, which were prepared with the same tool.

Photo 4 shows that the proportions of the cleat joint were exactly one third of the total thickness of the top so that the coving bit used in the router to form the edge decoration would line up exactly with this feature. The cleats were glued with PVA applied to the extreme edges and central spot only. Although the purpose of a cleat might be seen as an endeavour to prevent movement entirely, there is some sense in not applying glue across the whole width so that some movement of the wood about a centre line can take place.

With the top made the radiusing of the ends was carried out, and the underside and top surfaces skimmed-off with a fore plane before sanding and wax polishing. The routing of the edges was also done before polishing. The underframe was married to the top (Photo 2) with steel slotted fixing plates secured with roundhead screws running over a plate washer.

Photo 3. 'through mortise and tenon with an overhang housed-in above. . .'

PINE DINING TABLE

To my surprise the ironmonger informed me that these fixing plates are no longer obtainable with double slots (to accommodate different fixing positions in relation to the grain). I had therefore to modify the side plates with a rat-tail file to allow for sideways movement.

With Mr and Mrs Markham seated at either end of the new dining table and the children spaced along the sides I left them, satisfied with their promise that they would polish the top regularly.

Photo 4. 'proportions of the cleat joint were exactly one third of the total thickness of the top. . .'

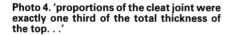

AT HELL'S GATE

WOODWORKER contributors get around. Harold King has recently been at Hell's Gate — the Canadian version we hasten to add, which is on the Fraser river and named after Simon Fraser the explorer.

Mr King says Hell's Gate is a deep and wild canyon which for many years has been a timber-felling area. And the lumberjacks are still tough. Indeed, as a hobby they sculpt timber using only a chainsaw and many of the old hands demonstrate their skills at fairs, stampedes and shows.

'Having tried a chainsaw I shudder to contemplate carving or doing anything else with the frightening gadget,' comments Mr King who notices that the competitive classes at this year's Woodworker Show include WB4 for carvings 'worked exclusively by power tools.' He adds: 'This could offer some surprises. I will not be entering a chainsaw carving, but a lumberjack may know of Woodworker Show!'

Henry Stadlbauer's chainsaw-only sculpture of explorer Simon Fraser who with the help of the Thompson Indians, pioneered a route in 1808 through the Canadian Rockies to Vancouver. Of Hell's Gate he said: 'It is a place where no human being should venture.' Mr King found that today's road makes access much easier. The life-size sculpture is on show at the viewing platform at Hell's Gate on trans-Canada highway 1, 130 miles east of Vancouver.

Round figures

Richard Piner talks through the making of this classic circular table

This table is designed to stand comfortably in a pine-furnished room — but it could just as easily be made in a hardwood, and perhaps more accurately too.

The legs are made from material 2in thick, the stem from a piece 3½×4in, and the 7in-square block from more 2in stuff — all scrap roof joists. The top is from 1in shelving, cleaned up, and with one tongued-and-grooved centre joint. The two bearers below are in oak, for extra strength.

Once cramped and glued, the top was cut to 3ft diameter with a jigsaw; imperfections were taken out by mounting it in a vice and doing some careful work with a Surform. Stroking with the hand indicated raised and otherwise imperfect sections.

The stem section was reduced to a rough 3½in square, mounted in my lathe and roughed out to 3¼in plus round. The

dimensions were carefully marked out, first in pencil and then with a parting-off chisel. The rest was straightforward. I left a little more than 2in in length at the top of the stem, which was useful later when gluing.

I then carefully marked out three flats at the base of the stem, each at an angle of 120°, and formed them with a width of 1¾in, the same as the width of the legs at this point. Careful marking was needed for the dovetail mortise — but not until the dovetail was formed on the legs, because I matched one to the other.

I had made an accurate template in hardboard for the legs. Having transferred its outline to the timber, I used a bandsaw to cut the legs to shape. The direction of the grain is most important. I then pencilled a centre line for each leg, top and bottom, as a guide for the even shaping of each side. Shaping was done with various Surforms and rasps or files — holding the leg in a vice and taking care to do each large section first, so giving plenty of hold for shaping the toe section. I made sure there was a smooth taper all round, and a good swelling for the toe is all-important. I included the foot pad as part of the leg, but it could be added later if that were easier.

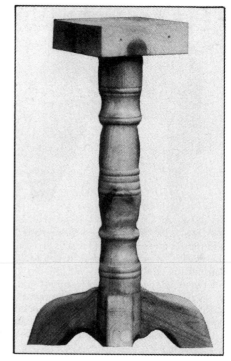

● *The turned stem carries a solid square block on to which the top is fitted. A combination of turning, hand shaping and nicely dovetailed legs*

The square block, 2in thick and 7in square, was carefully centred on the face-plate, and a 2in hole was turned to take the 2in section at the top of the stem. A good fit here is essential.

Two bearers were made from 1in oak, 26in long and nearly 2in thick at the centre — tapering to almost nothing at the ends, as they do not need to be seen.

Having ensured that each leg was a good fit in the stem (with room for the glue!) I mounted the stem and the legs on to a good flat surface and, using a large try-square, checked that when all was assembled the stem was vertical. In the absence of a square you could use a plumb-line.

The legs should be pushed well home against the shoulders. The lot was then glued together with Araldite. The square block was glued to the stem; again you should take care to see that it is pushed down on to its shoulder. I had previously taken the square to the underside of the top, marking the centre of both the top and the block for positioning later.

With the top still reversed, I positioned the stem and legs, and screwed one of the bearers into place. At least six screws each side are required to prevent any movement — but only insert two for the moment. The other bearer is then screwed into place, taking care to 'pinch' the block for added stiffness. The top is fastened to the block with two long screws each side; I deliberately made the table not to tilt.

I finished by careful sanding at each stage and when assembled, and I polished it with a good hard wax (leaving at least two days between applications) to provide an attractive depth of colour. ■

● *For well-balanced proportions, the diameter of the top should be no more than 1in larger than a circle round the feet. An absolutely vertical stem is also vital, demanding great care when gluing the feet up*

Stem

2″

2″ dia. top

2¼″

3¼″ dia.

7″ square block

3″ dia.

2½″

3″ dia.

2¼″ dia.

5″

2½″ dia.

3¼″ dia.

2″

2½″ dia.

3″

3″ dia.

1″

3¼″ dia.

leg

4¼″

dovetails

• *The legs are shaped with hardboard template and bandsaw, and jointed into the stem with long dovetails. The oak bearers for the top are screwed to the block, their ends tapering to nothing at the outer edge*

Leg

9½″

⅝″ dovetail

centre line of stem

1¾″

14⅝″

1¼″   1¾″

Top and bearers

1″ pine top 30″ dia.

bearers taper at outside edge

2 bearers oak 26×1″

7″ square block

stem

Chris Nussbaum's diary of the London College of Furniture C&G 564 cabinetmaking course

Each year students on the 564 cabinet-making course are set a relatively small piece of work to produce, embodying all or most of the practical techniques they should have acquired; our task this year is a 'correspondence cache', a portable writing/storage unit 375×330×250mm.

Designed by David Starling

Some of us have provided our own materials, so the piece is being constructed variously in ash, American oak, lacewood and English walnut. The main features are the inclined front, with forward-sloping drawer-front at the bottom, and backward-sloping flap above it which opens (pivoting along its bottom edge) to reveal a shelf, the front portion of which is canted to form a continuous sloping surface with the flap when it is fully open and resting on a table or desk.

The carcase is constructed with secret-mitre dovetails along the top edges, rails lap-dovetailed front and rear in the base, with sides and top grooved to take a veneered ply back. The shelf, which is assembled from two pieces edge-jointed at an angle, is housed and through-tenoned to show the quality (or lack of it) in the joints, which are optionally wedged. The traditional drawer construction, with its inclined front, gives us opportunity to practise our canted dovetails.

The flap is a framed fielded panel, which is simple enough, but it embodies the *pièce de résistance* of the design — the hingeing system. A rule joint is cut along the front edge of the shelf and the bottom rail of the flap with a pair of matched cutters, to give identical convex and concave surfaces. Two tiny wooden 'hinges' (rosewood reinforced with brass) are mortised into the shelf and pinned through the end of the flap to give a pivoting action. In this way the rule joint stays perfectly tight with the flap closed or open, shelf and open flap together forming a continuous sloping surface — in theory!

A break from this strenuous benchwork has been provided by a 24-hour 'work-in' in the college by a large number of students. This was organised as a protest against the Inner London Education Authority's attempt to force the college to join a new amalgamation of art and specialised colleges called the London Institute.

It was a great success — musical-instrument students producing a lute in 24 hours, other students repairing toys and equipment from a local school, and our own 564 group producing a real Rolls-Royce of a go-kart overnight, which will be donated to a local playgroup — when we've finished playing with it! ∎

Little rockers

Two makers present their delightful designs for cradles — each offering a very different challenge

Paul Davis writes: The weather was unexpectedly cold and wet, and a number of outside jobs had to be put off. I decided it was time to honour a promise to my wife to make a cradle for Anna, our month-old daughter.

The materials I had set aside were two well-seasoned through-and-through boards and a few scraps from a massive fireplace mantel, all in wild cherry. The idea was to combine a scrolled outline with the traditional dovetailed hopper construction of the French *petrin* or dough trough. Despite its apparent simplicity, this gave rise to a few posers; and then a further problem required solving — what do you do with a cradle these days once the baby has outgrown it?

After I had modified the dovetail joint to allow for the scrolling and profiling of the upper edge of the carcase, and joined a couple of pieces of beech to test the theory, I was ready to go. The answers to the other questions came as I went along.

The dimensions of the carcase were chosen so that it would fit round a 70x35cm pram mattress lying on the base 18mm from the bottom. The measurements given are the overall *inside* measurements, to take into account the 15° chamfer around the bottom.

The 27mm boards were planed down to 18mm — partly for aesthetic reasons, but also because they had spent a while propped up in a sawyer's shed and were badly warped. Unless you are lucky enough to have clean, straight boards that will allow you to cut out each of the components in a single piece, it would be advisable to cut out the scrolled parts before edge-jointing the various bits to make up the sides and ends. The offcuts from the scrolling can be used as softening and to keep the cramps in place. Note, however, that the ovals that form the handles come below the straight shoulders, and you should not attempt to cut out a single curved segment to add to straight-edged ends. In my case, the oval cut-outs also coincided nicely with a couple of unsightly knots.

The modified joint is dovetailed up to about 20mm from the top. The uppermost cuts are not raked, but made parallel to the straight edges of the board, and I mitred the two pins rather than chop one part out to take the other one entire. Thus the profiling can be done along the inside edge of the carcase as well as the outside (see the drawing). Again, be careful, as no angle in this kind of joint is square, so the mitres are not at 45°.

Making a mock-up of one of these corner joints in beech or any scrap wood can prove invaluable to get the hang of cutting at odd angles and to make sure you've got your

geometry right before making mistakes with the real thing. A quick 'on site' way of finding the angle at which the endgrain should be cut is to take a piece of paper or plywood and draw on it two straight lines intersecting at right angles. Stand — or rather, firmly support — along one line a thickish (25mm or more) piece of wood which has been trued up and had the

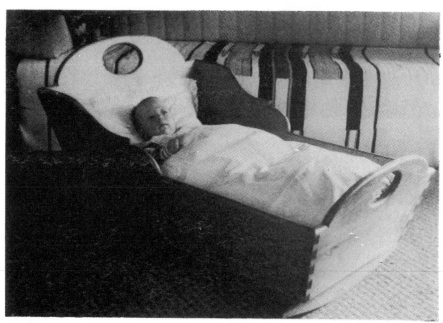

● *Wild cherry was the material for this dual-purpose cradle – the rockers are detachable so the container doesn't fall into disuse when its only or final occupant grows out of it*

bottom edge chamfered to the angle of slant you intend to use. Mark the points where the other line passes under the wood and, with a square, draw lines up both faces to the top, square edge. The line drawn across this edge which connects the two perpendiculars will give you the required angle. For a slope of 15° it should be a little under 93°.

● *Taking the rockers off is a simple matter of withdrawing four screws. The box dovetails (**below**) are canted – both boards slope; Paul Davis' description tells how to set about making these joints*

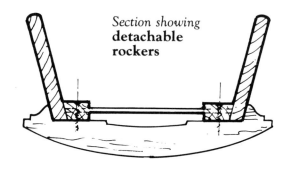

I t goes without saying that, since the dovetails are a salient feature of the whole piece which will be seen from all angles, they must be perfect. Do not be tempted to make the fit too tight, or the arrises may crumble and break off. Should the unthinkable happen and one or two dovetails be a shade loose, it is better to use a sliver or shaving of the same wood as packing than to try and hide the fault with a mastic filler.

Before gluing, the sawn scrolls should be cleaned up with a coarse file and scraper and the edges profiled. I used a portable router and an 8mm quarter-round cutter. The 2mm flat along the middle prevents the cutter from biting into the edge on the

Section showing **detachable rockers**

second cut and is quickly removed afterwards during finishing. The sharp inside angles were picked out with a *very* fine modeller's-saw-kerf bisecting them, and the rounding-off was carried up to the kerf with a few strokes of a chisel. It is a good idea, too, to do most of the hard finishing work on the inside surfaces before assembly.

When the carcase is glued up — if you use cramps, have wedge-shaped softening ready to hand — the ends of the pins and tails can be gently scraped down flush and the finishing completed.

It's at this stage that you may ask yourself what is to become of your efforts once the cradle's occupant has outgrown it a few months later. I made up a base from 6mm-thick pine slats loosely through-tenoned into two narrow 'stiles' which run the length of the carcase at the bottom and have the outside edges chamfered to the same 15° slant as the sides. This rather floppy structure was fitted flush to the bottom of the carcase; then the 'stiles' were pressed hard against the sides and screwed down at the corners directly on to the rockers underneath. This procedure firmly locks the carcase into position between the base and rockers; at some later date it can be re-covered intact and adapted for more permanent use as a magazine-rack or plant-trough.

Alternatively, if no further children are forthcoming, it can be lent out as a cradle for discreet publicity purposes. But don't let your friends use it for a dog's bed or a log-bin!

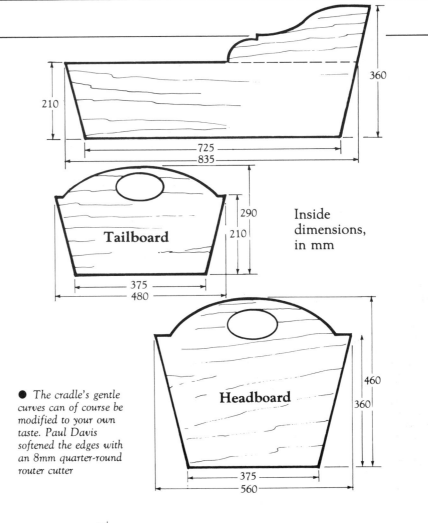

Inside dimensions, in mm

● *The cradle's gentle curves can of course be modified to your own taste. Paul Davis softened the edges with an 8mm quarter-round router cutter*

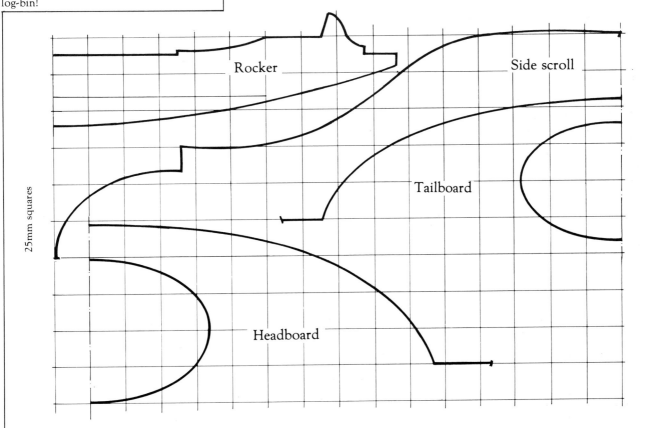

Peg-legs and sgabelle

Alan and Gill Bridgewater explore the other way of making chairs

When is a chair not a chair? And when is a stool not a stool? When it's a peg-leg, sgabelle, spindle, stick, spinning, Orkney or slab-back seat.

If you're still no wiser, picture the simple, traditional milkmaid's stool — three- or four-legged, it makes no matter. Add an upright plank back, a handful of wedges and a bit of shallow relief carving. Before you can say 'rustic and belonging to the peasant tradition', you have the basic, archetypal cottage chair.

Chairs of this type and character can't be described as belonging to specific countries or periods. All we can say for sure is that they are found wherever there is a peasant, folk-primitive, 'kitchen hearth' furniture-making tradition. In colonial New England there were beautiful plank-seated, stick-legged, wedge-tenoned chairs known as 'peg-legs'; in Renaissance Italy there were somewhat over-carved, three-legged, scroll-backed seats known as 'sgabelle'; closer to home, in Scotland and northern Europe, there were plank-backed chairs known variously as 'Orkney', 'spinning' and 'spindle' stools — and so we could go on, with examples from Russia, Scandinavia, Switzerland and Germany.

Peg-legs and plank-backs are essentially humble, rustic and home-made, and therein lies their naive and honest charm. What's more, of course, you don't need a fancy tool-kit, and there aren't any high-tech joints, screws, nails, glues or suchlike: just slab wood and simple, direct, easy-to-manage techniques. You won't finish up with a gesso-encrusted baroque cabriole-legged carver (or even, for that matter, a particularly comfortable chair); but you will be able to let rip with your own idiosyncratic design ideas, and get to grips with some honest-to-goodness making and carving.

We reckon that this project can be undertaken by the keen beginner in a couple of weekends.

Tools and materials

Before you start, throw away most of your pre-conceived ideas on how a chair ought to be made, and try to feel yourself into the shoes of a never-done-it-before pioneer or peasant woodworker. You're using 'in-the-rough' or found wood; you only have a few basic tools; and you are seeking, to the best of your ability, to make a simple, strong, serviceable and decorative chair.

Get yourself a slab of rough-sawn 1½in half-seasoned oak, and make sure that it's reasonably straight-grained and free from warps, splits, shakes and dead knots. A board 42in long, 12in wide and 1-2in thick will do just fine. Our chair, as illustrated in the gridded working drawings, has a seat

● She had a spinning-wheel – did the Queen have a plank-back stool as well?

12x13in; the plank back is 27in long including the tenon, and tapers from 6-8in wide at the top to about 4in wide at the tenon shoulders; and there are four tapered, octagonal-sectioned legs.

As for tools, you need a large coping- or

bow-saw, a mallet, a brace or hand-drill, a spokeshave or draw-knife, a straight chisel, a straight gouge, a V-section tool, a spoon-bit chisel, a spoon-bit gouge, and of course such 'around the workshop' items as pencils, a measure, a compass, a square, a cramp and rough working-out paper.

First steps and marking out

Have a good look at our working drawings and inspirational ideas, give your wood a last check, and then with the compass, measure and pencil start to set out the design, as illustrated.

Measure and mark the eight-sided seat slab, the four legs, the plank back and the set. When you're sure that all is correct, clearly label the blanks. If you like the overall design but would prefer a taller back, a wider seat or whatever, now's the time to adjust the chair to suit your needs.

Finally, cut out the blanks with a fine-toothed straight saw.

Setting out and carving

Before you start setting out the areas to be carved, take each piece, secure it to the

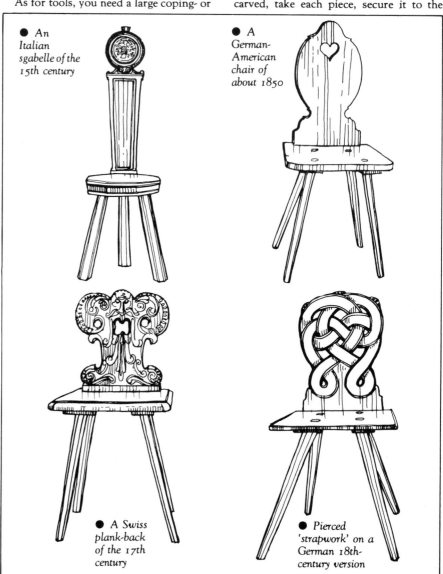

● An Italian sgabelle of the 15th century

● A German-American chair of about 1850

● A Swiss plank-back of the 17th century

● Pierced 'strapwork' on a German 18th-century version

● *The project's central feature gives it life . . .*

bench with the cramp, and with a shallow gouge bring its surface to a slightly rippled finish. Don't aim for a characterless 'plastic' smoothness — rather a soft, dappled and gently scalloped tooled texture.

Next, with a compass and straight-edge, set out the areas for carving. Have a good look at the gridded drawings and see how the design of the 9in-diameter seat roundel is quartered, and set back about 1¼in from the front edge of the seat slab. Notice also how the plank-back design is organised, pierced and contained within a border.

The plank back

Once you have drawn out the design you can start to work the back. With the wood secure in the vice, take the coping-saw and hand-drill and work the pierced heart motif. Drill a starter hole, and then (with the coping-saw blade at 90° to the working surface) cut out the heart. Work with an even and steady stroke, manoeuvring and turning the saw as you go.

Then clamp the wood flat and square on the workbench and arrange your chisels and gouges so that they are comfortably to hand. Re-check the design, and with a pencil re-establish its lines and black in the areas that need to be lowered.

Now take the V-section tool and start to outline the whole of the design — all the time working on the waste or ground side, and cutting into the wood about ¼in outside the drawn lines. As you work the V-section incised trench you will be cutting both with and across the grain, so hold the tool with both hands, one guiding and one pushing; work with short, shallow, controlled strokes, and be ready to stop short if you feel the tool running into the grain or skidding out of control. At this stage you shouldn't need to use a mallet; just put your shoulder behind the tool and try to cut a smooth V-section trench, not too deep.

When you've outlined the design, go round the drawn lines and 'set in' with the straight chisel and gouge. Hold the tool in

● *A little inspiration: some seats and backs in the European folk tradition*

one hand so that the handle is leaning slightly over the design, and cut into the lines of the motif with short lively taps of the mallet. Try all the time to keep the depth of cut constant, say ⅛-¼in, and aim to establish a clean, sharp-edged design. The setting-in should follow the V-trench and the edge of the design in a single, smooth and continuous line.

Some carvers lower or 'waste' the unwanted 'ground' of the design before they set in. Otherwise, you can do this now.

Take the spoon-bit gouge, cut a broad trench on the ground side of the V-section cut, and — when you have established the depth of the lowered ground — chop out the whole area. Try to leave the lowered ground smooth and even, but not so overworked that you can't see the tool marks. Finally, work round the now raised motifs and make sure the angles are free from bits and burrs.

Look at the acorns-and-oak-leaves design, as illustrated, and see how the forms

Peg-legs and sgabelle

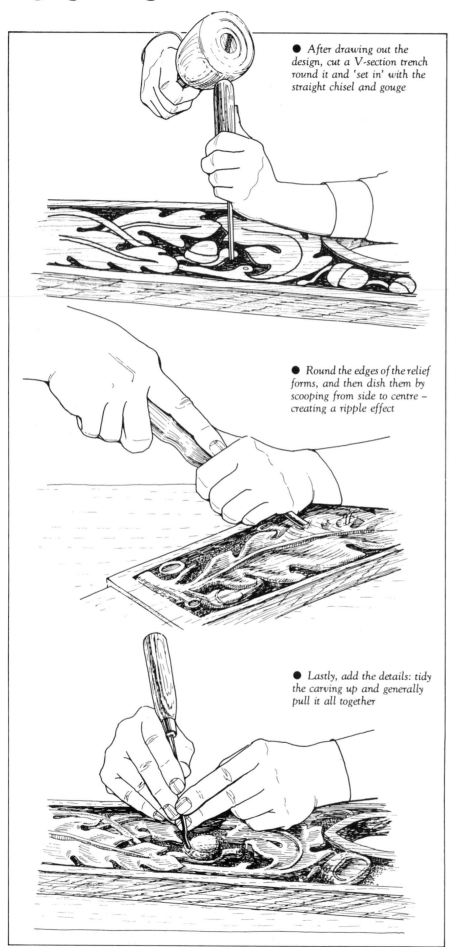

● After drawing out the design, cut a V-section trench round it and 'set in' with the straight chisel and gouge

● Round the edges of the relief forms, and then dish them by scooping from side to centre – creating a ripple effect

● Lastly, add the details: tidy the carving up and generally pull it all together

have been worked in rather a formal and mechanical manner. Take the straight gouge and work round the raised design, all the while cutting away and rounding the sharp edges. Don't even attempt to carve subtle realism and complex undercuts; rather go for swift and direct stylisation. When you have rounded the edges of the motifs, dish them gently — scoop out the wood from side to centre, all the time taking care that you don't damage short-grain areas or cut into the raised-leaf veining.

And so you continue to work: cutting and running the tools across the grain, and over and around the forms, until you feel that you have taken the carving as far as you want it to go. Don't fuss and worry the design; try to keep it simple and bold. When you have worked the plank back, work the seat roundel in like manner.

The mortises and tenons

If you look closely at the plank-back-to-seat joint, you will see that the tapered plank is tenoned and rebated so that it enters the seat mortise at an oblique angle of about 100-110°. Once the plank tenon and seat mortise have been cut and worked to fit, the rebated shoulders of the tenon need to be pared and bevelled until they strike the seat smooth and clean.

This done, cut a mortise in the plank-back tenon, at an angle parallel to the seat, and then cut and fit a wedge as illustrated.

Cutting and fixing the legs

Take the 14in-long leg blanks, a stick at a time, secure them in the vice and then shape

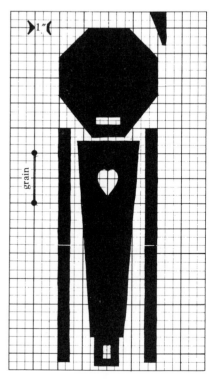

● This cutting diagram provides a well-proportioned layout for all the components of the chair

106

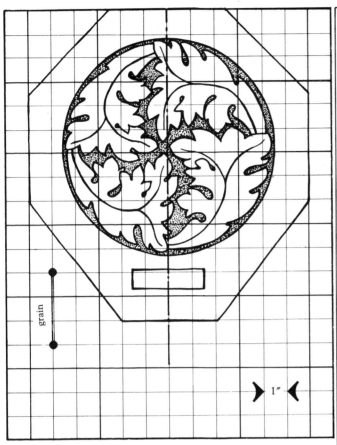

● Here is the seat design we evolved for this particular project. Again the secret of accurate setting-out is to use a grid. Apart from anything else, this ensures symmetry if the design calls for it

grain

1″

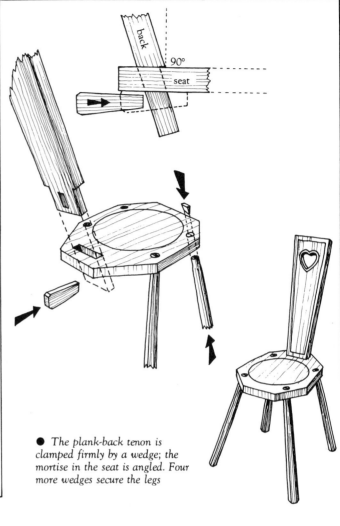

back

90°

seat

● The plank-back tenon is clamped firmly by a wedge; the mortise in the seat is angled. Four more wedges secure the legs

● Setting up the coping-saw for open-heart surgery on the plank back. The bow-saw is an alternative tool

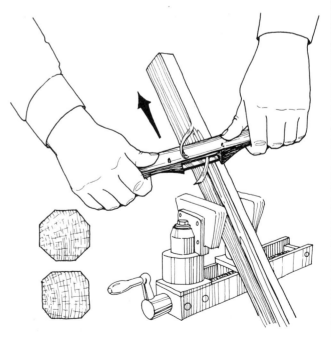

● A spokeshave, draw-knife or plane tapers the legs and takes them down to an octagonal section – regular or otherwise

Peg-legs and sgabelle

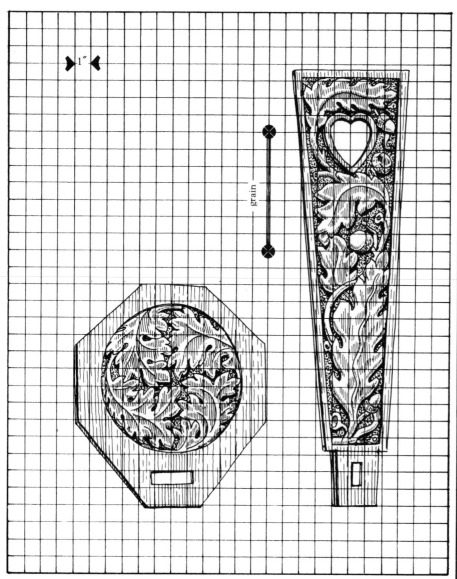

1″

grain

● *Here the seat roundel is drawn out next to its accompanying plank back. We went for an oak-tree theme, but don't let that stop you from casting as far and wide for inspiration as you like. The world's folk art offers a vast treasure-house of inspiration, and a great deal of that has found its way into books*

them with the spokeshave or draw-knife until they are gently tapered and octagonal in section. Aim to take the taper from about 1½in at the bottom to about 1¼in at the top.

When you've done four legs, place the carved seat slab face-down on the workbench and bore four angled holes. Then continue to work the tapered ends of the legs until they are a good stiff fit in the bored seat holes.

Finally, when the legs fit flush with the seat, make the joints as shown.

Getting it all together

When the legs have been wedge-tenoned into the seat and the plank-back tenon inserted into the seat mortise, its holding wedge can be banged home. Adjust the chair so that it sits firm and four-square, and go over your work with a small gouge tidying up sharp edges and making sure all

the surfaces have a dappled, tooled texture.

Finally, remove all the dust and wood fragments with a stiff brush, give it a couple of coats of beeswax, and the job is done.

On traditional peg-leg chairs of this character the carving is usually incised or shallow-relief, but of course there's no reason why the chair shouldn't be painted, chip-carved or whatever takes your fancy.

Some other points:
● When you come to fixing the leg wedge-tenons, make sure the little wedges are cut in so that they run across the grain of the seat, as illustrated.
● If you think the 1½in-thick slab seat looks a little on the heavy side, bevel the under-edge with a gouge so that edge-on the seat looks to be about ¾in thick.
● When you bore the leg holes in the seat slab, watch out that you don't split or damage the wood. It's a good idea to drill from both sides. ∎

Table-top seat_____

When is a table not a table?
When it's a settle — one you
can make with the help of
Vic Taylor's splendid
drawings

T he 'Monk's bench' is unusual as an
early example of dual-purpose furniture. In one guise it acts as a side-
table for serving food, and by re-arranging
and re-fixing the top it becomes a settle.

We can tell that it is intended as a side-
table because of the following two features;
first, the back edge of the top lines up with
the back edge of the cross-piece (fig. 2),
whereas there is an overhang at the front
edge; and second, there is a slot cut through
each cross-piece and a peg can be pushed
through to engage in a hole in the arm at
each end. This allows you to slide the top
towards you when sitting at the table and
gives you more leg-room — quite a normal
characteristic of this kind of table.

The individuality of the design, however,
lies in the fact that you can withdraw the
pegs, take the top off and re-position it as a
settle-back by inserting each peg through its
slot into a second hole bored through the
back end of each arm, as shown in the end
elevation, fig. 2. The result is a settle with a
wooden seat and back which will need some
cushions to make it comfortable.

The piece was probably made in the early
or mid-17th century; it's difficult to be precise as furniture of this type was usually
locally made by the village carpenter and
the woodturner, and popular designs continued to be made for many years after their
inception. Settles of this style are often
called 'monks' benches', but there's no
evidence that they were particularly
favoured by monks; anyway, most monas-
teries had been dissolved by Henry VIII and
the monks disbanded by the end of the 16th
century, many years before our design came
into existence.

Construction

The top couldn't be simpler. It consists of
three pieces of oak, laid alongside each
other and nailed to the two cross-pieces.
The inevitable has happened, of course, and
the pieces have shrunk across their widths
with resulting gaps and splits.

If you are concerned with authenticity
you can do the same, but shrinkage plates
(fig. 5A) would be better. Fig. 5B shows
how the plate is first screwed to the cross-
piece, sunk slightly below the surface (say
1/32 in or so) which means that the cross-
piece and the top will be in close contact.
Use a round-head screw to fix the plate to
the underside of the top; the slot will allow
movement without the top splitting.

Fig. 1 shows the various joints used. You
will see the framing uses mortise-and-tenon
joints, all pegged; the joints on the seat rails
are double tenons.

The wedged tenons on the tops and

● Having it both ways; a
flick of the wrist and the table
becomes a settle – and not
just for monks!

Methods of construction

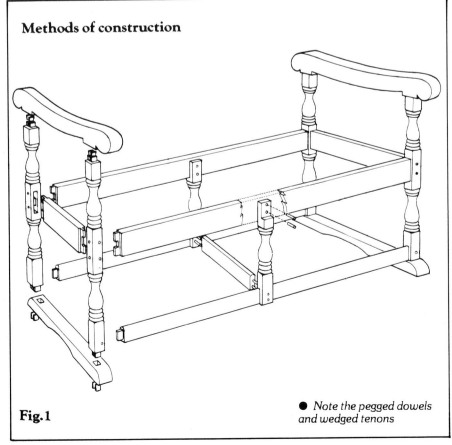

Fig.1

● Note the pegged dowels
and wedged tenons

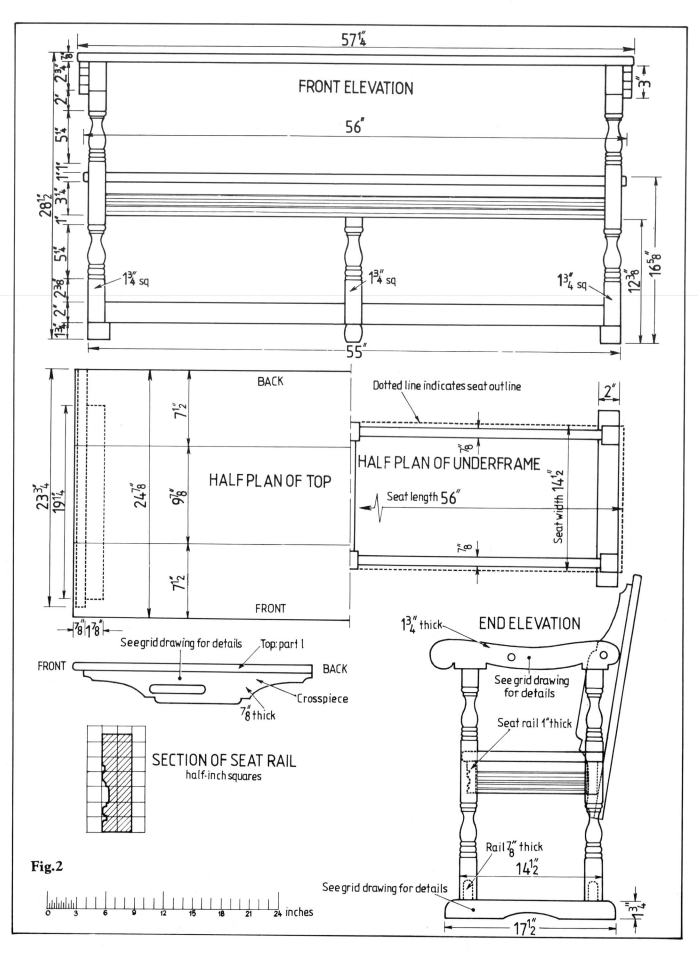

FRONT ELEVATION

57¼"

56"

3"

28½"

2⅜"
2"
2¾"
7⁄8"
5¼"
1'1"
3¼"
1"
5¼"
2⅜"
2"
1¼"

16⅝"
12⅜"

1¾" sq   1¾" sq   1¾" sq

55"

BACK

HALF PLAN OF TOP

7½"
9⅞"
7½"

23¾"
19¼"
24⅞"

FRONT

⅞" 1⅞"

Dotted line indicates seat outline   2"

HALF PLAN OF UNDERFRAME

⅞"
⅞"

Seat length 56"

Seat width 14½"

See grid drawing for details   Top: part I

FRONT   BACK

Crosspiece

⅞" thick

SECTION OF SEAT RAIL
half-inch squares

END ELEVATION

1¾" thick

See grid drawing
for details

Seat rail 1" thick

Rail ⅞" thick

14½"

See grid drawing for details

1¾"

17½"

Fig. 2

0 3 6 9 12 15 18 21 24 inches

110

Table-top seat

bottoms of the legs need cutting carefully. The tenons at the top ends are blind and call for a slightly different treatment from the bottom ones which are through tenons; fig. 4 shows both kinds, B at the bottom and C at the top of the leg. Points to note are:

● The saw-cuts to accept the wedges should only extend two-thirds of the tenon length.

● The mortise should be slightly splayed as shown to allow for the expansion of the tenon when the wedges are driven home, but the splay only extends for two-thirds of the mortise depth, the same as the length of the saw cuts.

● Judge the size of the wedges nicely. They mustn't be too thin to expand the tenon properly, nor should they be too thick so they force the tenon apart prematurely and jam it before it's fully home.

The tops of the intermediate legs are cut away to accept the seat-rails, and the joints are pegged right through (fig. 1). At the bottom they are bridle-jointed over the underframe rails as shown at fig.4A, and the joints are pegged right through with dowels, which also fix the intermediate cross-rail.

Like the top, the seat consists of two pieces nailed to the end seat-rails and notched round the legs. This is obviously another case for using shrinkage plates along the end seat-rails; fixing to the front and back seat-rail can be by pocket-screwing (fig. 5C), if you don't mind a gap opening up in the middle of the seat. If you prefer comfort to authenticity, pocket-screw at the front and use shrinkage plates everywhere else.

All the seat-rails had moulded faces, the profile of which is shown in fig. 2. This would probably have been worked with a combination of moulding planes and scratch-stocks, but life is easier for us, and we can use a spindle moulder or a router to speed things up.

The only other components are the two pegs (detail, fig. 3) which call for straightforward wood turning.

Furniture like this almost always began its life 'in the white' — free from any kind of polish. Hundreds of years' worth of wax polish would have been applied, of course, and you can do the same thing; use any good quality proprietary wax polish.

You can see from the main drawing that the piece has had some heavy wear, particularly on the front under-frame rails where the wood has been worn away to about half the original size. If you want to give your reproduction the same appearance you can use a rasp to simulate the wear, restricting it to the front under-frame rail and the edges of the legs, where feet would normally scuff the wood. The edges of the arms were also notched and bruised, and so were all the edges of the top.

● The design is reproduced by kind permission of Mrs Lyle, Barrington Court, near Ilminster, Somerset. ∎

Fig.3

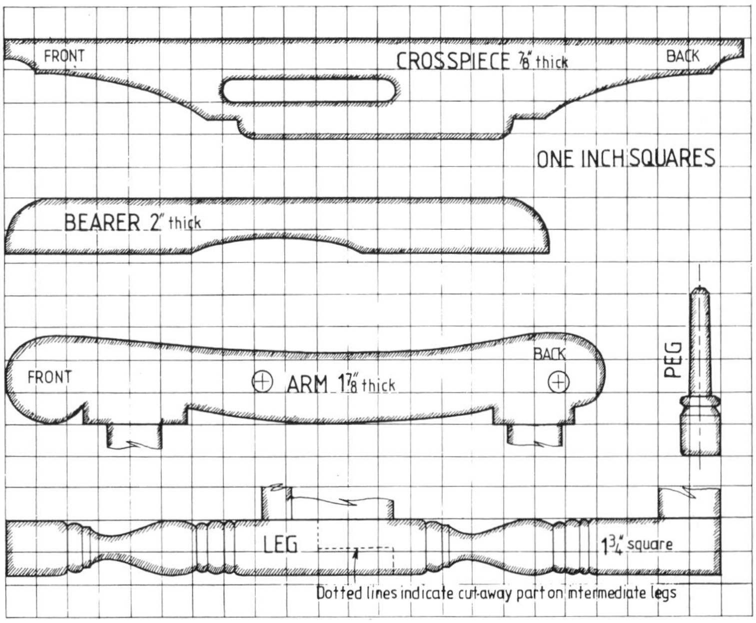

FRONT   CROSSPIECE ⅞" thick   BACK

ONE INCH SQUARES

BEARER 2" thick

FRONT   ARM 1⅞" thick   BACK   PEG

LEG   1¾" square

Dotted lines indicate cut-away part on intermediate legs

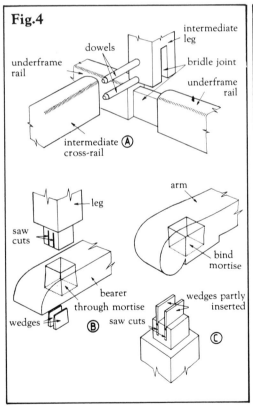

Fig.4

intermediate leg

dowels

underframe rail   bridle joint

underframe rail

intermediate (A) cross-rail

leg   arm

saw cuts

bind mortise

bearer

through mortise

wedges   saw cuts   (B)

wedges partly inserted

(C)

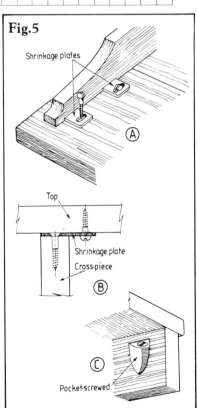

Fig.5

Shrinkage plates

(A)

Top

Shrinkage plate

Cross-piece

(B)

(C)

Pocket-screwed

Cutting list

All components in oak: all dimensions are finished sizes

Top	1	57¼in x	24⅞in x	⅞in	1454mm x	632mm x	23mm
Crosspieces	2	23¾	3⅛	⅞	603	80	23
Seat	1	56	14½	1	1423	369	25
Arms	2	19¼	2¾	1⅞	489	70	48
Legs	4	23	1¾	1¾	584	45	45
Intermediate legs	2	13	1¾	1¾	330	45	45
Long seat-rails	2	53¼	3¼	1	1353	83	25
End seat-rails	2	13⅛	3¼	1	333	83	25
Under-frame rails	2	53¼	2	⅞	1353	51	23
Bearers	2	17½	1¾	2	445	45	51
Intermediate cross-rail	1	11	2	⅞	280	51	23

No holds shelved

A multi-adjustable storage system without so much as a screw or nail to wall, floor or ceiling? A couple of simple ideas make Alan Blower's shelves a triumph of flexibility

photos Steve Mussell

● *Detail of the lowest shelf shows the cut-in overlap and adjustable foot*

Faced with building a shelf unit to cover a wall, I didn't want to take the usual approach and end up with square-ended sections, the normal type of shelf unit one comes across. No matter what goes into the design, they always somehow look the same; a variation on a theme of square box-like shelf sections. So after much doodling and pondering on how to break away from this, I decided to develop an idea that uses pillars braced floor to ceiling, the shelves resting on crossbars on the pillars. The original scheme I heard of used eight 2x2in pillars, with a section of shelves between each pair, but I re-thought it, and decided to use four 3x3in pillars, the shelves supported by a dowel passed through as a crossbar under the shelf (fig. 1). Putting the first hole at 7in from floor level, the second at 14in up, then every 6in up to a height of 75in, or 20in from the ceiling, gave 11 possible shelf levels.

The first problem with this is that once a shelf is on the first section, you can't have a shelf on the next section at the same level, or the shelves will clash at the pillar — or can you? Fig. 2 shows how I solved the problem, but it makes another in that you have to predetermine the arrangement of shelves to some degree. By making a couple of pairs that will meet on a pillar, they can be used to change the arrangement later — it was important that the whole unit be designed to be re-arrangeable.

Making the pillars

Being a great believer in the strength of laminated timber, I made the four 3x3in pillars from four lengths of 4x1in each, planed to $\frac{13}{16}$in, which gave me an extra $\frac{1}{4}$in when the four lengths came together as one. The extra $\frac{1}{4}$in proved useful, as though the pillars came out of the clamps reasonably straight, I still had enough to finish them to 3x3in dead straight.

Making the shelves

I decided to build up an approximate 12in width from 4x1in timber; the original length of shelf I planned would have given 35in between pillars, but the timber came in either 3m or 6m lengths, so to save wood I ordered the 3m and closed the pillars up to give 33in between them. A 3m length cut into three gave one at 35in and two at 41in for each shelf (fig. 3). Realising that once the three lengths were together it would be a difficult job to end-sand the centre piece, I did this on a disc sander before I glued up, to a dead 31¾in. The two outer pieces were cut at 41in, planed to 3¾x¾in, and once out of the clamps the four outer lengths' ends were trimmed to within $\frac{1}{16}$in, then disc-sanded to a dead 39¼in. I finished the shelves by putting a slight rounding on all four edges of each one. I allowed ⅛in round the pillars between pillar and shelf on three sides, and on reflection feel that $\frac{1}{16}$in would have been enough. If you go ahead with this project, I'd recommend you allow just that clearance. For the arrangement I have, I

continued

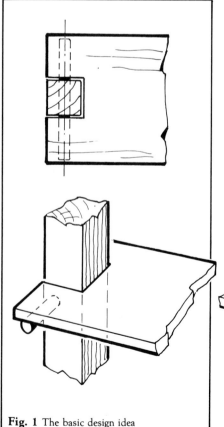

Fig. 1 The basic design idea

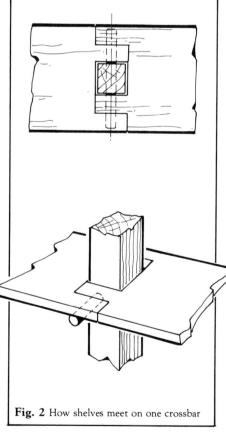

Fig. 2 How shelves meet on one crossbar

No holds shelved

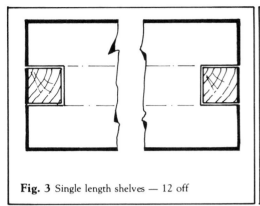

Fig. 3 Single length shelves — 12 off

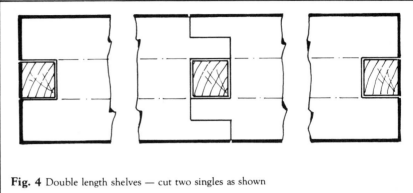

Fig. 4 Double length shelves — cut two singles as shown

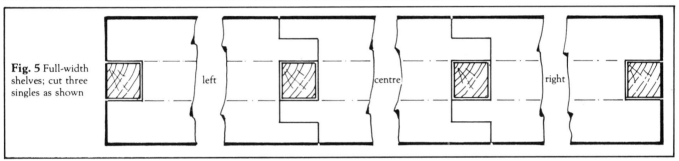

Fig. 5 Full-width shelves; cut three singles as shown   left   centre   right

made 12 shelves as shown in fig. 3, a pair as in fig. 4, and a set of three as in fig. 5 that go straight across the bottom to take large books and files. It makes a total of 17 shelves.

Drilling

For drilling the holes in the pillars I already have a very useful jig I made myself some years ago that fits on to my pillar-drill table (fig. 6), and for a job like this it really came into its own. Once the pillars were marked for holes, the drill table arranged to allow the length of the pillar to go through the jig unhindered, and a pile of offcuts ready to hold up the pillar to the same height when drilling, I found little problem completing the task. The critical part is that the holes are true through the pillar; I checked this by putting a dowel in a hole I'd drilled and trying a T-square on it off the pillar.

I know I'm not the only one that's been driven half mad trying to match imperial drills to metric dowel and vice versa, and not all dowel, as we know, comes perfectly round. But having acquired a good 1in drill-bit I got the dowel matched on the second attempt, and although it was a little tight, I made a simple tool to sand out the holes a bit. This is merely an offcut of dowel turned down a fraction, rolled in 150-grit abrasive paper with lots of glue, and covered in elastic bands overnight. It did the trick.

Bracing

The bracings I used are really adjustable feet with a threaded M10 pin moving in a threaded spiked collar that hammers into the endgrain. They are like the ones you find on bed legs or adjustable-height kitchen units. Rocking-type hard rubber-pad feet have 15mm nuts incorporated in

the top to screw the foot in or out of the spiked collar and adjust height. I drilled a ⅜in hole in each end of the pillars, tapped the spiked collar in round it, then threaded the rubber pad in. It doesn't matter if the hole isn't dead square, as the pads will adjust. A word of warning — look for these fittings and buy them before you make your height calculations and start cutting and drilling the timber!

Construction

Bracing each pillar, I packed 3x3x½in softwood pieces between pad and floor and pad and ceiling. Once the first pillar was in

place, slightly tightened and lined up with a spirit level, I put the second pillar in line with it, using a 33in offcut between pillars and another of 4¾in to the wall. And so on until all four pillars were up.

No floor is dead flat, and my living room floor is no exception. It posed the problem of getting the shelves level, but I found that the pillars, once they were up, would turn on the pad fittings. Turning a pillar to the right raises it by winding it up the top fitting and off the bottom one, and this allowed me to raise or lower each pillar fractionally to get the shelves dead level. You only have to make sure the bottom pad fitting is

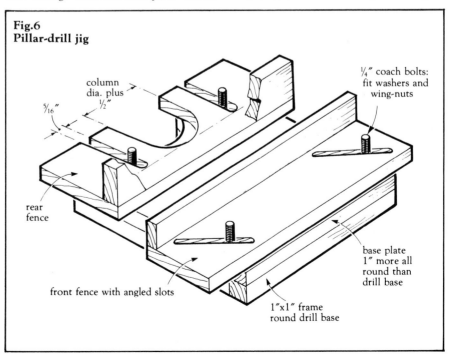

Fig.6
Pillar-drill jig

column dia. plus ½"

5/16"

¼" coach bolts: fit washers and wing-nuts

rear fence

front fence with angled slots

base plate 1" more all round than drill base

1"x1" frame round drill base

unscrewed just a little before starting. After I'd completed the unit and added some weight in the form of books, the top fittings needed tightening a little as the pillars sunk into the carpet. After this I found I only needed to adjust it a little just twice, once after a week and the second time about 10 days later. Before it went up and the arrangement of shelves was decided, I expected to have a lot of empty holes about, but surprisingly enough there aren't. There are more empty holes in the two end pillars for obvious reasons, but on the arrangement I have there are 13 empty holes in all, out of a total of 44.

Conclusions

I built the unit to go against a wall in my living room, but it can also, of course, be used as a room divider. The spacing of the pillars doesn't need to be constant; one could for example have the first two pillars 30in apart, then the third 18in or whatever from the second pillar — however you want it. Of course the finish is entirely optional. I used a polyurethane finish to match my existing furniture, but it could be painted to blend in with a colour scheme.

I live in a small modern block of flats with concrete floors and ceilings, which allow the unit as it stands to work. If you live in an older house it might not be so easy — you'd have to redesign to line the pillars up with the joists and beams. First question — do the joists and beams line up? No doubt 'plates' of, say, 4x2in between pillars and floor and ceiling would spread the weight; 4x1in might be enough. But then you have great lumps of wood on floor and ceiling, which would give it a heavy look. Your problem!

Although building the unit involved a lot of work — planing up 102 metres of 4x1in

sawn was just a part of it — the entire unit, which covers a wall about 8ft high by 11ft wide, has over 46ft of shelf space between pillars, and it stands solid without a screw, nail or joint. It cost me less than £85 to build. But the nice part (next to the building) was that it has put me in domestic good books for some time to come! ∎

● **Above**, the installation is decorative enough on its own, but of course it'll hold a lot more than this. The feet work fine on strong walls and ceilings, but load-spreaders would be necessary in old and infirm structures

● **Left and above**, shelf and vertical member meeting details. The clearance round the pillars could have been less, says Alan

A MEETING TABLE

Before re-opening her furniture restoration business after having children, Anna Cunnyngham went back to school: a table for the local Quaker Meeting House was her exam project

I had put my furniture restoration business in mothballs to have a family. Now my children were at school and I found I had time during the day at last.

But getting back to business after eight years is not easy. I found my self-confidence was damaged. I had to do something about it and decided to look for a teacher.

Evening classes were out of the question – child care problems and fatigue were the main deterrents – so I enrolled in the local comprehensive school sixth form to study A-level design. This was new ground for me, since I had avoided commission work in the past, sticking strictly to restoration work. At the school I found exactly what I wanted: a teacher, colleagues, fellow students, a well-equipped workshop and a scheme of work which would open up an exciting new aspect of furniture making.

Now, two years later, we've taken our exams – it felt like graduating – and the students who worked together are setting off in a variety of directions: art school, university, colleges of further education . . . and for me, opening a business.

The course took us through a rich variety of design activities to establish a strong familiarity with the design process. The culmination was a major project to be completed by the end of the second year, and I decided mine would be a piece of furni-

ture. But not for my own home, for there wasn't the room for any more stuff.

Now the local Quakers (Religious Society of Friends) were building a new meeting house in the city and were going to need lots of furniture. I approached them and they offered me the chance to design and build a table for their meeting room.

This was a many-layered challenge; the piece had to be robust, good looking, and fit in with the style of the room and the aesthetic tradition of a Christian denomination known for their simple, domestic-style worship. The background research took me to the meeting house architect, to' neighbouring meeting houses, and to local craftsmen and furniture factories. From some I got advice, from others practical help: one firm allowed me to run the assembled tabletop through their 4ft-wide drum sander, so I brought both surfaces to level in half an hour instead of half a week.

Before I started work I used an IBM PC computer to construct a critical path analysis of the project. With some help from

an expert, I got the machine to spit out a plan of work – resources needed, tools, machines, space and estimated time to be spent on each part of the job. This plan kept me in line, making sure I had everything I needed at each stage, and I actually finished the job two weeks ahead of time with no ugly surprises on the way.

I used American cherry. The design is slightly unusual in that the base frame supports the top along its diagonals, not its edges; this reflects the strong diagonal emphasis of the room itself. The repeat pattern of verticals in the base frames echo the repeated verticals of the window frames, giving a certain Japanese flavour to both room and table.

I used very straightforward mortise-and-tenon joints for the base frame, with bridles where the two frames crossed. After assembling and gluing one frame flat, I offered the second up to it and assembled and glued it with both standing. The top has eight dry-jointed grooved boards with 8mm ply fillets, enclosed in a frame glued at the corners with tongued mitres. After polishing

the top and base frame, I used buttons to fasten them together.

Base frame

I planed all members to size, and then carefully stacked the timber to avoid warping. I cut the base frame joints on a mortiser and bandsaw and then shaped the leg tapers before smoothing the inside surfaces and giving them a coat of sealer to make cleaning off the glue easier later on. I dry-assembled each frame separately and flatted the outside surfaces; I found I was catching the heel of the plane on the areas behind which I was working, so I used single, light strokes to avoid this. I left cutting the bridle joints till last so they would keep crisp.

Then I glued up the first frame; this has bridles opening upwards so the second frame can rest down on these during its assembly. Once the glue was set on frame one I assembled and glued frame two around it, with the frames both upright.

Making the top

The top has 12 pieces, eight boards for the panel and the mitred frame around. Shooting the butted edges took a lot of vigilance over how much I was taking off. As I shot each board I laid it with its fellows to check if there were any discrepancies in the overall dimension. If there was a slight discrepancy with

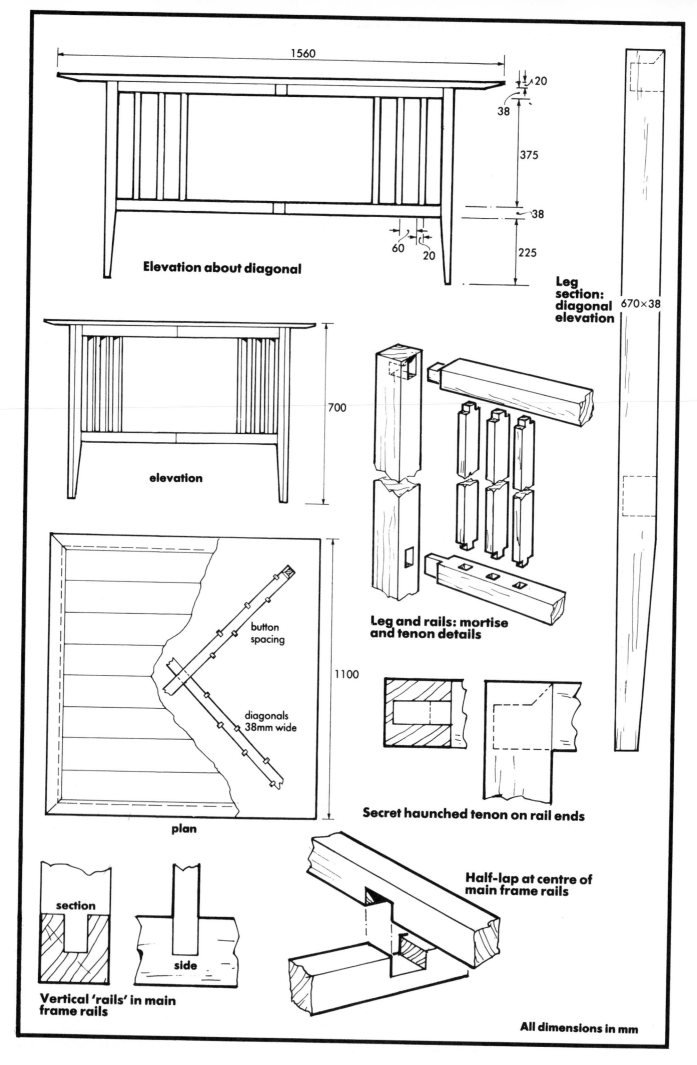

1560

20

38

375

38

225

60   20

Elevation about diagonal

Leg section: diagonal elevation

670×38

700

elevation

Leg and rails: mortise and tenon details

button spacing

diagonals 38mm wide

1100

plan

Secret haunched tenon on rail ends

Half-lap at centre of main frame rails

section

side

Vertical 'rails' in main frame rails

All dimensions in mm

one board, I compensated for it with the next. The result was that I kept a constant width down the table top. I had previously grooved the boards to accept the ply fillets. As I fitted the boards together, I allowed about ½-1mm space between each for possible swelling. I also put a light chamfer on those edges which butted against each other to highlight the top's construction and to disguise alterations in spaces between the boards as they shrank and swelled in changing conditions.

Happy with these panel boards, I turned to the framing. I had originally planned the tongues in the mitres to come well out to the edge of the table. But I wanted to put a deep chamfer on the table edge and was in danger of exposing the tongue. So I redesigned the tongue so it was stubbier and ended further from the table edge. At the same time, I made the chamfer a bit shallower. This redesign allowed the chamfer to pass to one side of the joint (see opposite).

I assembled and glued just at the corner mitres, leaving the rest dry to slide within the frame.

Flatting the whole surface might have taken me days, but a local furniture factory allowed me to put the top through their drum sander, which did the job in 20 minutes. I used a belt sander to take residual scratches off. However, flatting the table top removed most of my chamfers, so I recut these using a chisel and straight edge – quite a tricky job.

Finishing

I did the initial finishing of top and frame separately, using a coat of shellac sanding sealer and then three successive coats of Rustin's Plastic Lacquer, cutting down between each coat with 0000 steel wool.

I had already cut 24 buttons, and also button holes in the top horizontal rails of the base frames. I located these holes carefully so they lay beneath the centre of a board and not a join; the drawing overleaf shows how they are staggered. The holes nearest the centre of the table were cut to a snug fit, loosening them progressively as I got further from the centre; this compensated for the increased lateral

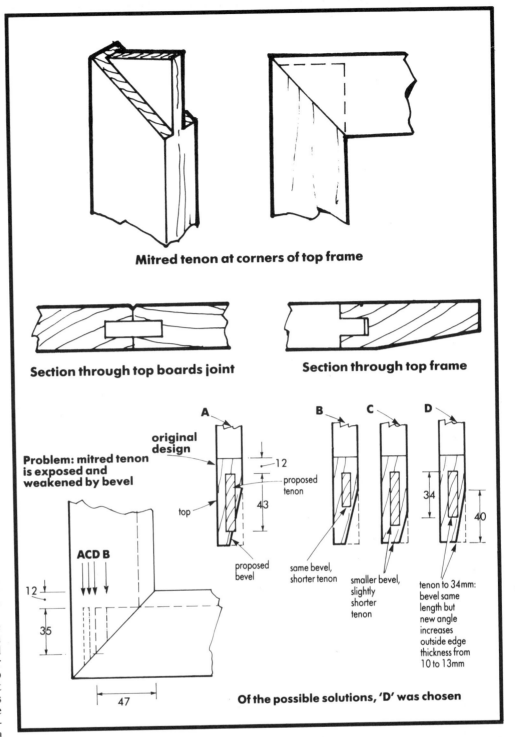

Mitred tenon at corners of top frame

Section through top boards joint

Section through top frame

Problem: mitred tenon is exposed and weakened by bevel

original design

proposed tenon

top

proposed bevel

same bevel, shorter tenon

smaller bevel, slightly shorter tenon

tenon to 34mm: bevel same length but new angle increases outside edge thickness from 10 to 13mm

Of the possible solutions, 'D' was chosen

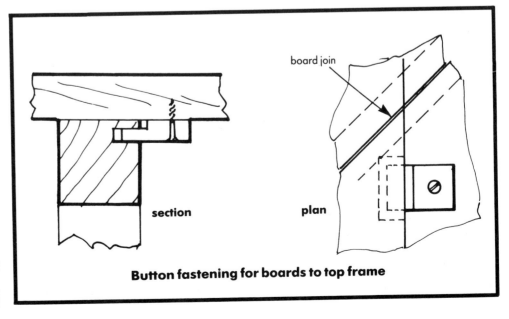

board join

section

plan

Button fastening for boards to top frame

movement expected towards the perimeter of the top. I placed the top in position over the frame, set the buttons loosely in their slots, and then fixed screws through the buttons into the underside of the table.

I finished by waxing all over; this caused a build-up of unsightly white deposit in the grooves at first, but I used a soft tooth-brush to clear this out.

Conclusion

I delivered the table in time for Easter Sunday and it seems to have met all the Quakers' re-quirements.

My experience shows that daytime secondary school courses can open up significant opportunities for people, especially women, who want to get back to work and need a renewal of confidence and skills to do so. I renewed both, and next month I'll be opening my own restoration business again. This time round I'll be able to accept design-and-build commissions too.

Has your local secondary school a similar course they might throw open to mature students? It's worth enquiring.

Cutting list

Final dimensions

Top planks	8	1005mm	×	123mm	×	20mm
Top framing	4	1100	×	65	×	20
Legs	4	685	×	40	×	40
Horizontal rails	4	1210	×	40	×	40
Vertical rails	12	415	×	40	×	20

● Anna Cunnyngham did her A-level Design course at Stantonbury Campus, Milton Keynes, Bucks.

Photo Karen Read

VIENNA TIME

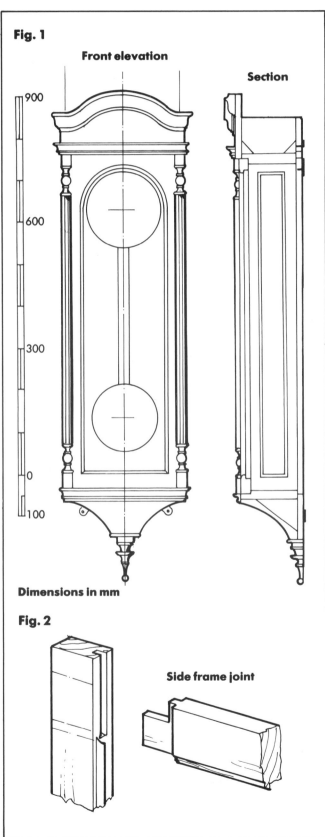

Fig. 1

Front elevation

Section

900

600

300

0

100

Dimensions in mm

Fig. 2

Side frame joint

Bill Walker's Vienna Regulator clock-case is a timely opportunity to develop your hand skills – and there's veneering too, if you want

I built this clock case to house a movement I purchased in a sale. Some parts – weights, dial and pendulum – were missing, so I bought these, made some minor repairs to the movement, and then set it up on a temporary backboard so I could work out the internal sizes for a case.

Having got my measurements, I drew up a full-size front and side elevation (rods) on a white-painted piece of hardboard; from this I worked out a preliminary cutting list. I used sycamore, both solid and veneer, but many other cabinetmaking hardwoods are suitable.

Use wood at least 12mm thick for the back, and choose perfectly flat material because the movement fixing bracket is screwed to it and the whole weight of the clock is suspended from this fixing. You can use solid wood, or plywood veneered on both sides to keep it balanced.

Side frames

For the side frames I used haunched mortise and tenon joints (fig. 2). I cut the mortises and sawed the tenon cheeks along the grain, but left cutting the shoulders until I had planed the rebates and ovolo mouldings. The mouldings can be scribed or mitred. I rebated the back stiles of these frames to take the back of the case. Before gluing, I cleaned up and polished the inside faces of these frames.

Bracket base

Main components of the base are the front and two side pieces, each cut out of 20mm wood with a concave hollowing. A triangular back piece and turned finial complete the construction (fig. 3). The cross-section of the main curved shape is shown in fig. 3C; I didn't set it out geometrically, but drew it experimentally freehand on a piece of thin plywood. When I was happy with the shape, I trimmed the ply to the line and

used it as a template on the full-size drawing; I also used it to test the shape when cutting the wood to this section, which I did in one length using a round-soled wooden plane. Gouges and a curved scraper will do the job. I tested the curve frequently, but it isn't such a difficult task as you might think.

Having completed the hollow along the board, I turned it over and marked the shapes of the front and two sides on it. In fig. 3D the developed shape of one side or half of the front is shown by ABCD; the mitre bevel is given by the angle YEF.

Cut the triangular back piece and rub-joint the pieces together; if they fit well no cramping is needed. When the glue is set, strengthen the inside with shaped blocks along the joints.

You can make the bracket from the same solid hardwood as the rest of the case, or you could use a softwood and veneer it. If you choose to veneer, strictly speaking the veneer should be mitred at the joints, which means the whole length would have to be veneered before the pieces are cut and mitred together. This doesn't allow for discrepancies in the shape of the section and you wouldn't be able to clean up or modify the shape if the pieces aren't exactly the same shape at the mitre. If you apply the veneer after the bracket is made up, veneer the sides first and trim flush before applying the front piece. Make sure there are no irregularities, bumps or hollows in the surface, testing the shape with the curved template and with a steel straight-edge parallel to the grain. Tooth the surfaces and size with thinned scotch glue. Make sure that the metal strip of your veneer hammer is perfectly smooth, with no sharp corners. The glue must be hot and thin, and warm the back before you start: never try to carry out this work in a cold workshop – you need a room temperature of about 70°F or more to ensure adequate work-

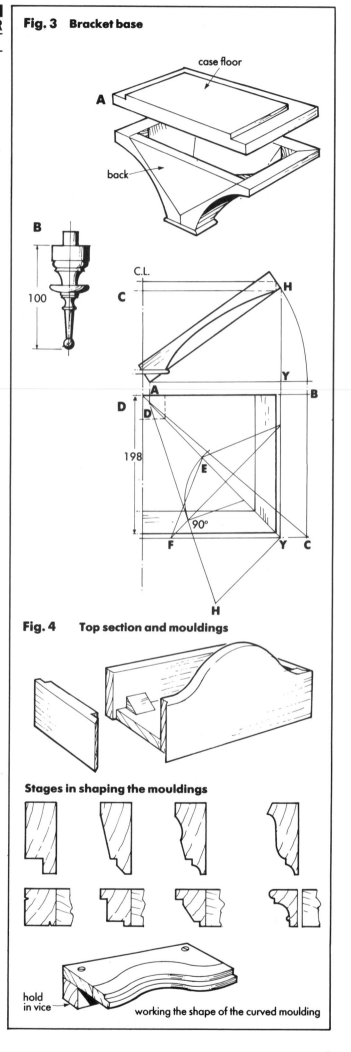

Fig. 3 Bracket base

case floor

A

back

B

100

C.L.

C

H

Y

B

A

D

D

198

E

90°

F

Y

C

H

Fig. 4   Top section and mouldings

Stages in shaping the mouldings

hold in vice

working the shape of the curved moulding

ing time and to avoid chilling the glue.

Veneering the bracket in this way does leave a visible butt joint along the corners which shows at the sides when the case is completed, but it won't be prominent unless you tell someone.

Complete the bracket base construction with the rebated floor piece, external moulding and turned finial.

Top section

The top section or cornice is a simple box construction (fig. 4) which you can make either from your chosen hardwood or veneered softwood, with mouldings added afterwards. The 'ceiling' piece is similar to the case floor piece, rebated on three sides. I mitred and rebated the joints at the front corners to avoid showing endgrain; you can do this whether you work from the solid or use veneer. The stages I used in making the mouldings are shown in fig. 4, which also shows a method of working the curved front moulding from the inside curve.

Columns

For the turned and reeded columns (fig. 5), first remove a quarter section on the circular saw or with a narrow cutter in a plough plane or portable router. Glue the piece back using tissue paper in the joint so you can remove it easily later. I formed the reeded columns by hand planing, holding the wood in a long V-block; you can use a small wooden round plane or a scratch-stock for the hollows. Finish the columns by turning and polishing before removing the quarter-piece insert, very carefully using a wide chisel.

Assembling the case

Join the side frames to the cornice top and bracket base (fig. 6) using two dowels to locate the parts and a counter-bored screw to hold them together. Then fit the back into the rebates and secure with screws all round. Test-fit dry before gluing.

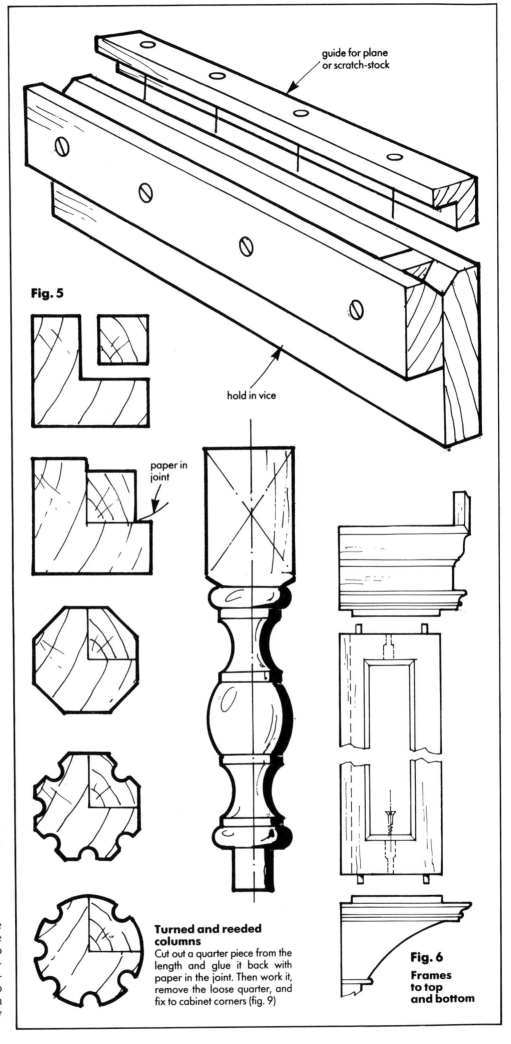

Fig. 5

guide for plane or scratch-stock

hold in vice

paper in joint

Turned and reeded columns
Cut out a quarter piece from the length and glue it back with paper in the joint. Then work it, remove the loose quarter, and fix to cabinet corners (fig. 9)

**Fig. 6
Frames to top and bottom**

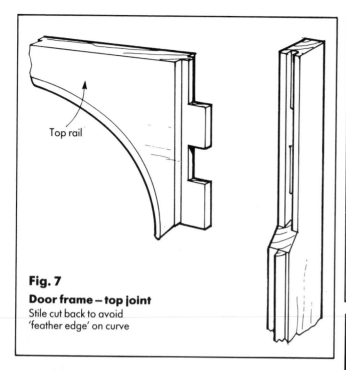

Fig. 7

Door frame – top joint
Stile cut back to avoid
'feather edge' on curve

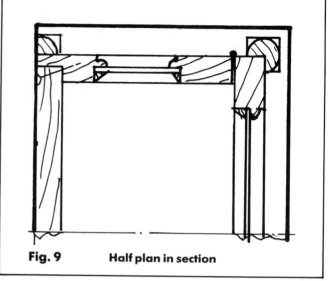

Fig. 9   **Half plan in section**

Door frame

The door frame is constructed using haunched mortise and tenon joints (fig. 7). The top rail joint is set deeper into the stile to avoid short grain at the springing of the curve. Complete the shaping of the rail mouldings and rebates after making the joints.

Fit the door and hang it using two solid drawn brass hinges. I made a brass turn catch to secure the door (fig. 8), but you can buy such fittings.

Glue the threequarter-sections of the reeded columns to the door frame (fig. 9), and the quarter-sections to the back stiles of the case side frames.

Fixing, glazing and finishing

To secure the clock I screwed three brass mirror plates to the back, one centrally at the top and two smaller ones either side near the bottom. The top plate bears the whole weight of the

case and clock, and should be fixed to the back of the case, not the cornice (fig. 1).

Drill and plug the wall for a substantial screw – say 2½×12 – for the case to hang on; you then fix it absolutely plumb through the two smaller plates at each side.

The glass in the side frames and door is 2mm thick, bedded into the rebates with putty and fine pins. Finish the putty with a neat fillet, which can be lacquered over when it is dry. Before puttying the glass in, make sure the rebates aren't bare wood but have been well sealed with polish. The case can be finished with several coats of white shellac polish or 'pre-cat' lacquer applied with a brush or rubber, which can then be cut back with 000 wire wool and wax polish to give the desired surface appearance. And very nice it looks too. ■

● Clock movements are available from a number of suppliers, many of whom can be found in WOODWORKER classified.

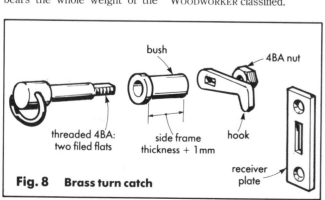

bush

4BA nut

threaded 4BA:
two filed flats

side frame
thickness + 1mm

hook

receiver
plate

Fig. 8   Brass turn catch

Cutting list
Thicknesses nett: lengths are given with allowance

Back	1	800mm ×	220mm ×	12mm	Solid or veneered ply
Side frames					
Stiles	4	800	40	15	
Rails	4	100	40	15	
Door frame					
Stiles	2	800	40˙	15	
Top rail	1	250	130	15	
Bottom rail	1	250	40	15	
Bracket base					Solid or veneered
Floor	1	250	130	20	Rebated at front/sides
Sides	2	600	160	20	Shaped in one length
Front	1				
Back	1	200	100	12	Veneer if required
Bottom	1	60	30	5	
Finial	1	120	40	40	
Cornice					
Ceiling	1	250	130	20	Rebated at front/sides
Front	1	250	130	12	
Sides	2	120	60	12	Veneer if required
Back	1	250	60	12	
Straight moulding	1	260	40	15	For two pieces
Curved moulding	1	300	150	15	
Front columns and mouldings					
Turnings	4	100	25	25	
Columns	2	600	25	25	
Top moulding	1	600	20	15	Cut from wider piece after mouldings are made
Bottom moulding	1	600	20	15	

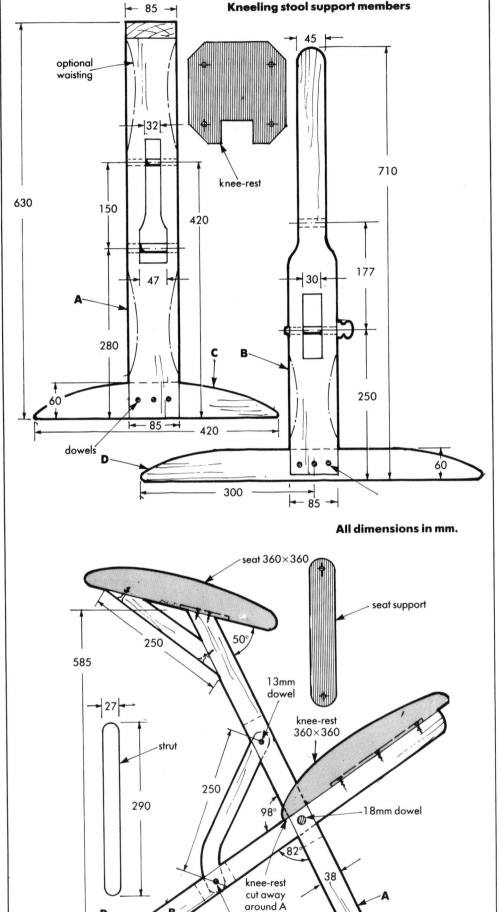

Kneeling stool support members

optional
waisting

knee-rest

A

C

B

dowels

D

All dimensions in mm.

85
32
150
420
47
280
60
85
420
630
45
710
30
177
250
60
300
85

seat 360×360

seat support

13mm
dowel

knee-rest
360×360

50°

18mm dowel

98°

82°

38

A

knee-rest
cut away
around A

13mm dowel

D

B

C

dowels

585

27

strut

290

250

250

I had never sat on a kneeling stool before, but I liked the look of the one I came across in a Sunday magazine – what's more, it seemed simple to make! I'd always thought that modern stool designs cling to convention rather than aim for comfort and efficiency; so I leaped at the chance to try my own hand.

Unfortunately, all I had for guidance was the magazine pictures, so my biggest problem was calculating angles for the supports, seat and knee-pad. First, I worked out rough proportions from the photos, estimated the angles, and made a working drawing.

I decided on a seat height of 23in – kitchen stool height – but the measurement you use should be dictated by the height of your work surface. For normal desk level, make the seat about 18in from the floor. Then I calculated the angle of the knee-pad and seat by sitting at that height on an ordinary stool, bending my knees back in an approximate posture, and measuring the leg and thigh angles. Finally, I transferred these measurements to the drawing.

I used oak because I already had some salvage timber from a dismantled veranda. It proved superb: hard, but precise to work. If you're buying timber, beech would be a cheaper alternative. You could also try using a contrasting wood for the floor members and seat brace for an interesting effect.

I cut the main members first, using a router to make the slot until I could enter a saw and elongate the sides. If you don't have a router, first drill the ends with an auger bit; then extend the slot with a bow saw and panel saw.

Make sure you plane the face side accurately and square up whole members before drilling holes for the pivot dowel point and strut brace. These holes should be drilled at exactly 90° to the outside faces to avoid any twisting on the two main members when assembled. The main pivot fitting should also be a close fit to prevent wobble between the shafts, and seat instability.

Cut and rebate the two floor

NATURALLY

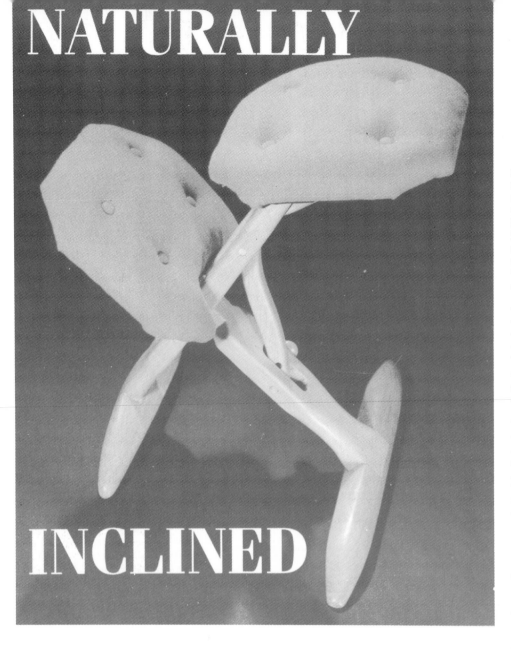

INCLINED

**Sitting could be a new experience
with a kneeling stool,
said to aid posture.
Follow Geoff Hopcraft's design
for an unusual addition
to your sitting room**

move around. Then tack lining material tightly round the foam, from the underside. You can use old sheeting for this, or special lining material can be had from your local upholsterer, who will also supply the covering material, and even cover your buttons with matching or contrasting cloth.

Next, fit the covering cloth in the same way; then use a long upholstery needle to pull the thread through (after looping it through the button wires) to the back of the ply bases. Form a slip-knot around a tuft of material, and pull up enough to give a cushioned effect on the top surface. Finally, sew and tack black base material across the under part to cover tacks, thread and tufts. (I attended upholstery classes, so perhaps have a slight advantage here – but your local upholsterer could do this part for you, if you don't feel confident enough to tackle it.)

This stool is really a prototype. If I produced another, I'd make the following modifications to the original design. I would:
- cut the slot in the seat member just long enough to allow the knee shaft through
- fillet the seat support to the underside instead of using a separate strut
- make the main members more shaped, so they have smoother lines and blend better with the crosspieces
- fit a screw jack (perhaps from a chandler?) between the main members to make the stool adjustable (this wouldn't alter the stool's general height)
- broaden the knee-pad, or cant up the sides slightly to support the knees better, as I find the knees tend to spread apart when in use. ∎

bars, making sure they fit accurately into the main members. Set three dowels in from the underside for final strength; drill these through with the floor bars cramped up tightly. Shape the adjustable strut in the curve shown, then drill accurately with the two holes and five components fitted up dry (minus the dowels). When you're sure everything fits well, dismantle and shape the parts according to your own ideas – here's your chance to be creative!

Cut the knee- and seat-pads from 5-ply and screw from the top through to the bearers, allowing plenty of screw length and grip. Shape seat and knee platforms according to taste. I felt I had to fit a seat support strut; you could flare out the upper part of the seat member (though this would mean wood of extra section), or else blend a fillet into this area.

For all timber shaping, I used a plane, a flat and a curved spokeshave – plus plenty of garnet paper and elbow grease! Lastly, I applied three coats of sanding sealer; gave a final wax polish using steel wool; and finished off with a cloth polish.

To cover the seat and knee-pad, first trim foam blocks slightly larger than the surface areas; then drill blocks with 1/2in holes for the button threads. Drill 1/4in holes in the ply bases to correspond. Fix blocks to bases with contact adhesive so they can't

Cutting list
(planed sizes in mm)

Seat member (A)	1	630mm ×	85mm ×	38mm
Knee-pad member (B)	1	710	85	38
Seat member floor bar (C)	1	440	65	60
Knee-pad member floor bar (D)	1	600	60	60
Adjustable strut	1	290	27	27
Seat support strut	1	250	67	30
Seat & knee-pad (5-ply)	2	345	345	
Dowels (pivots)	2	10mm diameter		
	1	18mm diameter		
Dowels (base plugs)	6	10mm diameter		

GOTHIC STAND

Jim Robinson designed this useful portable bookstand to supplement more permanent storage systems

When you have children studying for exams, books scattered at random around the house can be something of a problem. Static bookshelves, though necessary for long-term storage, don't always fill the need when several books are in constant demand. With this in mind, I designed a portable bookstand based on the style of the Gothic period. Oak is the timber usually associated with this period, but I had a small quantity of reclaimed sweet chestnut, which is still within character.

You need a total of six pieces of timber for this project. The wood I used for the two end pieces was 1in thick, painted on one side and varnished on the other; so I planed both sides clean and finished with a thickness of ⅞in, which was just about right. Then I cut each piece to 8¾×30in.

Next, I marked out the decoration on the panels with a pair of compasses, using the measurements shown on the side elevation in fig. 1. The shaping on the outside of the panels can be cut with a bandsaw, but the cloverleaf design and the hand-hole are all pierced work. This means you'll need to drill a hole through the waste wood before cutting to shape with a coping saw.

If you take care to keep the saw blade at right angles to the wood, little cleaning-up will be necessary after sawing. I used a half round file, followed by garnet paper for a good finish.

For the decorative edge around the outside of the end pieces and around the inside of the clover pattern and handhold, I used a ¼in-radius self-guiding rounding-over cutter in a router. However, if you don't have a router, you could work a rounded edge by hand, omitting the small step, and the result should be quite acceptable.

To make the shelves and back support, I used four pieces of wood each 25¼in long; this allows a ⅝in depth for each housing joint and finishes with a useful shelf length of 24in. This length can be varied to suit your particular requirements, but be warned that if you make the shelf much longer than the 24in I used, the system will be too heavy to be portable. Since this bookstand is intended to be moved around a lot, I decided that a joint somewhat stronger than a simple housing joint was necessary. I introduced a series of tenons into each joint, which increased both the rigidity and the total gluing area.

Next, I marked out the position of the shelves and back support on the inside face of the

ends, as shown in section AA, fig. 1. Remember that the two ends aren't identical because there's a left-hand and right-hand face. The back support is at right angles to the shelf and is held in this position during final assembly by gluing and screwing with three 1in × no. 6 brass screws. The book shelf is angled at 20° to the horizontal, as shown.

Then I cut the housing joint and mortises to shape with a ⅜in router bit, using a batten held in position with G-clamps as a guide. I trimmed the edges and corners square before marking out the tenons to be cut on the shelf. I find it easier to mark the tenons out from the mortices because it's easy to over-run with a hand-held router; though if this happens, the tenons can still be cut to a good fit. The back support doesn't have any tenons cut in and the housing consists of a simple 4×⅝in trench made with a ⅜in router bit. These joints can quite easily be made without a router, but might take rather longer.

Before final assembly (fig.

2), I had a dry run when the three screws could be driven home in the correct position. Then I took the shelves apart and glued and screwed the back supports to the shelves. I glued the housing joints on both surfaces with Cascamite glue before cramping home, taking care to avoid marking the chestnut by using soft wood scraps between the cramp heads and the bookstand ends. Make sure you remove any excess glue before it dries.

The stand is then ready for finishing. I found a good finish was Rustins Danish oil. I don't strictly follow the instructions, but give three thin coats at one-hour intervals, followed by a fourth coat after allowing 24 hours to dry. This is then finished after a further 24-hour period by a good wax polish, lightly applied with Scotchbrite cloth to remove any roughness caused by dust particles.

Now you should have no problem persuading your offspring to keep their books tidy! ∎

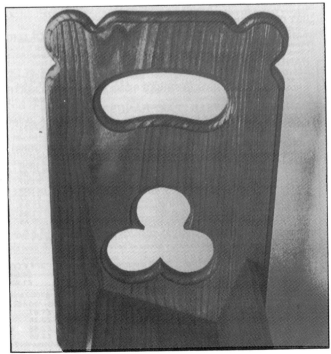

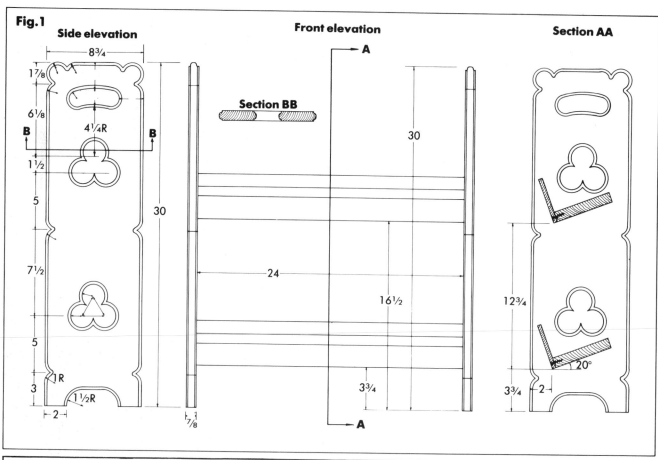

Fig.1

Side elevation **Front elevation** **Section AA**

Section BB

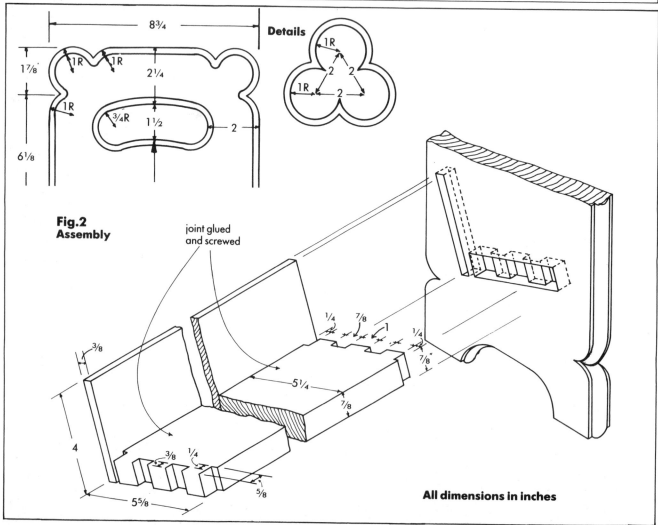

Details

Fig.2
Assembly

joint glued
and screwed

All dimensions in inches

SITTING OUT

If you're planning your Spring garden – and its furniture – here's a sturdy, weatherproof seat from John Cole

The first garden seat I made survived for about 20 years. I made it from some abandoned scaffolding planks, and the only reason it ended up on the bonfire was its unsuitable joinery system. I'd used one-inch dowels, wedged and glued, and despite occasional preservative treatment, these dowels were the points where rainwater penetrated the planks, and rot eventually took hold.

But when I looked around for a replacement, it soon became obvious that a ready-made item of the size and quality that I had in mind was going to be very expensive. Those I looked at

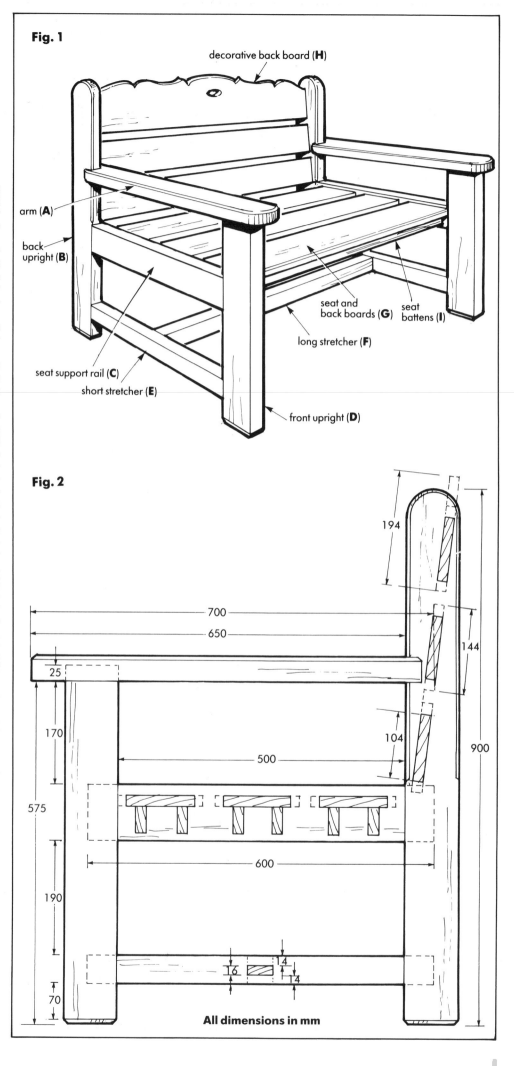

Fig. 1

decorative back board (**H**)

arm (**A**)

back upright (**B**)

seat and back boards (**G**)

seat battens (**I**)

long stretcher (**F**)

seat support rail (**C**)

short stretcher (**E**)

front upright (**D**)

Fig. 2

194

700

650

25

170

144

104

500

575

190

600

900

16 · 14 · 4

70

All dimensions in mm

cost anything from £200 to £1,000, while the cheaper end was plain rubbish. It was a clear case of do-it-yourself or do without.

I decided to go for a fairly traditional-looking design with sufficient length for a person to lie on, basically the outdoor equivalent of a generously proportioned three-seater settee. This design could also easily be adapted for a two-seater, or even a garden or patio armchair. The decorative top board is purely to add a cheerful touch to what would otherwise be a rather plain outline.

My first instinct was to go for a good durable home grown timber, such as elm, that would mellow over the years; we would grow old gracefully together. My local timber merchant, who specialises in English hardwoods, soon dispelled any such thoughts in that direction, but suggested that a suitable compromise might be iroko – which he referred to as poor man's teak. By this time, I had a preliminary design and a cutting list, and the garden seat I wanted to make in 'poor man's teak' was still going to cost well over £100.

This was still more than I was prepared to pay. I've also since learned that the use of tropical hardwoods is detrimental to the environment, in that it contributes to the destruction of the earth's rain forest areas. Not a happy thought, so I decided to settle for softwood treated with wood preservative and finished with the new 'stretchy' exterior wood paint. The final cost of the seat, including timber, glue, preservative and paint, worked out in the region of £45, which I consider very good value for money.

As with any purchase, it does pay to shop around. Present your cutting list, and ask for a price. Prices will vary and so will the quality of the wood: you may think it worth paying a little extra for better quality.

Once you've decided where to buy, be as selective as possible. Explain what you want the wood for and reject anything you regard as unsuitable. You'll have to accept knots, but not loose ones, or ones which

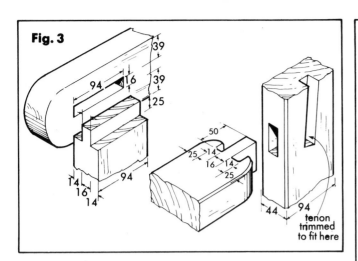

Fig. 3

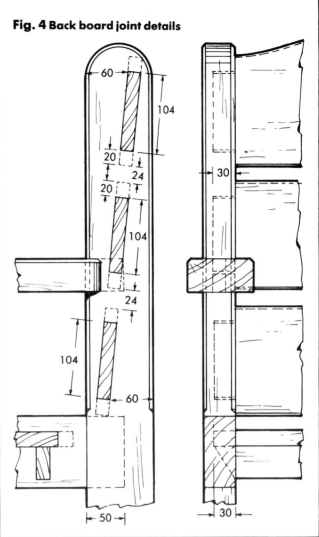

Fig. 4 Back board joint details

weaken the structure of a piece of wood. Avoid twisted or warped wood, or wood with splits or excessive surface damage from the planer, and look for the closer-grained and heavier pieces. The finished job will only be as good as the material you start with, so good hunting!

Construction

There are 26 joints, all stopped mortise-and-tenons to combine strength with weatherproofing, and glued with the waterproof version of Resin W – look for the blue container, not the green. I used a router bit in a drill chuck in a vertical drilling stand to provide a controlled system for cutting the housings. I cut the tenons on a saw bench, though these could all easily be marked out and hand-cut by anyone not having access to suitable machinery.

The rounding on the arms and the back uprights (figs 3&4) was done on a bandsaw and finished, clamped in pairs, with a plane, though these could also be jigsawn or chiselled. The joint where the arm enters the rear upright (fig 3) is designed to give maximum strength, even in the event of the arm being sat upon. It has proved to be more than adequate to the task.

The three seat boards each have two strengthening runners added (fig. 5); without these the seat would have been too

springy. These runners are simply glued and tacked in position with a 2in oval nail every 300-550mm. You'll need about 36 nails. The ends of the runners are angled at 55°, which makes a very satisfactory seat joint (fig. 6).

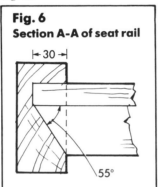

Fig. 6
Section A-A of seat rail

I chamfered with a plane the front seat board, the rear uprights above the seat, the upper edges of the arms and all the feet – most important this, as it prevents damage in the event of the seat being dragged over rough ground.

Before assembly, make the decorative back board (fig 8) by drawing free-hand in pencil on one half only of the two inches allowance on the top board; follow the curve with a bandsaw or jigsaw. Then carefully re-assemble the cut-away pieces on the other half of the board and hold in place to form a template for drawing the other side. The hole is an optional extra done with a large brace and bit and converted to an oval

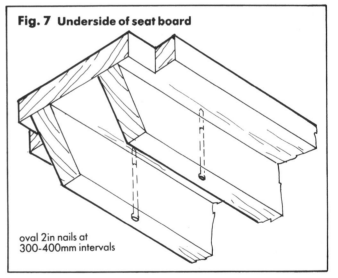

Fig. 7 Underside of seat board

oval 2in nails at
300-400mm intervals

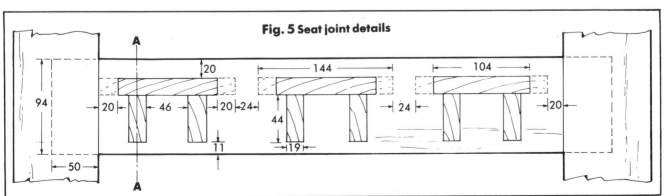

Fig. 5 Seat joint details

Fig. 8
Varied curves for the back board: 20mm grid squares

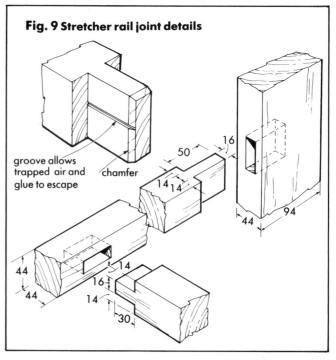

with a woodcarving gouge. Any suitable curve can be used for the top board and there are plenty of sources of inspiration, such as Welsh dressers and old picture frames. A final clean-up with either spokeshave, rasp or similar tool is all that's needed.

Method

First check the overall length of all pieces, including tenons. You should have 23 pieces of timber: two sets of five for the end frames; the six seat and back boards (one wider to allow for the decorative cutout); six seat-strengthening runners; and one stretcher rail. Even if you bought your wood cut to size, it's important to carefully check it before commencing work. A timber merchant will often leave excess material on a piece if there's no saleable value in the offcut, and it's very annoying to only discover this after you've lovingly cut your tenons.

Then mark out, glue and nail the reinforcing battens on the underside of the seat boards. Make a stack of the three and place weights on top until the glue dries. Mark out and cut the rounded arm fronts and the top rear uprights. Leave the rounding where the arm joins the rear upright at this stage. (A suitable size paint tin can often make a handy circle template.)

The mortise and tenons should be marked out and cut next. Do this as carefully as possible, numbering each pair as they are fitted so they can be assembled correctly at the gluing stage. Try to aim for a good push-fit by hand. If they are too tight as a dry fit, it will be hard to knock them all the way home with the additional resistance of the glue.

Finally, chamfer the necessary edges, round the rear ends of the arms, and complete the decorative back board as described previously.

Assembly

This is best tackled in two stages. First, assemble and glue the two end frames, ensuring that they are perfectly square. Knock all joints well home using a mallet, but always interpose a piece of scrap wood to prevent marking of the finished surface. Next, when the end frames have dried (preferably overnight), you can assemble the back and seat boards and the stretcher rail. I found the best method was to place one end frame on the floor and insert the boards vertically, remembering to check the numbers. Then, having well glued the mortises in the other end frame, it was simply a matter of locating the seven pieces and knocking the now top frame fully home. Put the seat on its feet on a level surface, and check that everything is square and all the joints are fully home: it will be too late once the glue has set.

Now for the finishing. Use a suitable filler, or make your own with glue and sawdust, to make good any less-than-perfect joints or any other imperfections. Once dry, sand the whole seat, with an orbital sander if possible, or by hand with a sanding block.

Next, apply a generous soaking of clear wood preservative, giving special attention to end grain. Find some suitable dishes for the feet to stand in, pour in a generous amount of preservative, and leave overnight to soak up as much as possible. The feet will be most vulnerable to rot, especially if the seat stands on a lawn. Give a second all-over application for good measure and allow to dry out thoroughly for three days to a week before proceeding to the next stage.

Before gloss painting, I used pink acrylic primer, simply to ensure that it would be completely covered by the final white gloss coat. This is a good

Fig. 9 Stretcher rail joint details

groove allows trapped air and glue to escape

chamfer

50
16
14 14
94
44
44
16
14
44
14
30

time to attend to any final imperfections that might need a bit of filler. A rub-over with fine paper between coats is also useful.

The final step is the gloss coat. The new formula Cuprinol exterior paint I used wasn't so smooth and shiny as traditional gloss paint (it's more akin to emulsion paint), but hopefully its long lasting properties will

compensate for any lack of finish. A second coat will do no harm.

You've now reached the most enjoyable stage of all – evaluation. This consists of sitting in the sun on your new garden seat, a glass of your favourite lubrication to hand, and just the hint of an expression of satisfaction as you contemplate your handiwork and plan your next project! ∎

Cutting list
All sizes are planed all round.

A	Arms	2	44mm	×	94mm	×	700mm	F	Long stretcher	1	44mm ×	44mm ×	1800
B	Back uprights	2	44		94		900	G	Seat and back boards	5	19	144	1800
C	Seat support rails	2	44		94		600	H	Decorative backboard	1	19	194	1800
D	Front uprights	2	44		94		600	I	Seat battens	6	19	44	1800
E	Short stretchers	2	44		44		600						

A WINETIGHT CASE

David Hodge's case for the popular but ugly 3-litre winebox will make that extra glass an irresistible proposition

I can't claim the idea of a wooden case for a winebox is mine. I saw something like this in a country pub a few years ago, and I haven't seen one since, but I was taken with the idea enough to make one. The silver-lined cardboard boxes are nothing to write home about aesthetically, however hard the packaging designers try, and a case like this is a good way of bringing your wineboxes in line with the style of your living room. You don't have to hide it – which may, perhaps, mean that the contents disappear more quickly!

Construction

The construction is extremely simple – a box, the back of which slides in a groove to get the wineboxes in and out, and the bottom of which is really a raised shelf. You can make it how you like; on mine, the 6mm ply panels fit together in rebates and grooves. The dimensions I give suit most of the boxes on the market, but check your favourites before you start; I allowed extra height inside, be-cause it is easier to get the box in and out if you can tilt it a bit.

I veneered the basic carcase to match my sideboard before applying the mouldings; veneering the top came after the mouldings were glued on, so I could run the veneer across the flat top of the moulding for a neat finish on the edge. The back cover slides in grooves in the hardwood edging I used on the back exposed edges of sides, shelf and top; it's held by a turnbutton fixed under the shelf.

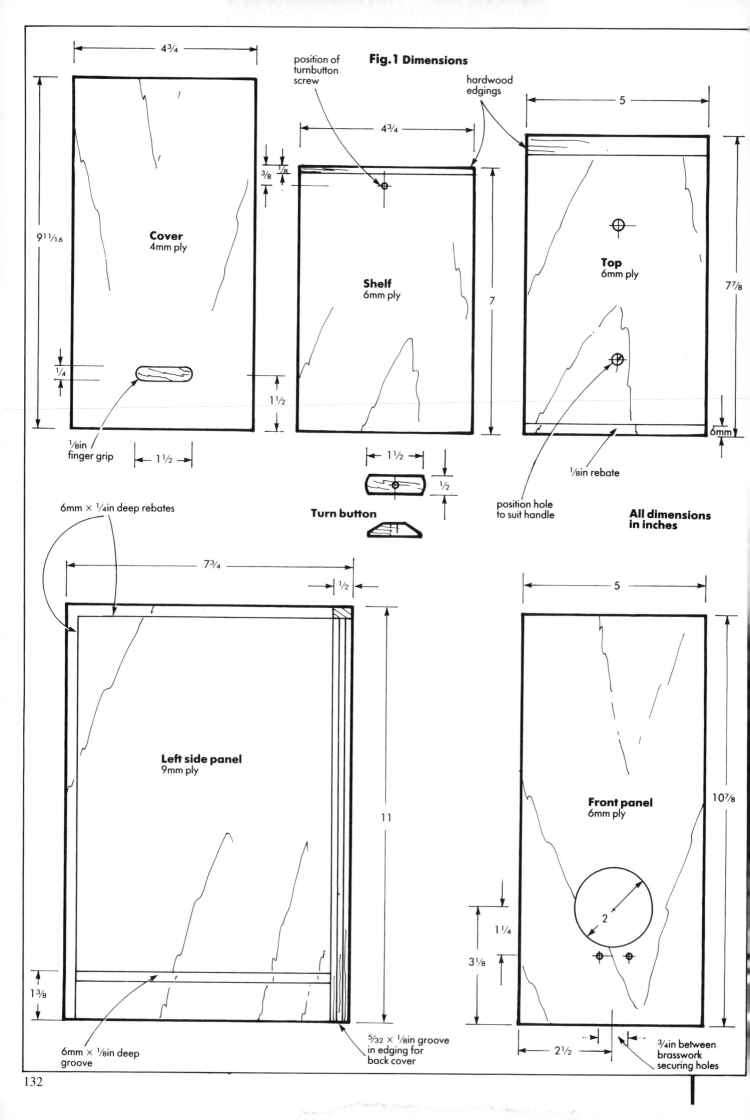

Fig.1 Dimensions

Cover
4mm ply

4¾

9¹¹⁄₁₆

¼

¹⁄₈in finger grip

1½

1½

position of turnbutton screw

Shelf
6mm ply

4¾

³⁄₈ ¹⁄₈

7

hardwood edgings

Top
6mm ply

5

7⁷⁄₈

¹⁄₈in rebate

6mm

position hole to suit handle

Turn button

1½

½

All dimensions in inches

6mm × ¼in deep rebates

Left side panel
9mm ply

7¾

½

11

1³⁄₈

6mm × ¹⁄₈in deep groove

⁵⁄₃₂ × ¹⁄₈in groove in edging for back cover

Front panel
6mm ply

5

10⁷⁄₈

2

1¼

3¹⁄₈

2½

¾in between brasswork securing holes

132

Brasswork

A brass carrying handle – which also helps when you want to tip the box to get the last few glasses out of the tap – is held to the top with 4BA screws going into nuts underneath in counterbored clearance holes; the brassware which holds the box tap in place is slightly more complex, but hardly a great challenge. I used 19swg sheet, but only because that is what I had to hand. The dimensions suit most tap heights, but if you find variations you can elongate the hole and provide a second position for the fittings to hold the brassware.

A 2in hole is cut in the front panel for the tap, the barrel of which sits in the cutout in the lower plate. The upper plate slides down over the neck of the tap; it moves behind the bottom plate, which is held by two no.6 × ½in roundhead screws, and packed out the thickness of the upper plate plus a little. Either use thicker plate to pack, or the same thickness plus a shim. You don't want too good a fit here or spilt wine will gum the whole thing up.

Finishing touches

Finish should be alcohol-proof – I used polyurethane rather than the more visually appropriate french polish – but Danish oil or teak oil, meticulously rubbed down with 0000 wire wool or 1000-grit wet 'n' dry between coats, are good alternatives.

Trim the bottom edges with green baize or felt to protect the surface of your sideboard as you pull the case forward to get the glass under the tap; and remember that when you load a box the tap unit must be pulled fully out through the cardboard, past the second flange.

When you have finished the wine, you can take out the inner foil bag and inflate it for the kids' amusement – or use it as a handy beach pillow! ∎

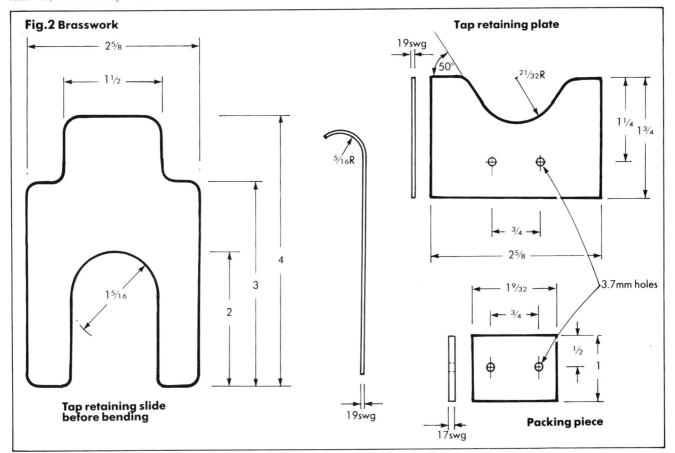

Fig.2 Brasswork

Tap retaining slide before bending

Tap retaining plate

Packing piece

STANDING REFLECTIONS

Jim Robinson explains the making of this attractive mirror for your dressing-table or chest

F or this dressing-table mirror I used pine, but any close-grained hardwood is suitable. Pine used to be rather looked down on, but is now popular: it's cheaper than hardwood, more durable than chipboard, and of course less draining on tropical rainforests.

Turned parts

Begin by turning the two pillars, three feet and two knobs (fig. 2). For the pillars, you'll need two pieces of wood, 20in long, finished size $1\frac{3}{4} \times 1\frac{3}{4}$in. Square the ends and draw diagonals to locate centres ready for mounting on the lathe.

Fig.1 Front and side view

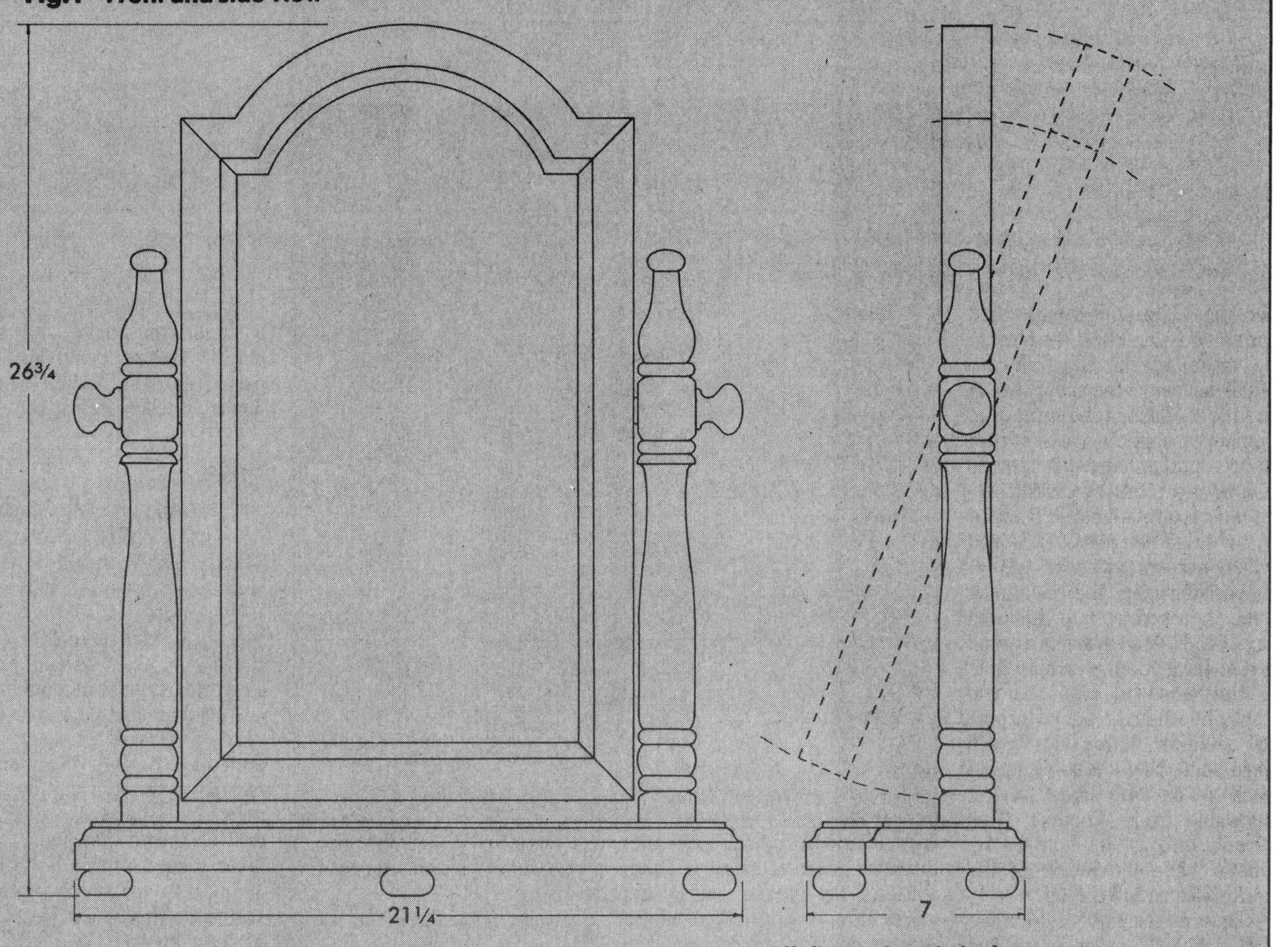
26¾
21¼
7
All dimensions in inches

Fig.2 The turned parts

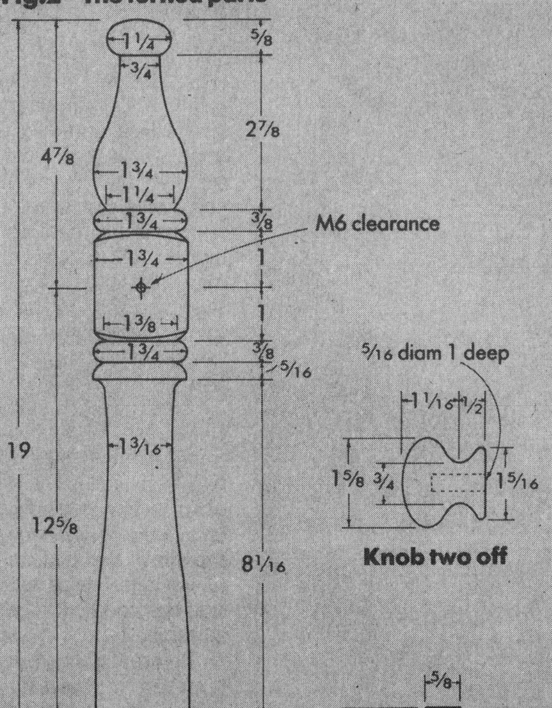
1¼
¾
⅝
2⅞
4⅞
1¾
1¼
1¾
⅜
M6 clearance
1¾
1
1
1⅜
1¾
⅜
5/16
5/16 diam 1 deep
1 1/16
½
19
1 3/16
1⅝
¾
1 5/16
12⅝
8 1/16
Knob two off
⅝
¾
¾
1¾
1⅝
1⅜
1¾
7/16
1¾
1
1¾
7/16
1¾
1
1
1½
Foot three off
Pillar two off

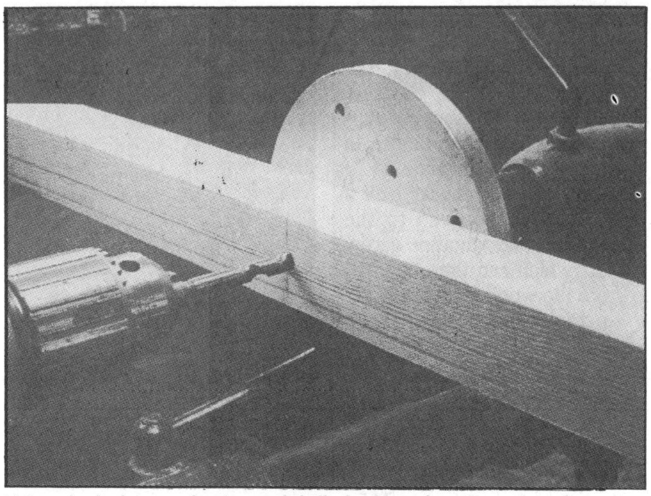

Using the lathe as a horizontal drill, the faceplate is mounted on the tailstock, the workpiece held flat against it to ensure the squareness of the hole (above)

Before turning, I drill a clearance hole for the M6 rod, perpendicular to the surface. If you've no bench drill, convert your lathe to a horizontal drill by mounting the face-plate at the tail-stock end (Coronet have a No.1 morse taper, threaded to take their faceplates, for this purpose).

Next, mount the wood between centres and draw a line all round to define the ends of the two sections to be left square; when the lathe is revolving these lines will be clearly visible. Now push the long corner of the skew chisel gently into the wood on the pencil lines; by pushing the point in again from each side, a V-groove will form, which can gradually be deepened and slightly rounded to the depth and shape required. Take only thin slicing cuts with a sharp tool to achieve a good finish. Practice first on scrap wood if you're not used to this operation.

Now turn all the round sections to a cylinder with a roughing gouge. You can do all the rest of the turning with the skew chisel, except for the concave shape just below the upper square section. If you feel more confident with a small beading chisel,

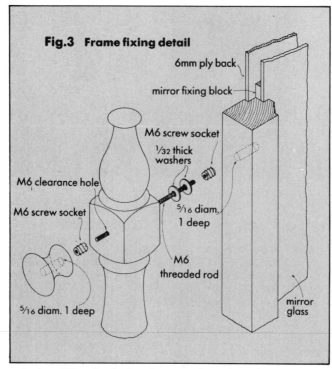

Fig.3 Frame fixing detail

6mm ply back

mirror fixing block

M6 screw socket

1/32 thick washers

M6 clearance hole

M6 screw socket

5/16 diam, 1 deep

M6 threaded rod

5/16 diam, 1 deep

mirror glass

use that. The 1in-diameter pin turned on the lower end could be varied to suit the drill size you'll be using for the holes in the base. Turning the three feet is simple, especially if you turn them together between centres before separating by parting off.

The frame is held in position by a small length of M6 rod which screws into the frame, passes through the clearance hole, then screws into the knob (fig. 3). If you're using a good dense hardwood, a simple hole in the wood to take the rod might be enough, but with pine or a softer hardwood, you'll need something a little stronger, such as an M6 screw socket (available from Woodfit). This screws into a pilot hole in the wood, while the inside of the socket has an M6 thread.

Before turning the knobs, drill a hole ⁵⁄₁₆in diameter and 1in deep into one end of a 1¾×1¾×2in piece of wood. Screw the socket into this hole; then if you insert a small piece of M6 rod into this socket, the blank can be held in a chuck at the headstock for turning, supported by a revolving centre in the tailstock until finishing off. If you don't have a chuck, drill a piece of wood screwed to the faceplate to take another screw socket, which can then be used to drive the wood for turning.

At first, I had problems getting the sockets into the slot in line; I solved this by screwing a wing-nut and the socket on the

The knob is held in the lathe chuck by a spare piece of thread rod (below)

end of an M6 rod, aligning the threaded rod vertically, and starting the socket into the wood by screwing in the wing-

Starting the screw sockets into a hole using a length of studding and a wing-nut (below)

nut. Once the socket was started correctly, I continued with a screwdriver.

Finally, finish the knobs using

a finger-nail gouge and skew chisel. Before removing each part from the lathe, sand it down with 320-grit paper.

Base

Transfer the outline shown in fig. 4 on to a piece of wood about 1½in thick, then cut to shape with a bandsaw or bow saw. After smoothing all the edges, you can add a moulding with a router; I used a self-guiding ogee cutter, but you could work a plain chamfer by hand instead. Next, drill three holes in the underside to take the feet and two holes through the full thickness for the pillars. Before drilling these, however, it's a good idea to have a trial assembly, to adjust for any slight variations that might have crept in along the way.

Frame

The frame (fig. 5) consists of two sides and a bottom made from 1¾×1½in material, and a top part cut from a piece 4¾× 1½in. Once you've cut all parts to length, cut 45° mitres on the ends; only part of the top piece is mitred, to match up with the mitres at the top of the side pieces. If you have a circular saw, you can cut mitres accurately, using a mitre gauge and a saw blade with as many teeth as possible to give a smooth finish.

To draw the outline of the shape for the top, make two cardboard templates by drawing two semicircles of 4¾in and 6½in radius respectively. Position them on the wood (fig. 5) and draw the outline. Cut the top piece to shape with a bandsaw before gluing – afterwards it can't be done.

Before gluing the frame together, it's best to drill the hole in each side piece for the screw insert (section EE, fig. 5). This hole must be vertical, so again I used the lathe as a horizontal drill, with the work held against the tailstock-mounted faceplate. At this stage, it's also best to insert the M6 screw socket (fig. 3).

The frame is now ready for gluing together; I use a urea formaldehyde resin glue. My simple and cheap cramping arrangement consists of a thick

Fig.4 Plans and cross sections of base

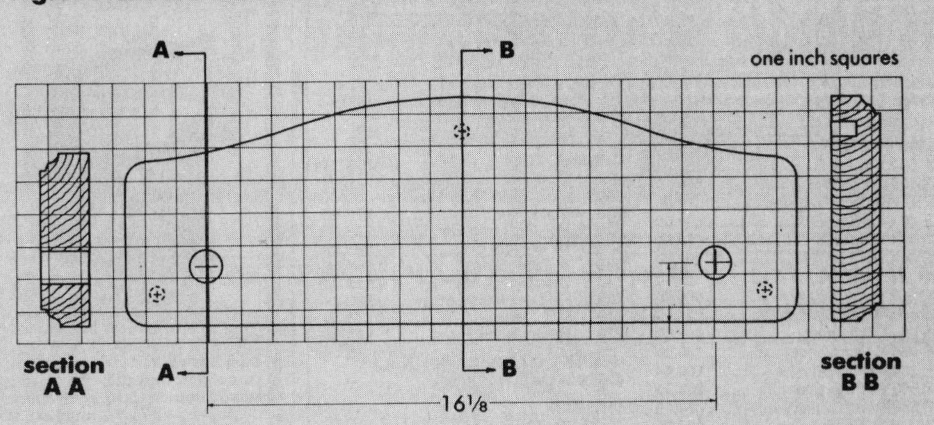

A
B
one inch squares
section AA
A
B
section BB
16⅛

Fig.5 Details of Frame

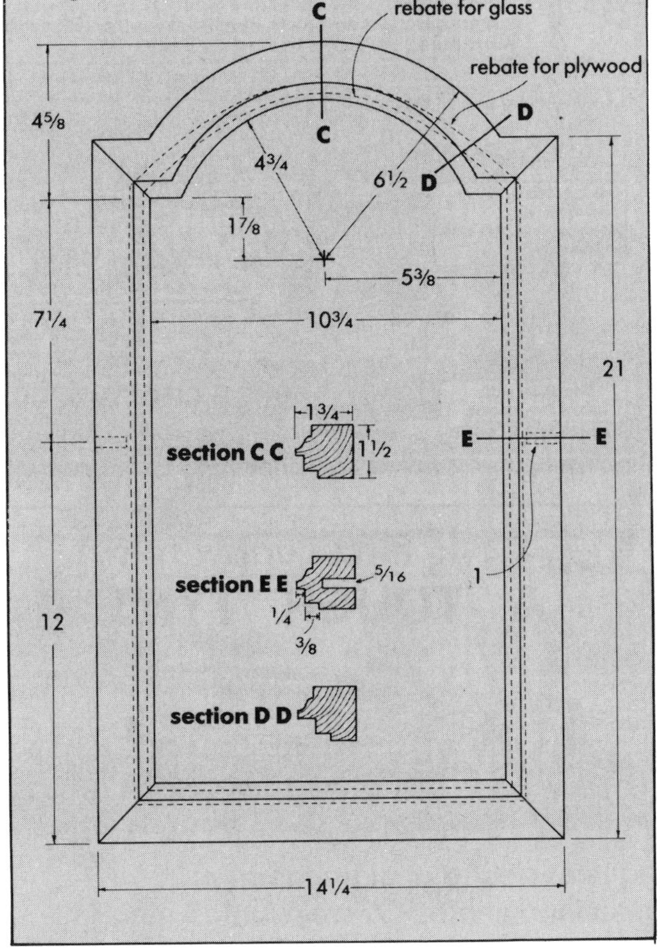

C
rebate for glass
rebate for plywood
D
C
4⅝
4¾
6½ D
1⅞
5⅜
7¼
10¾
21
1¾
section C C
1½
E
E
section E E
5/16
1
¼
⅜
12
section D D
14¼

cord tied around the frame, with six square blocks of wood inserted between the cord and timber at the centre of the sides and bottom. I then slide the blocks outwards, to tighten the cord and compress the joints.

If the mitres are well cut, with the right type of glue, no joint reinforcement should be necessary; the mirror fixing and backing also help stabilise the frame. But if you're worried, you could always strengthen them by pinning or inserting loose tongues into saw cuts.

After the glue has hardened for 24 hours, a moulding can be worked on the inside. I used the same router cutter as on the base, but extended the moulding into the mitre by hand to avoid the rounded-corner machine look. In fig. 5, the inner dotted line gives the outline of the glass rebate, and the outer one shows the rebate for the ply back (see also sections CC and DD). I shaped the glass rebate to this line to simplify mirror cutting, avoiding the need to drill through the mirror at the internal corner before cutting the mirror.

My local glass merchant cut the glass from a sheet, using a template I provided, less ⅛in all round than the size actually required, to allow for the cutter thickness. I cut most of the rebate for the mirror with a self-guiding rebate cutter, but some of the deep curved section had to be extended by hand. I then used the same router cutter to take out the plywood rebate.

Finishing

After sanding, it's best to apply the finish before final gluing: this avoids unsightly surplus glue marks. The pine could be left natural and waxed with a clear wax, but I prefer a mellow, stripped-pine look, using just a very light stain. Apply evenly and remove any excess before allowing it to dry. Any raised end grain can now be lightly sanded, before finishing with old pine wax or Briwax P7. For the first coat, use a piece of Scotch-brite de-nibbing cloth; for further depth, apply a second coat of polish with a cloth, before finally buffing up.

Assembly

Fit the mirror in the frame; to hold it in place, use softwood square-section fixing-blocks, lightly smeared with PVA glue, then pinned. Make sure the blocks are flush with the rebate to take the plywood backing, which is then pinned or screwed into the outer rebate, to finish slightly below the rear of the frame.

Next, fix the pillars to the frame, using the M6 threaded rod screwed into the screw sockets inserted in the knobs and frame. Use washers, built up to about 1/16in thickness, to separate the pillar from the frame, to allow the frame to tilt without rubbing. Now check to see if any adjustment needs to be made to the pillar-hole spacing in the base.

After drilling these holes and finishing the base, first glue on the feet, then the pillars. It's best to glue the pillars in place with the mirror in position, to ensure the clearance holes for the M6 rod in the pillars are in line.

Finally, I don't believe in distressing furniture to make it look old; but if you feel like hitting this piece with an old chain – do mind the mirror! ■

The frame cramped using a loop of cord and wooden blocks, which apply the tension

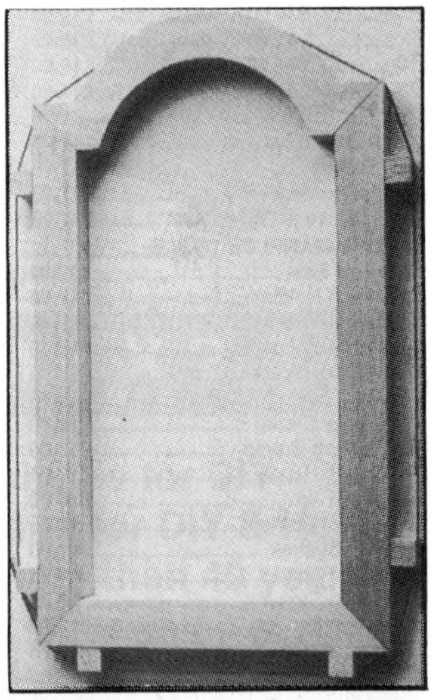

Cutting list
(Allowances made on length)

Pillars	2	20in	×	1¾in	×	1¾in
Knobs	2	2	×	1¾	×	1¾
Feet	3	2	×	1¾	×	1¾
Base	1	22	×	7¼	×	1½
Sides	2	21½	×	1¾	×	1½
Bottom	1	15	×	1¾	×	1½
Top	1	15	×	4¾	×	1½

6 mm plywood back
Scrapwood for mirror fixing blocks
Length of M6 threaded rod
4×M6 screw sockets
Mirror (cut to size)
Washers; wing-nut

Decorative Dovetails

With a plank of wood sawn into three, and a little ingenuity, Neil Wyn Jones makes the simplest of stools interesting

The tapering of the sides is essential to this elegant design (above), and it doesn't present too many problems in production

I designed this stool to be a relatively inexpensive piece for an exhibition. My original estimate of a selling price of around £60 was considerably out, for despite being small pieces, each uses over half a cubic foot of timber and involves much hard work. However they are extremely useful and honest pieces as well as being almost indestructable.

Since the first prototype we have produced a couple of dozen in various timbers, mainly ash, elm and oak. Indeed a stable, well-dried board is essential to make the stool, as any move-

ment after construction will open up cracks around the joints.

First make a template for the ends including the dovetail joints, the tails being graduated from small in the middle to large at the outside, making an attractive feature of the joints.

Mark out the three pieces on the board, so the grain flows through the stool (fig. 1). Having crosscut the board into three, thickness the top piece down to 32mm, and taper the sides from a thickness of 40mm at the bottom to 32mm at the top.

The first stool I made, I tapered by hand as my planer

Fig.1 Elevations and cutting plan

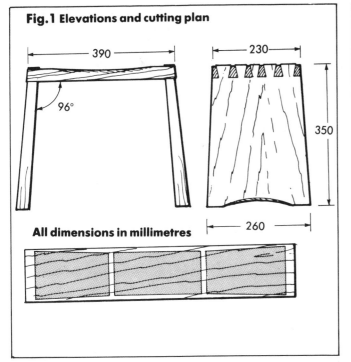

390

96°

230

350

260

All dimensions in millimetres

Fig.2 Cramping block

6°

was out of action, though subsequently I made a jig to do this through the thicknesser (fig. 3), which saves time. With the sides tapered, mark out the profile using the template, marking round the dovetails as well. Set a sliding bevel to 96° and mark round the ends and then across the back (fig. 5). The sides are then cut out on the

Having removed the waste of the tails and cleaned them up, mark out the top (fig. 4) and cut it down to size. The ends of the pins are left 5mm proud so the joints may be 'raised' when finished. Having transferred the profile of the tails on to the ends of the top, carefully remove the waste. This is hard work, and it is worth taking great care, as

the accuracy of the joints can make or break the overall appearance of the stool.

After making sure the dovetails fit satisfactorily, make the hollow in the top, taking the bulk of material out by using a belt sander with very course paper across the grain, and finishing

with a cabinet scraper, spokeshave (to round the edges) and glasspaper. With all three sections cleaned up to 180 grit paper, glue up the stool using three sash cramps and cramping blocks (fig. 2). When dry, carefully sand down the dovetails, leaving the joints standing 3mm proud of the surface and then chamfer round each edge.

This is very time-consuming, and cleaning all the glue off is very painstaking, but the effect of the raised dovetails is well worth it and also means any movement in the wood doesn't show as obvious cracks around the joints. After chamfering the outside edges, and the radius around the bottom, finish off with 240 grit garnet paper, and half a dozen coats of tung oil. ∎

Fig.3 Thicknesser jig

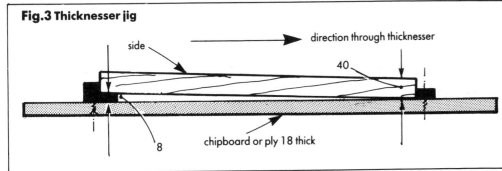

side

direction through thicknesser

40

8

chipboard or ply 18 thick

bandsaw, but remember to set the bandsaw to 96° when cutting around the bottom of the ends, to mirror the angle through the dovetails.

Fig.5 Marking round tails

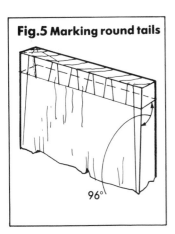

96°

Fig.4 Top markings

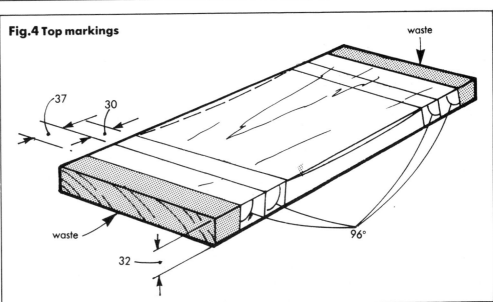

waste

37

30

waste

32

96°

Wedged Wood

In making this simple bookcase Dennis Sutton finds an easy way to make a quantity of wedges, and, by a mistake, discovers an alternative design

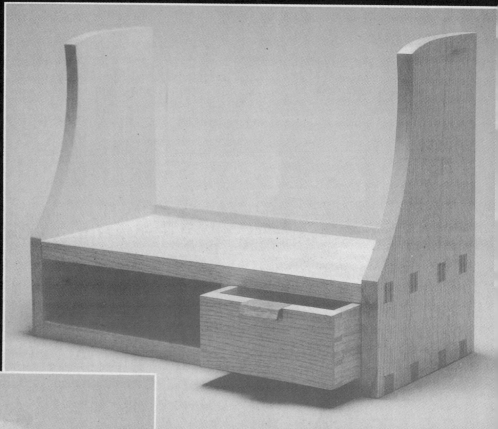

H aving finished David Savage's course for fine cabinetmaking, which I had extended to 18 months to enable me to fit a project of my own into the course, I arrived home to start erecting, fitting out and equipping my own workshop, bringing with me my tool cabinet in oak which was only about 60 per cent complete.

My own workshop took me about 2½-3 months to complete before it was ready for any serious work because I was

The original design in American red oak has two drawers, with wedged tenons for the shelf. Note the double wedges: these must be hammered in together to ensure one slot is not closed. The tenons and dovetails should match (below left)

determined to get it completed to my own satisfaction, and not fall into the self-deceiving notion that I would leave that job and do it later, because once I started woodwork again I would never get around to the workshop. After all this time of not doing any fine woodwork I felt it would be wise to do a small project to get back into the swing of things before finishing my tool cabinet.

A few months earlier I'd designed a small bookcase with a small dovetailed drawer. This was done as an exercise for a friend to familiarise him with several different operations on different aspects of machining. Having said that, it is a good project to do by hand, as all the operations described can be done by hand or with the minimum of small machines, though it will take longer of course.

The bookcase is of a size to take reference books, rather than novels, and the small drawer and shelf are suitable for small items and give an overall pleasing effect. Whilst building my workshop I'd made some strong backs in American red oak and while working this wood I could envisage a red oak bookcase. There are two bookcases, one in American red oak, the other in afrormosia; the difference is in the drawer, as in one it is shallower and goes the full width of the opening.

Sides

Whatever wood you decide to use, spend some time looking at the grain for the sides, as it will show, so go for a good grain effect. Plane the wood to thickness, cut to length and width,

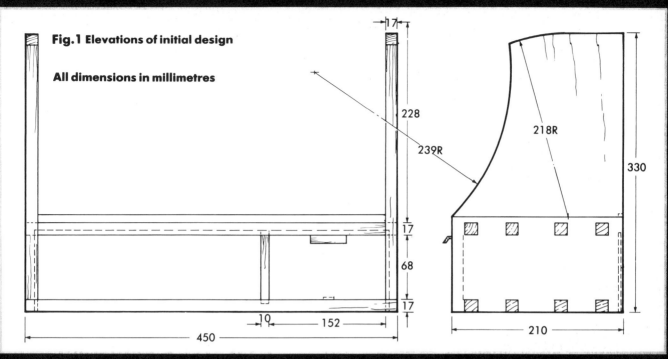

Fig.1 Elevations of initial design

All dimensions in millimetres

17

228

239R

218R

330

17

68

17

10

152

450

210

and mark out the two curves. It is important there is a good crisp point where the two curves meet. Next work out your dovetails and the through mortises and tenons. The bottom is dovetailed and the shelf jointed with wedged mortise and tenons in a stopped dado.

I do my mortise and tenons slightly unconventionally using a router against a fence to do the stopped dado which is 5mm deep and is stopped 15mm from the front, but is not stopped at the back of the bookcase. One way to mark out for the mortise is to cut the tenons previously;

The obvious difference of the afrormosia bookcase is the long narrow drawer. It was the result of a mistake when cutting dovetails, but the accident was turned to advantage

one holds this upright in the dado and tries to mark off around the tenons inside the dado; a most difficult operation.

Alternatively after doing the dado, leave the fence in position, with the workpiece sitting on a piece of ply or scrap as you are going to plunge through. Re-set the router to just break through the workpiece, mark off your tenons in the dado, and position the router over the mark, and set up a second fence against the router. Do not move the router, except to plunge it, during this operation. Using slight pressure against both fences, plunge the router through the workpiece, (you will hear a crack as it breaks out) repeat this operation for the remaining mortises, and for the other end. Don't forget though, this dado is opposite (left-hand/right-hand). Square off the corners of the mortises; the dado gives a good landing for your chisel on the inside.

Plane the shelf down to a good push fit inside the dado; take your time over this operation, a loose fit will completely spoil the appearance of the bookcase. At this stage I apply coloured spots to the different joints, which I learnt about in David Savage's workshop and is an excellent idea; self-adhesive coloured spots can be bought in about 10 colours.

Clamp one side, dado side down, on the bench. Select the end of your shelf, which fits into that side, making sure the front of the side and the front of the shelf are together; lay the end of the shelf half over the mortise holes, clamp the two together, and mark the mortises on to the shelf using a knife. This ensures the tenons are going to be exact for the mortises. Repeat for the other side. Set the gauge for the depth of the tenons – the thickness of the sides minus the depth of your dado – mark sides with a gauge, transfer the marks using a square along the edge and down one side, and mark the waste with pencil. Repeat for the other end. Cut out the waste, and then fit the shelf. The shelf is wedged so a little later you will need to cut wedge slots and wedges.

Next comes the marking out of the dovetails for the bottom, which are cut so that the bottom knocks on from underneath. This means the dovetails can be in line with the tenons when

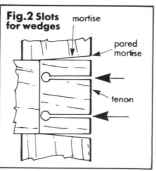

Fig.2 Slots for wedges
mortise
pared mortise
tenon

viewed from the side, but don't forget the tenons are wedged so the dovetails are to be the width of the wedged tenon, not the width as it appears unwedged; usually you are going to increase the width of the tenon by about 2mm. Knocking on from underneath also makes for an easier glue-up, as you can do it in two goes; first the shelf, then the bottom later.

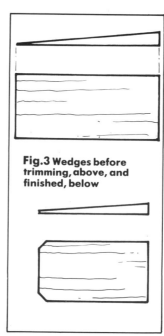

Fig.3 Wedges before trimming, above, and finished, below

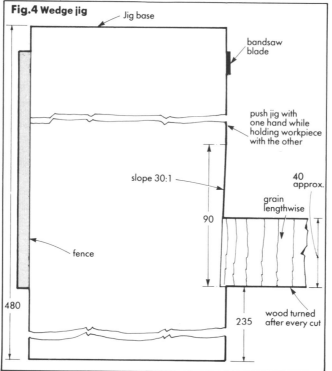

Fig.4 Wedge jig
Jig base
bandsaw blade
push jig with one hand while holding workpiece with the other
slope 30:1
40 approx.
grain lengthwise
90
fence
480
235
wood turned after every cut

Wedging

I don't think it will go amiss to talk a little about wedging, as it is most important to get it right. The marking is straightforward: put the shelf end up, and straight, in the vice, mark in 5mm from either side of the tenon and 3mm up from the dado shoulder line, scribe down to the shoulder line, and where the two lines meet drill through with a 3mm drill. Next saw down the line into the drill hole (the hole is to stop your wedge splitting the

shelf) and repeat on the other side.

Having to make 16 wedges, it is worth making a jig using MDF (fig.4). Use wood for the wedges the same thickness as the shelf and don't forget the grain must run lengthwise down the wedge. Put the jig on your bandsaw so that the notch-free side of the jig is against the fence, with the notched side running along the blade and the taper running away from you. Put the piece of wood into the notch, with one hand holding the

wood and one pushing the jig, and push through the blade, turning the wood over each time, to stop you eventually running into short-grain. Do this again, and keep repeating until all the wedges are cut; for safety reasons I use a longish piece of wood, but it is not a difficult operation.

Once all the wedges are cut you need to do a little work on them; measure the saw-cut that the wedges will fit, measure down the wedges to just under this measurement and mark and cut the wedges off at this mark. Then cut the shoulders of the wedges off with a chisel for easier entry.

Next rout a groove under the shelf and at the rear of the sides 5mm wide, 5mm deep so that the cutter is 9mm from the back edge. Whilst with the router at hand cut the stop housing for the drawer divider, 10mm wide, 5mm deep and stopped 10mm from the front. Also rebate the top of the shelf at the back for the book stop, by 10mm.

The next router operation is the drawer stop in the base, which is central on the drawer position, and is simply a small groove using a 3mm router cutter, 5mm deep×20mm long, 20mm back from the front, which is the thickness of the drawer front. Later on put a piece of wood into this to act as a drawer stop, it only needs to stick up about 3mm, enough to clear the drawer bottoms.

Once satisfied with all the joints, shape the sides, cutting out the major waste on a bandsaw but a coping saw would do equally well. To clean up to the line, I put a drum sander on the spindle moulder, but again this can be done by hand. It is very important where the two radii meet to keep the angle very crisp; when it is assembled, this will be an eye catcher, so be extra careful.

Clean all of the inside surfaces, going through the normal grades of paper, being careful to protect the joint faces with masking tape. Put the tape across the front of the stopped dado for the drawer dividers, prior to gluing, and polish all inside surfaces. Ensure anything going to take glue is covered with masking tape, as glue does not stick to polish.

For the glue-up itself, when you do the shelf, only put glue on the shoulder, not the tenons;

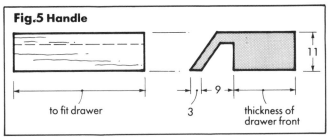

Fig.5 Handle

to fit drawer

9
3
thickness of
drawer front

11

the reason for this is your tenons are going to be wedged, and will need to be free to move outwards during wedging.

During the wedging operation, always knock two in together, otherwise you will completely close the other wedge slot if you do one at a time. Put glue on the wedges, and alternately tap each wedge until the tenons have expanded into the mortises. When dry, cut off the wedges about 3-4mm above the surface. If they accidentally break below the surface they will cause problems.

The divider is made with the grain running top to bottom and is a push fit into the dado, the front shoulders being an exact fit; only glue the front shoulders, allowing for expansion of the bookcase front to back.

The drawer front is the same oak as the bookcase, but the sides and back are white oak, and the bottom cedar. The construction is a typical lapped drawer front. The handle is in brown oak to match the wedges.

Set your table saw at 25° to give a cut of 65°, having first planed your wood to the correct dimensions. Cut off the front at 65°, leave the saw at the same angle, reset the depth of cut to give a cut of 6mm, and bring the workpiece 5mm in for the second angled cut. Reset your saw to 90° reset the depth to give 6mm, and bring the workpiece another 3mm in for the third cut; bring the saw up to cut through wood and cut off to your required depth.

The drawer front is 20mm thick, so cut about 21mm to give leeway for clean-up. Cut the handle to the length required, very carefully mark out on the drawer front, and cut out this section of the drawer front. It is a good idea to mark this section slightly undersize, then your handle can be sanded to fit all around, before gluing it into the drawer front.

The back is made from one piece, rebated to fit the groove which is on three sides, allowing

about 2-3mm at the top for expansion. Two slots are cut at equal distance from the edges, to take brass screws; pare these slots to take a screw head. Finally clean up the outside. I finished mine with boiled linseed oil, keeping the inside polished as you don't want to get oil on your books.

Alternative design

The difference of the afrormosia bookcase is quite apparent, in fact I think this is a more elegant design, which came about by a stupid mistake on my part. I was cutting dovetails on one of the sides, it was only when I took it out of the vice that I realised I had committed the cardinal sin of having it around the wrong way in the vice. I thought long and hard on how to retrieve the situation and came up with the solution of cutting off the bottom 20mm of the sides, and biscuit jointing the bottom shelf to the sides, and as it was a narrower opening, fitted a full-width drawer. With it being a darker wood, brass knobs go well with it. Other than that the construction is the same, except that the wedges are not contrasting. Be warned though, afrormosia is a difficult wood to work, the grain is interlocked in places and it needs a lot of cabinet scraper and paper work on it. ∎

Wedged Wood

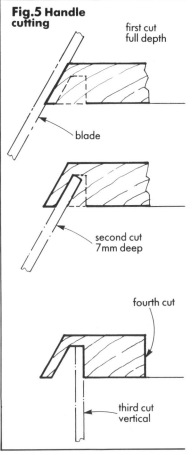

Fig.5 Handle cutting

first cut
full depth

blade

second cut
7mm deep

fourth cut

third cut
vertical

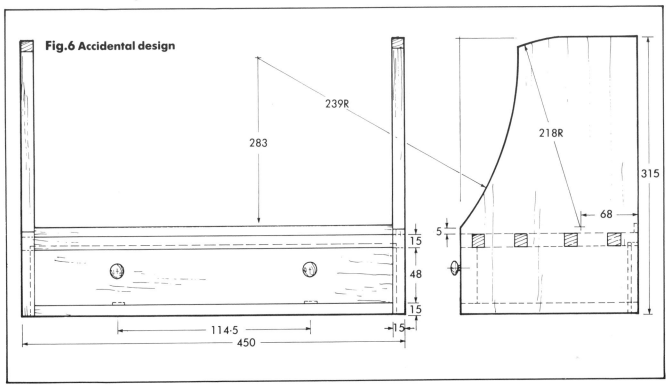

Fig.6 Accidental design

239R

283

218R

315

68

5

15

48

15

114·5

15

450

FRAME UP

David Hirst shows how to build and use an inexpensive picture framing jig

An economical yet effective picture frame making jig can be made from an offcut of kitchen worktop which may be obtained from a local DIY store or kitchen installer for a modest cost. Often a piece of worktop may be salvaged from a skip, the piece in the photograph was the cut out from an inset sink top, typical of pieces always scrapped.

Holes are drilled to a depth of

The final stages in the making of a frame, with wedges tapped in at the corners. Ensure the frame sits correctly

approximately three quarters of the thickness of the worktop on a 50mm grid to accept 8mm dowels. These holes do not have to be exactly positioned but care should be taken to ensure that they are at 90° to the surface.

A simple way of ensuring that the holes are all the same depth is to fit the drill or wood bit with a timber sleeve, formed from a piece of scrap timber two to three times the diameter of the drill square, and drill down the length of cut to leave the correct length protruding through the sleeve. This method of

drilling holes to a set depth is also useful when making dowelled or similar joints.

Cut eight pieces of 8mm diameter dowel to 75mm long and slightly bevel the ends to make fitting into the holes easy. Eight small wedges are cut preferably from hardwood, approximately 75mm long, 20mm wide and tapering from 15mm to a point is a good size. A few short ends of offcuts complete the kit, these provide packing pieces to enable frames of any size to be made.

When the pieces of frame have been cut to size and mitred,

set it up dry to ensure that the joints are a perfect fit.

Fit the dowel pegs into the board, in the holes nearest the frame being made, with the space between the pegs and frame is taken up with the packing pieces and wedges. At this stage the frame may be checked by measuring the cross diagonals, and then each joint inspected in turn, making any adjustments to joints not fitting perfectly.

When all the joints are satisfactory, the frame is glued and the wedges are tapped in turn, ensuring as this is done that the outside edges of the frame line up, and the frame is square by once again measuring the cross diagonals.

The advantages of this jig are that any excess glue from the back of the frame joints will not stick to the plastic top, which is flat so the frame will not be twisted, providing that at the gluing stage you ensure each piece of the frame is in contact with the base. ■

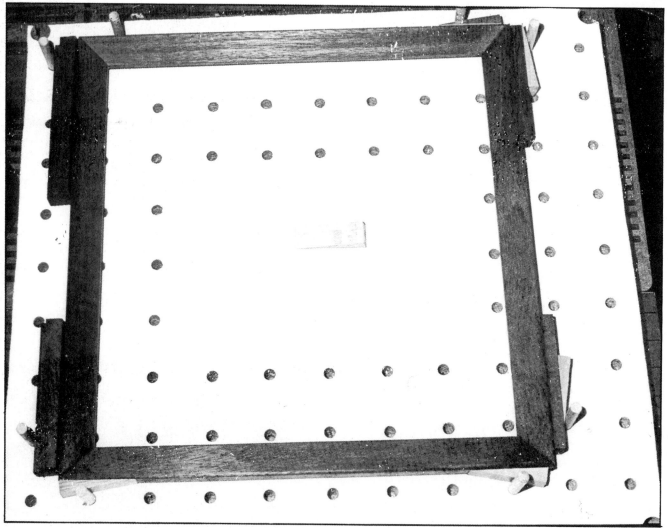

Popping Round

The noise of a lid being taken off a turned box has a special ring for the novice turner, but is simple to achieve, as Terry Porter explains

Making a box on the lathe is really not as difficult as it might at first appear. It's a matter of correct sequences, accuracy, patience and a need to develop an eye for proportion and form.

Boxes can be made up in segmental form and then turned. However, I want to concentrate on the procedures I have found effective – there are many ways to crack a nut – when turning a box from solid wood. If well seasoned, dense timbers, usually hardwoods, are the most suitable material for box-turning as they hold detail well and are less likely to distort, which is very important if you want to be able to remove the lid with ease every time. My first boxes were made from some old beech table legs. These were good for me to develop technique, but beech is visually uninteresting. I moved on to, dare I say it, boxwood, which turns beautifully and takes a good finish. In recent months I have been using more exotic woods such as pau rosa and jacaranda which present lovely natural colours and patterns.

If you want to turn a box from one piece of wood, the important thing is to achieve consistency in grain and colour between the base and the lid. First true up a blank between centres to create a cylindrical form. (The grain should be in line with the lathe bed).

If you intend to use a collet chuck turn a spigot at both ends to the correct diameter for your chuck. If you are using a three- or four-jaw engineer's chuck, as I sometimes do, then a true face at either end is all that is required, though spigots can be

used as the wood is held more tightly that way.

Having decided what shape the box is going to take, it is important to decide exactly where the lid is to be parted off. Good proportion is essential, so, disregarding what will become waste, ratios of $\frac{1}{3}:\frac{2}{3}$, or $\frac{2}{5}:\frac{3}{5}$ usually work well without making the box too top or bottom heavy.

Firmly mount the cylinder blank in the chuck using tailstock support with a revolving centre if you feel it is necessary, and usually select '3rd gear' at about 1200 rpm for smallish boxes.

Turn as much as possible of the finished shape of the box whilst still leaving the spigot on

Boxed box: a boxwood container (right) and a selection of boxes below). Note the proportions of lid and base

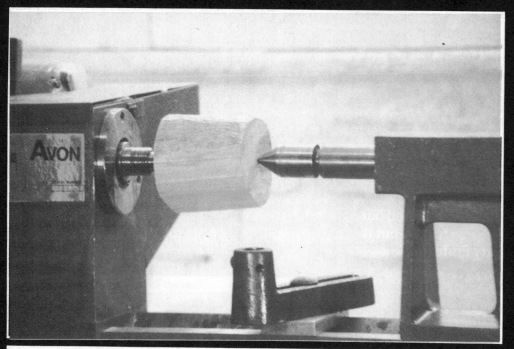

Popping Round

The blank on the lathe, between centres ready for roughing

the lid section for chucking later. Part off the lid using a fluted parting tool, which gives a very clean cut, or with a standard narrow parting tool. If you wish to keep the continuity of the grain on the two parts this cut should be as narrow as possible.

Mount the lid section in the chuck and hollow out the inside to the required depth and internal diameter. Allow enough wood for when the lid is finished externally later on. The sides of

Roughing out the blank. Note the light grip on the gouge

the first ⅛in of the inner edge of the lid should be square to allow true fitting to the base. The lid should be finished internally at this stage. (It's your last chance!)

Return the base to the chuck and proceed to hollow out the middle. Make a pilot hole using a Forstner bit mounted in the tailstock. If you have a bit of the correct diameter then the job can be done easily and quickly. If, however, like many woodturners you cannot afford a set of Forstner bits, use a flat bit to make a pilot hole, and then increase the hole using a round-nosed scraper. Remember, a flat bit has a point, so it is vital to allow for that in the depth of the

Spigots must be cut on the cylinder to fit the collet chuck

box. It is wise to mark the intended depth on the drill with tape so you don't end up creating napkin rings instead of boxes! The final cuts with the scraper will remove the hole made by the point of the flat bit. Of course, you may prefer a gouge to hollow out the box. We are back to cracking that nut again.

Finish the exterior of the base whilst bearing in mind the internal diameter of the lid. When cutting the recess for the lid to fit on, only remove about

¹⁄₁₆in from the height of the base initially until the lid fits snugly. This way, if you take too much off, so the lid is sloppy, you can remove the ¹⁄₁₆in and start again. At this lid-fitting stage it is important to keep trying the lid frequently between cuts until it fits. Remember, it's easy to take wood off but no so easy to put it back on, and a cut of ¹⁄₁₀₀₀in takes ¹⁄₅₀₀in off the diameter. When the lid fits, increase the depth of the part that goes into the lid to ¹⁄₈in or ³⁄₁₆in. If you have got it right the lid should come off with a 'pop' signifying some vacuum and a good fit.

To finish the exterior of the lid, put it on the box and turn it

to match the base. If the lid does not fit the box tightly enough for turning then a piece of tissue paper in 'the sandwich' usually does the trick. To ensure the lid doesn't come off during turning, gentle support can be given by using a revolving centre in the tailstock. Masking tape can be used to hold the lid in place while its top is being finished.

Before parting the box off finish the exterior by sanding down to about 280 grit or 400 grit if you want a really smooth finish. Briwax on fine wire-wool (0000) gives a fine satin finish. Friction polish and Danish oil are also finishes I use with success.

Remove the lid, and part the base off at a slight angle so the underneath is slightly concave enabling the box to stand well. The base can be finished by mounting the box in a four-jaw chuck on gentle expansion, or by creating a spigot from the waste and carefully jam-fitting the box on to it. You will then find that the first 'pop' from your first box is an especially lovely sound. ■

REVOLVING PATTERNS

Fascinated by the mathematics of the perfect square, Michael Hold designed a revolving bookcase with decorative top. He also found a way of disguising 15mm chipboard – so reminiscent of MFI furniture – with solid lippings

O f the requirements for a mobile bookcase probably the most important was that my wife wanted to find a place for all the books I like to keep within arm's reach of my favourite chair. About 20 to 30 books are kept within this range, so that my choice of reading is not constrained by the need to get out of my chair too frequently. It was clear that something had to be done when one day all the books which had, in my opinion, been stacked neatly around my chair, disappeared into a bedroom cupboard. The time had come when either I had to design and build myself a storage unit which could be placed next to my chair, or face a search of the house for my current books.

The bookcase had to be fairly easily moved and also compact; just over a metre or so of shelf space would be sufficient. A conventional set of book shelves would be a little unstable unless the castors could be widely spaced, so I decided upon a unit with books on all four sides. The books to be stored ranged in size from normal paperbacks

(180×120mm) to 320×250mm. Playing around on the drawing board led me to my final design. The shelves for the books are different sizes to make good use of the space, and relatively little volume is lost in the centre of the cube. I had to choose between a bookcase on castors or one which would rotate on a base with normal legs, and I selected the castors for three reasons. They allow the unit to be kept low; the shelves are easily moved; and finally I realised that the weight of the books in the unit would be up to 110 pounds, imposing large loads on any centrally pivoted unit, like the Victorian revolving bookstands. For some time I had been thinking of designs which would incorporate a pattern based upon a perfect square and a four colour inlay, and this seemed the ideal time to make use of this pattern.

At this stage I must explain briefly the perfect square and the four colour conjecture. In the mid-19th century, a mathematician named Francis Guthrie was colouring a map of the

counties of England when he realised that it was possible to colour the areas of the counties using only four colours.

Some simple maps can be coloured with three colours, but any map can be coloured with four. However he was unable to prove that this was the case for all maps, and a mathematician likes to see rigorous proofs for such ideas. Guthrie's thoughts set off a search for the proof which lasted until 1976 when two American mathematicians, Appel and Haken, at the University of Illinois announced that they had developed a new type of mathematical proof, using about 1,500 hours of a large computer's time to prove that the four colour conjecture is true in all cases. This method is so lengthy that it can not be carried out by a human being. Reading about this at the time made me think about using the four colours in some design project.

Some time later I read of another mathematical discovery which had been made by a similar method. This time a Dutch mathematician had used a highly sophisticated computer

program to discover the smallest perfect square. A perfect or squared square is one made up of smaller squares, no two of which are the same size. The one discovered by A.J.W. Duijvestijn is a square 112 units on a side and divided into 21 smaller squares. Seeing this reminded me of the earlier work, and the idea of combining the two into one design stuck in my mind.

Before embarking on a long drawing task to find smaller perfect squares please note that it has already been proved that there are no perfect squares made up of 20 squares or less and Duijvestijn proved that his 21 order square is unique, therefore no other square will ever be found that is made up of 21 or fewer squares. Use your time for woodwork not chasing elusive fame as a mathematician. If you wish to read more about the four colour problem there is an excellent book, 'Mathematics: The New Golden Age' by Keith Devlin, published by Penguin in 1988 and written for non-mathematicians like myself. There are many other books, in particular those by Martin Gardner, which are similar in their approach to

---

Fig.2 Plan section

450

180

450

180

202

470

dowelled joint

screwed and glued

dowelled joint

■ Teak lipping

▨ 15mm teak veneered chipboard

All dimensions in millimetres

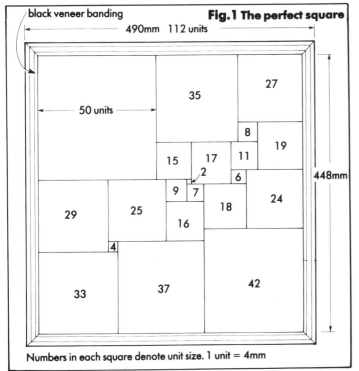

black veneer banding

Fig.1 The perfect square

490mm   112 units

50 units

448mm

35

27

8

15   17   11

19

2

9 7   6

18   24

29   25

16

4

33   37   42

Numbers in each square denote unit size. 1 unit = 4mm

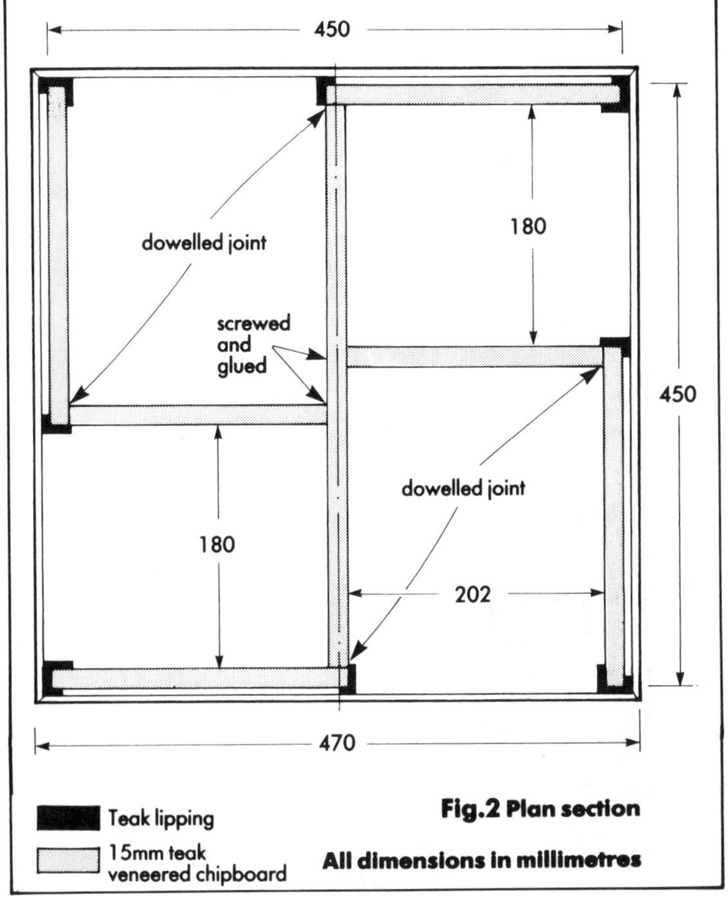

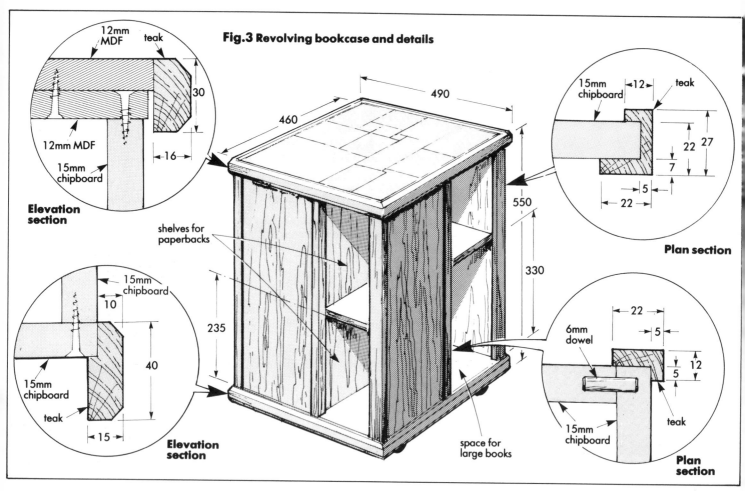

Fig.3 Revolving bookcase and details

mathematics for laymen and they may give you other ideas upon which designs can be based. Nine point circles, super-ellipses, many different spiral curves and lots of other shapes may inspire you. If you have children with access to a computer, they may be able to help you by writing programs to draw out the shapes. You could do this for yourself, but personally I prefer to use computers at work and do woodwork at home.

Given all the requirements described and the urgent need to make the bookcase, the design gelled quickly. The unit had to be square in plan, and the height had to be about 600mm to allow two shelves for paperback books and to bring the top to the right height for a glass near at hand when using the bookcase. Two opposite sides of the unit would have paperback-sized shelves and the others would each have a shelf for larger books and a small space for keeping pens, notebooks etc. . . The sides can be open showing the books or have solid panels. I chose the latter as I had some teak-veneered chipboard left from a previous

job. The colour and grain matched other furniture, and I had a plank of solid teak from which I could cut the edge mouldings. This had been bought before prices rocketed and we all became concerned about the depletion of the hardwood forests.

One problem that arises when using veneered chipboard in a design is that all the boards are 15mm thick and this gives an 'MFI' look to furniture, which is to be avoided; also the edges are easily damaged. To overcome both of these difficulties I used teak mouldings on all the chipboard edges that could be seen. These can be different thicknesses and they give a more solid look to the piece. If you are making longer shelves they also add considerable stiffness and reduce sagging under load, (before making a bookcase weigh some books to see what loads your shelves have to carry). All the mouldings were cut on a radial arm saw, but a router or saw bench could be used. Generally the mouldings have a 15mm groove so that they fit over the edge of the chipboard and cover any slight damage that has occur-

red during the sawing of the board.

The basic structure of the unit is particle board screwed together so that the screwheads cannot be seen on the finished product, and dowelled and glued in other places. The edge mouldings are added after the basic structure is complete. The base is screwed from below and a false top of 12mm MDF screwed on from above. The actual top was made separately and the pattern of squares made up from four different woods selected for contrasting colour rather than their grain.

There are many different ways in which the colours of the squares can be chosen, and the best method is to play around with the different veneers to ensure that two squares with the same colour only meet at points, never along an edge. When the veneering of the top was complete it was edged with a deep lipping that comes down over the edges of the false top and is fixed from below. This is a slightly complicated approach but it means that the top can be changed if you don't like the

four-colour, perfect square. It would have been simpler to have used one top made from thicker MDF and fixed to simple metal brackets. It has not been necessary to change the top, as the family like the design and visitors seem to enjoy puzzling over the significance of the pattern.

Design purists often quote the old maxim of the Bauhaus, "Form follows function", and there is no doubt that this can produce some beautiful pieces. However in this case I have not followed a set methodical approach, but taken a basic square pattern which I had wanted to use for sometime and then designed a functional piece of furniture around it.

Hence the design principles almost reverse the Bauhaus rule, as I looked for a function which could be performed effectively within a form. The unit has now been in use for over a year and fulfilled the objectives of the design. If I were to produce another one there would be some minor changes in details but the overall design would remain very much the same as featured here. ■